THE NEW SEX WARS

THE NEW SEX WARS

SEXUAL HARM IN THE #METOO ERA

BRENDA COSSMAN

NEW YORK UNIVERSITY PRESS
NEW YORK

NEW YORK UNIVERSITY PRESS
New York
www.nyupress.org

References to Internet websites (URLs) were accurate at the time of writing. Neither the author nor New York University Press is responsible for URLs that may have expired or changed since the manuscript was prepared.

Library of Congress Cataloging-in-Publication Data
Names: Cossman, Brenda, 1960–   author.
Title: The new sex wars : sexual harm in the #MeToo era / Brenda Cossman.
Description: New York : New York University Press, [2021] |
Includes bibliographical references and index.
Identifiers: LCCN 2021009011 | ISBN 9781479802708 (hardback) |
ISBN 9781479802746 (ebook) | ISBN 9781479802722 (ebook other)
Subjects: LCSH: Sexual harassment. | Sex crimes. | Sexual ethics. | Sexism. | Feminism.
Classification: LCC HQ1237 .C675 2021 | DDC 305.3—dc23
LC record available at https://lccn.loc.gov/2021009011

New York University Press books are printed on acid-free paper, and their binding materials are chosen for strength and durability. We strive to use environmentally responsible suppliers and materials to the greatest extent possible in publishing our books.

Manufactured in the United States of America

10 9 8 7 6 5 4 3 2 1

Also available as an ebook

For Bao and Leah

CONTENTS

INTRODUCTION   1

1 #METOO FEMINIST DEBATES: From Backlash to
Generation Gap   17

2 FEMINIST SEX WARS: Then and Now   43

3 #METOO AS SEX WARS   87

4 READING BESIDE THE QUEER/FEMINIST DIVIDE   117

5 REGULATING REPARATIVELY   163

CONCLUSION: Beyond War, beside Anger   197

Acknowledgments   207

Notes   211

Bibliography   237

Index   257

About the Author   269

INTRODUCTION

How should we regulate sexual harm? This question has been debated by feminists for decades. From the sex wars of the 1970s to the conflicts about #MeToo today, disagreements about sexuality, agency, and law have prevailed. The debates run deep, are often antagonistic, and are occasionally outright hostile. Well before #MeToo erupted, feminists were embroiled in renewed and contentious sexual politics over the regulation of sexual harm. High-profile criminal court cases, from the seemingly endless trials of Bill Cosby to Jian Ghomeshi's acquittal on charges of sexual assault in Canada to Stanford University student Brock Turner's reduced sentence for sexual assault, have mobilized outrage and protest. On university campuses across North America, debates have been raging about policies on sexual violence. In the United States, Title IX became a lightning rod of controversy, following the Obama administration's requirement that universities take immediate action to protect students from sexual harassment and sexual assault.[1] While many feminists have celebrated the new policies, others have taken issue with their potential overreach and negative stance on sex and sexuality. Some feminists decry law's failure to address sexual harm and want more law—broader definitions of sexual harm, more robust notions of consent, more effective enforcement and punishment. Others oppose the expansion of regulation; they worry instead about the overcriminalization of sexuality. These feminists not only resist an increasing reliance on the carceral state, which metes out punishment through its expanding penal system, but also argue that an overly protectionist approach to sex and sexuality is bad for women.

The feminist debate about regulating sexual harm was in full swing when #MeToo arrived. On October 15, 2017, Alyssa Milano began a viral sensation with her tweet: "If you've been sexually harassed or assaulted write 'me too' as a reply to this tweet." Within a day, Milano's instruction had been retweeted five hundred thousand times, and within days, millions of women from eighty-five countries had taken to social media with the hashtag. Activist Tarana Burke was credited with starting the Me Too campaign in 2006 to support Black women and girls who were survivors of sexual violence.[2] But the hashtag movement took on a life of its own. In the weeks and months that followed, powerful men like Harvey Weinstein, Charlie Rose, Matt Lauer—to name but a few of the most prominent—lost their positions as stories about sexual violence and harassment proliferated. Broader conversations ensued about the pervasiveness of sexual violence against women, the meaning of consent, and the role of law. The massive outpouring of #MeToo stories quickly met with pushback. Many decried #MeToo for going too far—although what they meant by "too far" differed. Some called it a sex panic, others the end of flirtation, yet others the death knell to due process. These criticisms from across the political spectrum did not exclude feminists, who also expressed discomfort and disagreement with elements of the #MeToo movement. The debate among feminists was quickly framed as a generational one, and media reports often amplified the nastier conflicts between millennials and second-wave feminists. However, age or generation alone cannot account for fundamental disagreements about sexuality, agency, consent, and law that swirl around #MeToo. Rather, these debates are better understood through the lens of Sex Wars 2.0— the continuation of the feminist sex wars of the 1970s and 1980s.

It was the dispute over sexual harassment on US university campuses that led Emily Bazelon, in a 2015 *New York Times Magazine* article, to declare the "Return of the Sex Wars." Her article focused on feminist disagreement around sexual harassment, with high-profile feminist legal scholars Catharine MacKinnon and Janet Halley as the antagonists, representing opposite sides of the debate.[3] Bazelon draws a direct line from contemporary debates within feminism around sexual harassment and sexual assault to the highly polarized and antagonistic debate of the late 1970s to the early 1990s, which divided feminists over issues of sexuality, sexual representations, sexual activity, and women's agency.[4] The feminist sex wars lined up along a series of axes—danger/pleasure, victim/choice—as radical feminists insisted on sex as a site of danger and victimization of women while sex radicals emphasized sex as a site of pleasure and female autonomy. While the disagreement cut across a broad swath of issues, including prostitution, sadomasochism, and trans women's place within the feminist movement, the focus of the debate was on pornography. On one side were anti-pornography feminists, informed by the work of Susan Brownmiller and Andrea Dworkin, who identified pornography as a key site of male dominance and women's subordination.[5] On the other side were sex-radical or sex-positive feminists like Gayle Rubin, Ellen Willis, and Carol Vance, who criticized the sexual negativity of the anti-pornography position. Rubin, Willis, and Vance, among others, argued against what they saw as a deeply conservative sexual morality and were critical of support for state censorship of sexual representations.[6]

Bazelon's article rightly—if superficially—connected the dots between the intellectual history of the sex wars and the current feminist debates around sexual harassment on campuses. Picking up on Bazelon's observation, *The New Sex Wars* seeks to provide an in-depth and critical analysis of the contemporary regulation of sexual-harm debates. Three decades ago, the debates focused on pornography and prostitution. Today, they focus on sexual harassment, sexual assault, sexting, revenge porn, and polygamy, although debates around sex work continue. *The New Sex Wars* brings these intellectual inheritances into sharper relief and reveals the underlying investments at stake. Current feminist debates fracture along the axes of sexuality, consent, and law that figured in the early sex wars and are all too often similarly characterized by unproductive partisanship, hostilities, and standoffs, with caricatures and denouncements flung across the divide.

Contemporary sex and sexuality are not only debated among feminists but are also central to the complicated relationship between feminist and queer intellectual projects. Queer scholars and activists have mounted challenges to the contemporary terms of sexual governance, focusing on the multiple ways in which nonnormative sexualities are subject to increasing surveillance and regulation. From the criminalization of HIV and consensual teenage sexuality to child pornography laws, they explore how sex panics play into conservative regulatory discourse. The sex-radical critique of the earlier sex wars, epitomized by the work of Gayle Rubin,[7] has morphed into queer critiques of the current sex wars. David Halperin and Trevor Hoppe's *War on Sex* captures much of the queer iteration. Some of the #MeToo detractors similarly fall within this intellectual frame. Masha Gessen in the *New Yorker* expressed apprehension about #MeToo veering towards a sex panic and concern that campus sexual-violence controversies and policies often run the risk of "blur[ring] the boundaries between rape, nonviolent sexual coercion, and bad, fumbling, drunken sex. The effect is both to criminalize bad sex and trivialize rape."[8] Gessen's queer critique lines up with the sex-positive feminist position in the sex wars in general and in #MeToo in particular. Together, they express ambivalence and/or opposition to the criminalization of sexuality.[9]

In this book, I track these theoretical, political, and regulatory disagreements and demonstrate the enduring and unresolved nature of the debates with a view to thinking differently about the legal regulation of sexual harm. *The New Sex Wars* makes space to think through sexuality, consent, and law, disarticulated from the binary antagonisms of the sex wars. Rather than making a partisan intervention, I reveal the complexity of claims on both sides, and recognize the validity of seeming contradictions. The theoretical frameworks I bring to bear on current iterations of the sex wars build on sex-positive feminism, queer theory, and anti-carceral feminism, making room for the more dissident voices of the Sex Wars 2.0 and affirming the importance of a critique of dominance feminism and its hold on the public and legal imagination. I thereby build on my earlier interventions in the sex wars,[10] which were distinctively partisan, arguing in sex-radical and civil-libertarian terms against the deployment of obscenity law to regulate the alleged harms of pornography.

In *The New Sex Wars*, I return to those debates but with a different analytic sensibility that makes room for questions foreclosed by a "for or against" frame. Building on feminist interventions that have offered more nuanced retellings of the sex wars,[11] I explore how approaches to the regulation of sex and sexuality that eschew either/or thinking can envision sexuality, agency, and law as zones of ambivalence. How might we think through the precarity and indeterminacy of consent while also demanding something of it? How might breaking out of the antagonism of past sex wars and contemporary debates produce a more complex understanding of sexual harm and allow for more creativity in using law to address it? While I continue to be skeptical of broad definitions and expansive legal regulation, I seek ways out of the intellectual impasse.

More specifically, I will bring a reparative reading, inspired by the work of Eve Sedgwick,[12] to the feminist disagreements about the regulation of sexual harm. Sedgwick argued for a different kind of critical reading strategy, one not based in the paranoia or the hermeneutics of suspicion that, in her view, dominated critical theory. Instead of always looking for the hidden truths that lie beneath texts, Sedgwick argued for embracing uncertainty through a deliberate form of reading that did not already know what it was looking for. For Sedgwick, one must be open to surprise, to seeing things differently, so that "the reader has the room to realize that the future may be different from the present."[13] She does not reject critical readings but rather suggests the need to "interdigitate" these two very different strategies. I delve into reparative reading in more detail in chapter 4, but my approach throughout is informed by an emphasis on reading generously and keeping multiple perspectives in view. While much of what follows in *The New Sex Wars* would be categorized as paranoid—finding hidden truths about sexuality, consent, and law that lie beneath the sex wars, then and now, and #MeToo—a reparative reading can allow us to break out of these limiting debates.

I take each side of the sex wars seriously in their identification of harms and regulatory modes. My reparative approach examines law's failure to address sexual harm as well as the critique of overregulation. I argue that reading these claims beside each other, interrogating how the under- and overcriminalization of sex can both be valid, allows for the recognition of multiple harms, unrecognized sexual injury *and* over-regulation. Both sides of the sex wars have tended to fetishize criminal law. Even when activists are focusing on civil laws of sexual harassment, there is a conflation with the modalities of criminal law. One way out is to displace the centrality of criminal law and consider alternative modalities of regulation. Do we need more law to regulate sexual harm? Yes and no. But most importantly, we need to fundamentally rethink the legal apparatus to better redress sexual harms without relying on the criminal law or its carceral logics as extended to the realm of civil law.

Chapter 1 explores the emergence of the #MeToo movement and the feminist debates that surfaced within it. #MeToo garnered general consensus in the face of the most obvious sexual misconduct. Harvey Weinstein and others who engaged in sexual assault and quid pro quo sexual harassment, demanding sex in exchange for fame and fortune, were the undisputed villains. But, as #MeToo allegations against the rich and famous continued, not all of the stories fit the archetype of assault and harassment. The further away from that archetype the allegations were, the more the feminist consensus of harm faded. From the accusations against Senator Al Franken[14] to the Catherine Deneuve open letter denouncing #MeToo as a witch hunt[15] to the full-throttle clashes following the publication of the Aziz Ansari story,[16] the chapter tracks the evolution of the feminist disagreement about #MeToo. It focuses on the narratives that emerged, in particular the way #MeToo disagreement got framed as a feminist intergenerational feud: millennials versus second-wave feminists. While some feminists resisted this generational narrative,[17] the chapter explores how both mainstream and social media fixated on the disagreement as a younger versus older catfight.

Chapter 2 begins to challenge the intergenerational narrative of #MeToo. It begins by turning to the feminist sex wars of the 1970s and 1980s, highlighting the divisions over sexuality, consent, and law. The story of the sex wars is often remembered in the popular imagination in starkly oppositional terms, with radical feminists and sex-radical feminists lined up along a series of axes: danger/pleasure, victim/choice, oppression/liberation. While these axes capture something of each side's relative emphasis, they also tend towards caricature. Neither side was as one-dimensional as this story suggests. I pay particular attention to the debates in relation to law—a critical component of the narrative that has been given shorter shrift. The sex-wars story is often cast as one between radical feminists who advocated censorship and sex radicals who opposed it. However, this version of the story only reflects the final stage of the sex wars, when anti-pornography feminists lined up against anti-censorship feminists over the Civil Rights Ordinance, and law itself became a site of struggle over the meaning of pornography and sexuality. In fact, radical feminists were divided within their ranks over the question of legal regulation and censorship. Furthermore, the focus on censorship left many questions of law's role in the legal regulation of sexuality unexplored and unresolved. While lawyers and legal academics did not play a prominent role until the final stage, nascent and divergent theories of law emerged on both sides—differences that carry forward into the current feminist contestations.

The chapter then turns to more recent iterations of the sex wars, what I have termed Sex Wars 2.0. Debates today track the same feminist disagreements about sexuality, consent, and the role of law but through a more current set of issues. Feminists continue to battle over sex work, but a younger generation has also shifted the battle lines to college campuses, revealing the pervasiveness of sexual violence, with others provocatively pushing back against the vision of young women as victims. Feminists are debating issues of sexual harassment, sexual assault, polygamy, sexting, and "revenge porn." I focus primarily on the question of sexual harm in relation to sexual harassment and sexual assault that falls out from Title IX and campus sexual violence. Unlike in the earlier sex wars, the debates do not fit a simple binary of "for or against" particular sexual practices. On one side, feminists seek stricter enforcement of existing laws, as well as harsher civil and criminal penalties for both sexual harassment and sexual assault. These feminists point out the pervasive nature of sexual violence against women, the underenforcement of existing laws, and the lax penalties against even those convicted. On the other side, feminists are critical of overly broad definitions of sexual harassment and sexual assault and the potential overreach for criminal and civil remedies. Unlike in the earlier debates, where feminists on this side were in favor of pornography and sex work, the feminists in Sex Wars 2.0 do not support sexual harassment and sexual assault; rather, they contest the sexual behaviors that constitute it and the expansive use of the criminal and civil justice system to address these behaviors.[18] Some argue that the definitions of sexual harassment on campuses and beyond are too broad and risk capturing consensual sexual behavior.[19] Other feminists focus on the definition of consent and question the feminist enthusiasm for affirmative consent.[20] I argue that the same unresolved issues around theories of sexuality, consent, and the potential use of law that defined the sex wars of the 1970s and 1980s continue to plague debates about the regulation of sexual harm today. While the issues have changed, the underlying disagreements remain remarkably similar.

Chapter 3 returns to the #MeToo feminist debates. Seen through the lens of the Sex Wars 2.0, they reproduce the same disagreements, fracturing around sexuality, consent, and the role of law in regulating sexual harm. This lens better captures the stakes of the feminist debates, their historical continuity and substantive investments. At their root, the conflicts revolve around competing feminist understandings of the role of sexuality in women's inequality, the degree to which women exercise sexual agency, and the role of law in addressing sexual harm. Simply put, feminists are divided about what constitutes sexual harm and how it should be regulated. I argue that contemporary #MeToo feminists are the intellectual inheritors of the radical feminists of the 1970s and 1980s and the dominance feminists of Sex Wars 2.0. #MeToo feminists emphasize sexuality as oppressive and dangerous to women; they seek to reveal the extent to which sexual danger remains real and ubiquitous for women. The #MeToo feminist detractors, by contrast, are the intellectual inheritors of the feminist sex radicals of the sex wars, then and now. They emphasize the importance of sexuality as a site of pleasure and empowerment. Similarly, there are clear echoes of the radical feminist critique of consent in the context of heterosexuality. MacKinnon's ghost—the impossibility of consent when sexuality is constituted in and through women's oppression—haunts the discussion, in its substance and its caricature.[21] Many #MeToo feminists post Ansari have sought to promote a discussion of sexual interactions that are "dubiously consensual."[22] In contrast, among the #MeToo detractors, there are clear echoes of the sex-radical emphasis on the importance of recognizing sexual agency in women's lives and not overly determining women as victims of predatory male heterosexuality.

The chapter focuses in particular on the controversies around the role of law in the #MeToo movement and its lack of a clearly articulated theory of law. Indeed, one of the most notable features of #MeToo's early days was the extent to which it played out in nonlegal forums, from social media to board rooms, bypassing courts and legal actions. This speaks volumes about law: the sheer exposure of the pervasiveness of sexual violence in women's lives is a performance of law's spectacular failure. The chapter highlights two major points of feminist contention around law in #MeToo: the due process critique and the question of sexual misconduct. Both the procedural issue of the relevance of due process and the substantive issue of the scope of behavior captured by #MeToo are related to underlying disagreements about the relationship between law and sexual harm. But, I also argue that deep tensions arise from the role of law within both the #MeToo feminism camp and the feminist detractors—tensions that reside in the underlying power of law as the exclusive arbiter of sexual violence. Both #MeToo feminists and their feminist critics challenge the law's power while also reinforcing it. They do so in different ways that evoke the complexity of feminist disagreements that have come before.

In Chapter 4 I turn to the controversy that emerged when Avital Ronell, a professor at New York University, was accused of sexual harassment by her graduate student Nimrod Reitman. The incident was first labeled as a kind of #MeToo reversal, as in the *New York Times* headline, "What Happens to #MeToo When a Feminist Is the Accused?"[23] Charges of feminist hypocrisy abounded, particularly in light of a letter in defense of Ronell signed by prominent feminist scholars, most notably Judith Butler. Like #MeToo more generally, the Ronell controversy was initially framed in generational terms, as millennials versus second-wave feminists were replaced by graduate students and precariously employed academics versus senior, tenured academics. Relying this time on a distinctively queer diagnostic and proscriptive lens, I argue that, once again, the generational reading misses the underlying disagreements about sexual harm and its regulation. I reframe the controversy as an eruption of the feminist sex wars, now with a feminist/queer divide, and break open the divisions and antagonisms across the sex wars, #MeToo, and the Ronell controversy by using Eve Sedgwick's practice of reparative reading and reading beside.

The chapter returns to the Senator Al Franken controversy. The second coming in the summer of 2019 hit with the publication of an article in the *New Yorker* by Jane Mayer,[24] who reexamined the allegations and reactions, suggesting that there had been a rush to judgment, in the absence of facts and fairness. Her article produced another feminist flashpoint. Paying particular attention to the role of the photograph that implicated Franken, I consider how a reparative reading of the Franken controversy that refuses a dichotomy might help us better understand the competing claims. The photograph showed Franken's accuser, Leanne Tweeden, asleep in a chair aboard a military aircraft, dressed in a helmet, fatigues, and a body armor vest. Franken leans towards

Tweeden, his hands hovering over her breasts. Curiously, the photo provided both supporters and detractors with incontrovertible evidence of "what happened" and intense responses to the other side's inability to see it. Reading both the controversy and the photograph reparatively, I seek to hold competing feminist and queer claims in view, simultaneously recognizing the harms of sexual misconduct and its regulation.

In Chapter 5, I focus on different ways to think about regulating sexual harms. The sex wars have been debates about law, about when and how to use it to redress sexual harm. On one side of the sex wars, feminists stake their claims around the harms of nonconsensual sex, and the failure of law to regulate it, often calling for more law—broader definitions of sexual harms, more robust notions of sexual consent, more effective enforcement and punishment. On the other side, sex-positive feminists and queer critics stake their claims around the harms of regulating consensual sex. They focus on the overcriminalization of consensual sexuality. To a large extent, theirs is a claim for less law, antiregulatory in impulse, equating regulation with criminal law. In this chapter, I interrogate law's failure to address sexual harm *and* the critique of overregulation. Building on the reparative reading of the previous chapter, I argue that it is possible to read these two claims beside each other in order to ask, for example, how the under- and overcriminalization of sex can both be valid. Reading reparatively, on the surface, seeing what is in plain sight, taking the intensity of the affective claims seriously, we can acknowledge the harms of overcriminalizing nonnormative, consensual sexuality. At the same time, we can recognize the failure of law to regulate and prevent nonconsensual sexual harms, and the extent to which harms go unacknowledged or unaddressed. This is not to suggest a complete commensurability in these claims; there are points of conflict and convergence, to be sure. But, we might begin with what can be simultaneously held in view: noticing, valuing, and sustaining the claims of those who aver harm while recognizing multiple modalities of harm. Yes, there is a harm, real or perceived. Its affirmation, through a reparative reading, need not implicate a particular regulatory response.

What if we explored the implications of the regulatory responses, while holding the multiplicity of harms in view? How can we affirm, make whole, one harm without exacerbating the other? I argue that a *reparative* justice model demands a more complete break from the criminal justice system. Criminalizing sexual violence has done little to reduce sexual harms or promote accountability. Regulating reparatively would mean exploring different ways of promoting accountability: listening, education, apology, and other potential modalities of repair.

In the final pages, I turn a reparative lens back to the sex wars themselves and the affect that has animated them. I take a closer look at the role of anger—feminist anger, in particular—and argue that we can put anger to use. Bringing the discussion of #MeToo back to where it started—with Tarana Burke—the conclusion gestures towards reading anger alongside the potential of cultivating other emotional responses to healing the trauma of sexual violence, individually and collectively.

I tell the stories of #MeToo and the sex wars, then and now, through what Sarah Banet-Weiser describes as feminist flashpoints: "Feminist flashpoints are media events that, at once, open up and constrain our thinking about feminist futures."[25] Building on the idea of #MeToo as a flashpoint in gender politics, Banet-Weiser describes these moments of popular feminism in terms of light and heat:

> They can light up an issue and show us the importance, the urgency, of feminist politics. They move feminism into the spotlight. They are also *hot* in that gendered abuses of power can ignite and encourage a quick response and commentary. These quick responses, often written from a moralizing perspective, are "hot takes," whose primary purpose is to attract attention. The hot take is uniquely suited for the digital domain, where, if successful, it goes viral, gets retweeted and memed.[26]

Banet-Weiser notes that feminist flashpoints obscure the complexities of the very issues they push into the light: "Feminism is flattened out, made into something that erases history and neglects to acknowledge its debt to other conversations and other activisms. The focus shifts to individual cases and individuals, on whom it is easier to pass judgment."[27]

Banet-Weiser's discussion of feminist flashpoints is located in the now of the Twitterverse, social media, and "going viral." The flashpoints of the past, while not as instantaneously explosive, were flashpoints nonetheless. They were moments when feminist issues—and internal conflicts—burst into view within both the feminist and mainstream press. The flashpoint might swirl around an individual, a protest, a conference, a law, to create a moment when feminism becomes simultaneously popular and contested.

Long underacknowledged in the sex-wars debates is race. The flashpoints of the sex wars, then and now, and of #MeToo, have reflected what Alison Phipps calls the political whiteness of mainstream feminism.[28] She builds on the work of Daniel Martinez HoSang, who has described whiteness as a political stance and perspective rooted in white racial identity. Echoing Martinez HoSang's work, Phipps notes, "It operates as a kind of absent referent, hailing and interpolating particular subjects through various affective appeals witnessed in claims to protect 'our rights,' 'our jobs,' 'our homes,' 'our kids,' 'our streets.'"[29] Phipps argues that mainstream anti–sexual violence feminism, and #MeToo in particular, is shaped by this political whiteness and the woundedness of white femininity. Feminist flashpoints have overwhelmingly told stories of white feminism, Tarana Burke notwithstanding. Indeed, Burke has expressed consistent frustration with the mainstream movement and has repeatedly tried to recenter the #MeToo conversation on marginalized communities that experience sexual violence: "The conversation is largely about Harvey Weinstein or other individual bogeymen. No matter how much I keep talking about power and privilege, they keep bringing it back to individuals. . . . It defeats the purpose to not have those folks centered—I'm talking black and brown girls, queer folks . . . people with disabilities . . . Native Americans."[30] As Phipps describes, Burke's relationship to mainstream #MeToo is complicated: "She has been credited as the movement's founder but at times tokenized and spoken over, and has consistently acted as its conscience and critic."[31]

Many feminists of color have pointed out the whiteness of the #MeToo movement, and the fraught relationship between mainstream anti–sexual violence feminism and marginalized communities. As Ashwini Tambe identifies, "We know the history of how black men have been lynched based on unfounded allegations that they sexually violated white women. We know how many black men are unjustly incarcerated. The dynamics of #MeToo, in which due process has been reversed—with accusers' words taken more seriously than those of the accused—is a familiar problem in black communities. Maybe some black women want no part of this dynamic."[32] The political whiteness of mainstream sexual-violence feminism—current and historical—has often facilitated its turn to the carceral state, a move at once exclusionary and alienating of Black and other marginalized women. While the role of law, and the tendency to resort to the criminal law, is part of what has been contested in all the sex wars, these debates have largely taken place within the confines of political whiteness. Telling the story of these feminist flashpoints runs the risk of reinscribing the racially myopic nature of the sex wars and their instantiation in #MeToo. I try to counter this by recentering the work of feminists of color, from Tarana Burke herself to abolition feminists like Beth Richie and Angela Davis, who have been doing anti-racist and anti-violence work for decades without flashpoints—or rather, without the feminist flashpoints of political whiteness that often take up the oxygen in the room.

Finally, a note about terminology. Discussing the "sides" of the sex wars is itself an ideologically loaded exercise. "Anti-pornography" suggests that the other side is pro-pornography, just as "sex-positive feminism" suggests that the other side is sex-negative. The terms "anti-rape" or "anti–sexual violence" imply that the other feminist side is pro-rape or pro–sexual violence. The idea of "feminist critics" of the former suggests that anti-rape feminists are not themselves feminist critics. I make an effort to deploy the terms most commonly used to describe each side, while recognizing the ways in which the terminology itself risks reinforcing the sex wars' divides.

And then there is the term "sex wars" itself, which typically refers to the intense feminist debates over sexuality of the 1970s and 1980s. I use "the New Sex Wars" and "Sex Wars 2.0" to describe the ways in which those same divides continue to haunt contemporary feminist debates to suggest that the current feminist contestations are the second coming of the sex wars. Such a telling obscures the ways in which the 1990s were characterized by their own version of feminist sex wars. As discussed in chapter 1, the 1990s saw another replaying of the sexuality debates and their danger/pleasure, victim/agency divisions. The 1990s also saw the emergence of broader cultural wars, with government efforts to censor and limit funding to artists, such as photographers Robert Mapplethorpe and Andres Serrano. Sex-positive feminists joined queer activists and others to protest the conservative attack on these artistic representations.[33] In many ways the sex wars have never gone away. They simmer beneath the surface, erupting from time to time. The term "Sex Wars 2.0" is not intended to erase this history. Rather, the 2.0 framing signals the nostalgia, the retro nature, the overuse of 2.0, as well as its distinctive features. As the *Oxford Living Dictionary* defines it, "2.0" is "used to denote a superior or more advanced version of an original concept, product, service, etc."[34] Its etymology is in Web 2.0—a transformation of web technology from a reading site to one in which the user participates through various forms of interface software, including social networking, self-publishing platforms, comments sections, and *like* buttons. While 2.0 as attached to various concepts indicates the idea of something new and improved, the designation is in fact passé. I intend for "Sex Wars 2.0" to capture how current feminist debates around sex and sexuality are already old, restagings of performances past, with a hint of nostalgia for the purity of bygone days. Yet, the very capabilities of the Web 2.0 have intensified the sex wars, enabling battles to be fought in real and viral time for all to witness.

Another limitation of the sex-wars framing is raised by Suzanna Danuta Walters in the introduction to a special edition of *Signs* devoted to their rethinking. She warns against the metaphor of war itself, and, together with other contributors, gestures towards ongoing deliberations within feminism as proof of the continuity of old debates: "One could make an argument that the fault lines between, say, the prostitution abolitionists and the sex worker advocates, or the 'yes means yes' anti-sexual-assault activists and their critics, or even trigger warning advocates and opponents show the continuing resonance of the sex wars."[35] The debates persist precisely, she argues, because the messy couplet of danger and pleasure remains central to feminism, which "can't really do its job if it's not talking about both." Walters proposes leaving the war metaphor behind because it created oppositional sides: enemies, not interlocutors. Walters states, "As in many internecine debates, the drawing of battle lines and asserting of oppositional stances left little room for waffling or even benign befuddlement. You were either anti-porn or pro-sex, as if these designations could capture the complex and often contradictory positions of both scholars and activists. . . . Too often (then and now) we marked each other as either 'with us' or 'against us'— and that meant we could not ever think these things *together* unless we were already on the same side."[36]

Indeed, we need to rethink the terms of the sex wars and the relationship between pleasure and danger in order to embrace the messiness and push "in directions that don't simply (obsessively) reinscribe these tiresome splits and divisions."[37] My ultimate objective is to reimagine the regulation of sexual harm through a reparative approach, taking a circuitous route through the terrain of the sex wars to get there. The contemporary feminist debates around sexual violence and #MeToo remain all too embedded in the well-worn fault line of the sex wars— divides that cry out to be left behind.

1

#METOO FEMINIST DEBATES

From Backlash to Generation Gap

On October 15, 2017, Alyssa Milano's #MeToo tweet started a viral sen-sation, shared five hundred thousand times within a day and used on Facebook by over 4.7 million people; within a few days, millions of women from eighty-five countries had taken to social media with the hashtag. While the phrase was coined in 2006 by Tarana Burke, a civil rights activist who founded the Me Too campaign to support Black women and girls who were survivors of sexual violence, in late 2017 "#MeToo" became a household word and a rallying cry against the perva-siveness of sexual violence. The tweet came on the heels of two explosive media reports by the *New York Times* and the *New Yorker* detailing over two decades of sexual-harassment and sexual-assault allegations against Harvey Weinstein.[1] Weinstein was fired within days, but the exposé of widespread sexual violence had only begun. In the months that followed, other powerful men—Charlie Rose,[2] Matt Lauer,[3] and Kevin Spacey, to name but a few—were toppled in the wake of public accusations of sex-ual harassment and assault.[4] The ubiquity of sexual violence in the lives of women blew up in mainstream and social media.[5]

But, #MeToo had critics from its inception. Some denounced it as a witch hunt.[6] Others decried it for going too far—although what they meant by "too far" differed. Yet others expressed concern over the flat-tening or lumping effect of #MeToo, particularly in the wake of alle-gations of sexual misconduct leading to the resignation of Senator Al Franken.[7] Commentators took issue with the fact that equating sexual assault with more "trivial" forms of sexual misconduct undermined the burgeoning movement. A fairness objection, focusing on #MeToo's disregard for due process, also emerged.[8] These critics were cast as part of the growing backlash to #MeToo.[9]

While these criticisms came from across the political spectrum, they included some self-identified feminists who expressed discomfort and disagreement with elements of the #MeToo movement. Cracks became apparent in the wake of the Al Franken allegations, but they erupted into full view after the publication of the Babe.net story detailing a young woman's date and allegations of sexual misconduct against Aziz Ansari.[10] Talk of backlash quickly morphed into the language of generational divide, as some younger feminists claimed that the problem was second-wave feminists. Mainstream media jumped on the generation-gap narrative. The backlash *to* #MeToo became a generational divide *within* #MeToo. This chapter tracks the emergence of feminist disagreements within #MeToo. It focuses on the critiques of the movement as articulated by those who self-identified as feminist but had misgivings about the direction, tone, and character of #MeToo. The disagreements came most sharply into focus through the Franken and Ansari controversies and accordingly, the chapter takes a close look at these flashpoints. #MeToo feminist responses ranged from dismissal of the criticisms as nonfeminist and part of the backlash to the framing of disagreements as generational.

The discourse played into well-worn tropes of the generation gap. Conflict between the Baby Boomers and every generation that followed is well rehearsed: the environmental controversies pitting millennials against Boomers and the viral sensation of the "Ok Boomer" retort exemplify the recurrent traction of old versus young. Feminism has long had its own discourse of divide, often articulated as waves. This chapter explores the genealogy of this divide. The idea of feminist conflicts within #MeToo as generational—between second-wave and millennial feminists—played into a readily available rhetorical device, establishing certain truth claims, relationships, and identities as natural or commonsensical. It is a claim that is simply too broad to be useful. As I will argue in subsequent chapters, the disagreements that came to light around #MeToo cannot be reduced to age or generation alone.

#METOO: FEMINIST CONTESTATIONS

#MeToo garnered the greatest consensus in the face of the most obvious sexual misconduct. The more monstrous and pervasive the behavior, the greater the consensus. Harvey Weinstein could emerge as the consensus villain, with multiple allegations of sexual assaults and classic sexual harassment, demanding sex in exchange for fame and fortune. Others who followed a similar modus operandi would also fall. Long-time CBS host Charlie Rose was fired after the *Washington Post* published the story of eight women who claimed he had made "unwanted sexual advances toward them, including lewd phone calls, walking around naked in their presence, or groping their breasts, buttocks or genital areas."[11] NBC fired *Today* anchor Matt Lauer at the end of November 2017, following disclosures that he would demand sex from female employees behind locked doors and reprimand those who refused.[12] Following years of rumors, Louis C.K. was accused by five women of repeatedly masturbating in front of female employees and associates.[13] He admitted to the conduct, his movie premiere was canceled, and his media company cut ties with him.[14] Kevin Spacey was accused by actor Anthony Rapp of making sexual advances towards him when he was fourteen years old.[15] Fifteen other men came forward with a range of accusations, from groping to exposure.[16] Netflix dropped Spacey from *House of Cards*, and Ridley Scott cut Spacey's scenes from the film *All the Money in the World*.[17]

But, as #MeToo allegations against the rich and famous continued, not all of the stories fit the archetype of sexual assault and sexual harassment. The further away the narratives moved from the archetype, the more the consensus of harm faded away. Masha Gessen in the *New Yorker* worried that #MeToo was at risk of blurring the boundaries between the likes of Harvey Weinstein and those who stood accused of less serious behavior. Gessen made clear, however, that she was against sexual violence, noting that she too had written "#MeToo." But, she expressed concern that #MeToo was becoming a sex panic, connecting it to the "war on sex" and the surveillance of sex through Title IX on college campuses. Foreshadowing the lumping critique that would gain ground, Gessen opposed "blur[ing] the boundaries between rape, nonviolent sexual coercion, and bad, fumbling, drunken sex. The effect is both to criminalize bad sex and trivialize rape."[18] The distinctions between "rape and coercion are meaningful, in the way it is meaningful to distinguish between, say, murder and battery rape."

On November 17, 2017, Senator Al Franken was accused of sexual misconduct by Leeann Tweeden in a radio episode and an affiliated article called "Senator Al Franken Kissed and Groped Me without My Consent, and There's Nothing Funny about It."[19] Tweeden wrote that Franken forcibly kissed her during a rehearsal on a 2006 USO tour, that he insisted on practicing the kiss: "I said 'OK' so he would stop badgering me. We did the line leading up to the kiss and then he came at me, put his hand on the back of my head, mashed his lips against mine and aggressively stuck his tongue in my mouth."[20] Tweeden released a photograph of herself asleep in a chair aboard a military aircraft, dressed in a helmet, fatigues, and a body armor vest. Franken is leaning towards her, hands spread over Tweeden's breasts, his face turned smiling towards the camera.

Franken first responded with an apology that did not fully address her accusations: "I certainly don't remember the rehearsal for the skit in the same way, but I send my sincerest apologies to Leeann. . . . As to the photo, it was clearly intended to be funny but wasn't. I shouldn't have done it."[21] He subsequently issued a longer apology in which he took fuller responsibility for his actions.[22] Other women, named and anonymous, came out with similar stories.[23] Senate majority and minority leaders Mitch McConnell and Chuck Schumer sent Tweeden's accusations to the Senate Ethics Committee for review. Other accusations emerged,[24] and more than two dozen Democratic senators—many of them women—urged Franken to resign.[25] On December 7, 2017, Franken resigned his Senate seat.

Whether due to the fact that he was a Democratic senator, with a history of supporting women's issues, the nature of the allegations, or just a rising backlash, Franken's fall from grace was more controversial than those of the men who fell before him. Many mainstream media commentators questioned whether Franken's conduct merited the resignation and surmised that #MeToo had gone too far. Bill Maher argued, "Al Franken doesn't deserve to be 'lumped in' with Roy Moore, Harvey Weinstein."[26] Andrea Peyser declared that "#MeToo has thrown trivial in with legitimate sexual assault," writing, "It's gone far enough. What started as a necessary mass-rejection of sexual harassment and assault is sliding into absurdity and irrelevance."[27]

While much of the critique came from decidedly nonfeminist voices, a few self-described feminists raised concerns. Bari Weiss of the *New York Times*, for example, tweeted, "Are others disturbed by the moral flattening going on? Glenn Thrush/Al Franken should not be mentioned in the same breath as Harvey Weinstein/Kevin Spacey."[28] Small cracks in the #MeToo feminist consensus began to appear. Kate Harding expressed her misgivings over Franken's resignation, writing that "I am a Feminist, I Study Rape, and I Don't Want Al Franken to Resign."[29] She argued that he should be held accountable in ways that would actually improve women's lives. He had done much good for women, and could do more without resigning.[30] Others expressed concern that Franken had been denied due process. Zephyr Teachout—a law professor and self-described feminist—wrote in the *New York Times* that she was unconvinced Franken should have resigned.[31] While proclaiming her passionate commitment to #MeToo, Teachout wrote, "Zero tolerance should go hand in hand with two other things: due process and proportionality." Both, she argued, had been undermined in Franken's case.

Emily Yoffe warned of the coming backlash to #MeToo if it was not careful of potential overreach.[32] Yoffe delved into the controversies around campus sexual violence and Title IX, arguing against running roughshod over the rights of the accused. She too worried about the "erasing of distinctions between the criminal and the loutish," in the wake of the allegations against Franken, an erasure she said equally characterized campus sexual-violence policies.[33] Yoffe raised many of the critiques that feminist legal scholars had been raising over the preceding years in relation to Title IX (critiques reviewed in the next chapter), and connected them to #MeToo. Yoffe argued that concerns about the absence of due process and overly broad definitions of sexual harassment, lumping serious with more trivial behaviors, applied equally to workplace sexual violence and harassment: "This amazing moment has a chance to be truly transformative. But it could also go off track if all accusations are taken on faith, if due process is seen as an impediment rather than a requirement and an underpinning of justice, and if men and women grow wary of each other in the workplace."[34]

The feminist misgivings, initially sotto voce, picked up volume in the early days of 2018. Daphne Merkin, in the *New York Times*, lamented the disappearance of flirting, the lumping of harassment and assault with vague "inappropriate behavior," and the absence of due process.[35] Merkin attributed these qualms to self-described feminists, herself included, who "publicly say #MeToo" but privately worry about the direction of the movement. Merkin insisted that she was of course against real sexual violence: "It goes without saying that no one is coming to the defense of heinous sorts, like Kevin Spacey and Matt Lauer. But the trickle-down effect of cases like those of Garrison Keillor, Jonathan Schwartz, Ryan Lizza and Al Franken, in which the accusations are scattered, anonymous or, as far as the public knows, vague and unspecific, has been troubling." Opposing serious sexual violence, but also flagging its dilution through the lumping together of the serious with the trivial and the ambiguous, would become a frequent refrain. Merkin also questioned the disappearance of women's agency, arguing that "we seem to be returning to a victimology paradigm for young women in particular, in which they are perceived to be—and perceive themselves to be—as frail as Victorian housewives."[36] And she worried about a repressive vision of sex resurfacing: "We are witnessing the re-moralization of sex, not via the Judeo-Christian ethos but via a legalistic, corporate consensus."[37] The solution, she said, is not "stripping sex of its eros. . . . [but] a broader and more thoroughgoing overhaul, one that begins with the way we bring up our sons and daughters."

Days later came the Catherine Deneuve open letter published in *Le Monde*, with one hundred French women denouncing #MeToo as a witch hunt that had gone well beyond sexual assault.[38] "Rape is a crime. But insistent or clumsy flirting is not a crime, nor is gallantry a chauvinist aggression."[39] The letter repeats the refrain of a movement gone too far: "As a result of the Weinstein affair, there has been a legitimate realization of the sexual violence women experience, particularly in the workplace, where some men abuse their power. It was necessary. But now this liberation of speech has been turned on its head." Echoing Merkin's concerns, the letter focuses on the puritanism of the #MeToo movement, its "Victorian moral outlook" and belief that "women are a species 'apart,' children with adult faces who demand to be protected." Women, they argue, should be able to distinguish between "an awkward attempt to pick someone up" and sexual assault. The letter defends the importance of sexual freedom for women, and argues that "the freedom to *bother*" is indispensable to sexual freedom. Of #MeToo, they conclude, "As women, we do not recognize ourselves in this feminism."

The #MeToo feminist response was swift.[40] A group of French activists signed another open letter written by prominent feminist Caroline de Hass, with a scathing critique: "Whenever women's rights progress, awareness is raised, resistance appears. In general, they take the form of '*it is true, of course, but . . .*' This January 9, we were treated to a '#Metoo, it was good, but . . .'"[41] They took issue with all of the claims, framed as backlash to the progress of women's rights. Sandra Muller, founder of the #BalanceTonPorc ("squeal on your pig") movement—the French equivalent of #MeToo—denounced Deneuve's letter. French feminist collective Osez le Feminisme also responded with outrage, tweeting, "Revolting. In the face of current awareness, women are defending the impunity of the aggressors and attack feminists."[42] The Deneuve letter was denounced by many within the #MeToo movement, well beyond

France.[43] Asia Argento tweeted, "Catherine Deneuve and other French women tell the world how their interiorized misogyny has lobotomized them to the point of no return."[44]

Beginning in late November, articles by #MeToo supporters began warning of the pending backlash from detractors. Most addressed non-feminist critiques.[45] The negative response was entirely predictable; as Jia Tolentino wrote, "Every woman I know has been anticipating a backlash since about thirty seconds after the Weinstein story broke."[46] But as more women joined in—including those who expressly identified as feminists—the backlash narrative was redirected at the likes of Merkin and Deneuve, who, some argued, were not feminists and never had been. Tensions were building, disagreements percolating, and camps dividing. But, the narrative was largely one of backlash—feminist or otherwise. Then came Stassa Edwards.

The Generational Twist

While conflicts had been simmering, the opening salvo in the feminist intergenerational feud belongs to Stassa Edwards's article "The Backlash to #MeToo Is Second Wave Feminism."[47] Edwards blamed "second-wave feminists" for having "rationalized, normalized, and coded abusive, predatory behavior as flirting, as courtship, as the simple reality of being female." She began her critique with yet another feminist flashpoint, Katie Roiphe's rumored exposure of the author of the Shitty Media Men list—a controversial and anonymous spreadsheet listing alleged perpetrators of sexual misconduct—in a forthcoming article in *Harpers*.[48] In response, Moira Donegan scooped Roiphe, outing herself as the list's author in a *New York Magazine* article.[49] Edwards speculated on the content of Roiphe's article, suggesting that, given her past writings as feminist provocateur, Roiphe was likely to downplay the harms of sexual harassment and write off #MeToo as feminist sex-panic hysteria. But, Edwards did not limit her criticism to Roiphe; she took issue with Daphne Merkin and the Catherine Deneuve gang, declaring that "the backlash to #MeToo is indeed here and it's liberal second-wave femi-nism."[50] It was those feminists who were responsible for trying to stop the #MeToo conversation, for "bringing the reckoning to a premature conclusion, suffocating this deeply-needed cultural moment,"[51] and holding onto old power structures. In a direct retort to the feminist crit-ics, and echoing the language of the Deneuve letter, Edwards concluded, "We do not recognize ourselves in your feminism." It is worth noting that Edwards puts equal blame on the "liberal" part of the feminism as she does on the "second wave" part. Whereas #MeToo feminists like Donegan were radical, the critics "smacked of this kind of limited lib-eral feminism, indebted as it is to the preservation of institutions and empowerment through them."[52] Radicals challenge power structures, liberals work within them. But these ideological differences between feminists were lost, and the take-away from Edwards's article was the deep generational divide.

Two days later, on January 13, 2018, two bombshells dropped—the Aziz Ansari story in Babe.net and an article by Margaret Atwood in the *Globe and Mail*. Edwards's generational narrative would quickly gain traction in their wake. First was Margaret Atwood, feminist literary icon and author of *The Handmaid's Tale*, who in an article titled "Am I a Bad Feminist?"[53] describes how she came to be accused of defending a sex-ual harasser, and labeled a bad feminist. The controversy swirled around a high-profile pre–#MeToo sexual harassment allegation at a Canadian university. In 2016, Atwood had signed an open letter to the University of British Columbia (UBC) criticizing its treatment of Steven Galloway, the former chair of the Department of Creative Writing, who had been accused of sexual harassment. The university had announced Gallo-way's suspension from teaching, based on "serious allegations," without further details. The university subsequently fired Galloway, following an investigation by a former judge, but did not release the findings of the inquiry. After seeing the report, the faculty association said that the inquiry had found all but one of the allegations to be unsubstantiated. The UBC accountability letter, signed by some of Canada's literary stars, raised concerns about the violation of due process and asked that an investigation be conducted into the university's handling of the case. The letter produced an uproar within the literary community, with hundreds of writers signing a counter-open letter. They denounced the signers of the UBC accountability letter for failing to express support for the complainants who had come forward.[54]

In "Am I a Bad Feminist?" Atwood returned to the Galloway/UBC accountability letter, but connected it to some of the disturbing trends she saw emerging from the #MeToo movement. Atwood accused her opponents of rushing to judgment and resorting to vigilante justice. Atwood pointed to the Salem witch trials—an analogy she had made in defense of signing the letter.[55] Her opponents—whom she calls "Good Feminists"—had taken exception to this. Atwood sought to clarify that she was referring not to the complainants as hysterical young women., but rather to the structure of the trials as "guilty because accused"[56]—a structure that tends to "kick in during the 'Terror and Virtue' phase of revolutions." Atwood's list of examples was provocative: "the French Revolution, Stalin's purges in the USSR, the Red Guard period in China, the reign of the Generals in Argentina and the early days of the Iranian Revolution."[57] This kind of vigilante justice, of "condemnation without a trial . . . begins as a response to a lack of justice" but can take far more sinister turns. She then turns to the #MeToo movement, describing it as "a symptom of a broken legal system," where women turned to the Internet and "stars fell from the sky." But, she asks, what comes next? "If the legal system is bypassed because it is seen as ineffectual, what will take its place? Who will be the new power brokers?" Her article had already pointed to ominous examples from the past. It will not, she says, be the moderates. Atwood concludes by returning to the idea that the letter represented a war on women. She exhorts feminists—good and bad—to "drop their unproductive squabbling, join forces and direct the spotlight where it should have been all along—at UBC."[58] Transparency and accountability need not be seen as antithetical to women's rights: "A war among women, as opposed to a war on women, is always pleasing to those who do not wish women well. This is a very important moment. I hope it will not be squandered."[59]

Twitter exploded in another feminist flashpoint. Feminists denounced the article and Atwood with it.[60] However, unlike those of Merkin, Deneuve, and the like, Atwood's feminist credentials were harder to dismiss; indeed, the critically acclaimed television adaptation of *The Handmaid's Tale* had taken her to new feminist heights. Instead, many countered with a direct response to Atwood's provocation: "Yes when you prioritize your powerful male friend over sexual assault/harassment victims you are in fact a bad feminist."[61] The title of an article in *Flare Magazine* declared, "Yes, Margaret Atwood *Is* a Bad Feminist."[62] The generational narrative quickly gained traction. Atwood was described as "losing her feminist lustre for many millennial feminists."[63] In an oft-quoted series of tweets, Erika Thorkelson wrote, "If @MargaretAtwood would like to stop warring amongst women, she should stop declaring war against younger, less powerful women and start listening."[64] Thorkelson stated the problem in starkly generational terms: "I realize that for a lot of older women, self preservation meant blinding oneself to the plight of other women. I realize that the skills that allowed you to make it to a position of power are the very skills that are making it difficult for you to feel empathy now."[65] It was older women—aka Atwood—who were not listening to younger women. In the media coverage that ensued, this generational narrative was repeated. Atwood's intervention would frequently be invoked as the embodiment of the problems of second-wave feminism and the generation gap of #MeToo.[66]

Then came the Aziz Ansari article about twenty-three-year-old "Grace," who accused him of sexual misconduct for repeatedly and aggressively pressuring her to have sex on their date, despite her discomfort.[67] She eventually left his apartment in tears and came to understand the experience as sexual assault. On January 14, Ansari released a statement in which he said that he and Grace had "engag[ed] in sexual activity, which by all indications was completely consensual," but that when he "heard that it was not the case for her, I was surprised and concerned."[68] By January 16, the Babe.net article had more than 2.5 million views. The sexual misconduct Grace described resonated with many women as the kind of sexual harm they regularly encounter.

But the article was also met with an outcry that #MeToo had clearly gone too far. Caitlin Flanagan in the *Atlantic*[69] and Bari Weiss in the *New York Times*[70] both denounced it. Flanagan called it "revenge porn," written with the intention to hurt and humiliate Ansari and destroy his career, "which is now the punishment for every kind of male sexual misconduct, from the grotesque to the disappointing."[71] Weiss similarly saw the article as an example of the excesses of #MeToo. While the sexual encounter may have been "lousy"—Weiss describes Ansari as "aggressive and selfish and obnoxious that night"—he did not have power over Grace: "Lumping him in with the same movement that brought down men who ran movie studios and forced themselves on actresses, or the factory floor supervisors who demand sex from female employees trivializes what #MeToo first stood for."[72] Not incidentially, Weiss referenced and linked to Atwood's "Bad Feminist" article, and its warning against casting women as victims incapable of agency.[73]

While critics focused on the Ansari sexual misconduct allegations having taken #MeToo too far, they also played directly into the narrative of a feminist intergenerational feud. Flanagan's opening lines described herself "as just too old" to understand, and described those who supported Grace's allegation of sexual misconduct as "a hit squad of privileged, white young women opening fire on brown-skinned men."[74] Then, there was the Ashleigh Banfield and Katie Way exchange. On January 15, HLN host Ashleigh Banfield read an open letter calling out Ansari's accuser for damaging his reputation over "a bad date." Banfield criticized Grace for failing to leave when the date became "overly amorous" and accused her of "chisel[ing] away at a movement that I, along with all of my sisters in the workplace, have been dreaming of for decades."[75] HLN subsequently sought an interview with Babe.net author Katie Way, who declined the offer but hit back. Way described Banfield as a "burgundy lipstick bad highlights second-wave feminist has been" that "no one under the age of 45 has ever heard of." Way, twenty-two years old, added that "no woman my age would ever watch your network." In turn, Banfield read excerpts from the e-mail on her January 17 show, saying that she did so because "this is not the way we have this conversation as women or men, we don't attack—as journalists, let's be frank—we do not attack people for their age or their highlights or lipstick, because it is the most hypocritical thing a woman who says she supports the women's movement could do."[76]

The generation war was on. Media reports repeatedly framed the controversy in intergenerational terms—millennials versus second-wave feminists.[77] The feminist public sphere also erupted.[78] From Twitter wars to media articles, millennial feminists fought back, adding fuel to the fire. Some, along the lines of Edwards, denounced the backlash as a response by second-wave feminists, whose time had come and gone. Laura Hudson, culture editor of *The Verge* website, tweeted, "I have great respect for the contributions that many older women made to the feminist movement, at times when it was harder than I have ever experienced. It is also time for them to listen, to learn, to step aside."[79]

Some high-profile second-wave feminists waded into the fray. Germaine Greer, in a January 2018 interview, said, "If you spread your legs because he said 'be nice to me and I'll give you a job in a movie' then I'm afraid that's tantamount to consent, and it's too late now to start whingeing about that."[80] While not defending the predatory behavior of Harvey Weinstein, she criticized women's failures to stand up to harassers, to "slap him down," in the moment. In her interview, Greer tried to advance her views on changing the law from rape to sexual assault, advocating "different degrees of gravity according to the amount of damage that you do." While this approach was already adopted in many jurisdictions, the argument got lost among Greer's battles with a younger generation of feminists over her anti-trans views and other more provocative statements: "Now it's becoming if you're in a position of power or influence, you can't make a pass at somebody, because it will be considered to be an inappropriate use of influence, force and so on. . . . How do you express

desire without putting pressure on people?"[81] Echoes of Catherine Deneuve and Bari Weiss were clear, but this time, the objections were expressed by an icon of second-wave feminism. Indeed, Greer expressed
disappointment that Deneuve had backed off her criticism of #MeToo
feminism. (Deneuve apologized to victims of sexual assault who were
offended by her letter, though she did seem to stand firm in her criticism of the movement as subject to abuses.)[82]

Others reinforced the generational narrative, while regretting some
of its tone. Kate Harding, who had been critical of the Franken resignation earlier in the #MeToo cycle, wrote, "The current feminist moment
is becoming marked by, among other things, an excess of intergenerational disrespect on all sides. Just in the last week, 78-year-old Margaret Atwood painted herself as the victim of a witch hunt by younger
feminists, and 22-year-old writer Katie Way condescended mightily to
veteran CNN journalist Ashleigh Banfield, because Banfield treated another young self-identified feminist shabbily on the air."[83] Harding, herself a feminist critic of some of the twists and turns of #MeToo, viewed
this generational conflict as painful but important. Her article was self-
reflexive. She described her growing awareness in watching the #MeToo
movement unfold: "I am now part of a generation whose practice of
feminism is not always relevant to younger women." Harding described
her discomfort—alongside that of "nearly every feminist I know over
40"—with the Babe.net story and the label of "sexual assault" to describe
the encounter, only to then further reflect on her own experiences of
sexual assault as a young woman. Harding sees continuity with today's
young feminists, who have taken the anti-rape lessons from the second
and third wave to heart and are coming of age "with much higher expectations than we had for bodily autonomy, for the right to sexual pleasure,
and for respect for their boundaries. Whatever intergenerational tension
this difference in our expectations produces, it can only be cause for
celebration."[84]

* * *

Not everyone bought into the generational-divide narrative. Some insisted that the backlash was not feminist at all. Claire Fallon of the *Huffington Post* denounced the likes of Roiphe, Flanagan, and Weiss as fake and deeply anti-feminist. In her view, they were engaging in a backlash to #MeToo disguised as feminism.[85] Similarly, Sady Doyle, in her article "It's Not (All) the Second Generation's Fault," attempted to trouble the generational narrative, denouncing Flanagan, Merkin, and Roiphe: "They don't appear to be second-wave feminists, or even just plain feminists, at all."[86] Atwood presented a slightly harder case: "Yes, there are some second-wave feminists participating in the #MeToo backlash—at least, there's one; Margaret Atwood is firmly in the second wave—but to the extent that these critiques resemble any of the feminist ideologies, they mostly resemble a warped, toxic take on the third wave's call for a sex-positive culture."[87] Doyle brought another generation into view, but simultaneously dismissed much of the backlash rhetoric as decidedly not feminist.

The debate raged on. Some claimed that feminist critics like Weiss and Roiphe were too young to be second-wave feminists.[88] Some pointed to the important contributions made by second-wave feminists. Doyle, for example, noted that younger feminists have been blaming so-called second-wave feminists for decades. "In the 1990s and 2000s, second wavers were cast as the shrill, militant, man-hating mothers and grandmothers who got in the way of their daughters' sexual liberation." Doyle went on to suggest that without second-wave feminism, there would probably be no #MeToo, noting the profound influence of Susan Brownmiller, Anita Hill, and Catherine MacKinnon.

Even in this more nuanced approach, second-wave feminism was being positioned as if it were itself homogeneous, obscuring the profound differences within it. Some #MeToo feminists directly addressed the limitations of the generational narrative. Michelle Dean, with her pointedly titled article "Who Are You Calling a Second Wave Feminist?,"[89] wrote, "The second wave wasn't a monolith."[90] Naming some of the feminists associated with the second wave—Betty Friedan and

Robin Morgan, Adrienne Rich and Gloria Steinem—Dean noted, "These women didn't necessarily like or agree with each other." While she did not mention the sex wars, Dean referred to the women-of-color critique that emerged within second-wave feminism as further evidence of the nonhomogeneity of this wave. There were important fractures and tensions within this feminism. In a nod to the earlier sex wars, Dean observed the debt that the current feminist moment owes to these earlier feminists who created sexual harassment laws: "Young feminists tend to dislike Catharine MacKinnon, the law professor who took on pornography, for perceived offenses against the 1st Amendment. They may not realize that it was also MacKinnon who, in the 1970s, wrote the legal theory later adopted by the Supreme Court when Mechelle Vinson sued her employer because her boss demanded that she sleep with him."[91] Others similarly challenged the problematic nature of the wave analysis. Constance Grady expressly stated, "The wave metaphor can be reductive. It can suggest that each wave of feminism is a monolith with a single unified agenda, when in fact the history of feminism is a history of different ideas in wild conflict."[92] While describing the three waves of feminism, and the ideas surrounding the emergence of a fourth in the current moment, Grady resisted casting the debates around #MeToo as a generational war. Instead, she concluded, "It is perhaps more useful to think of it as part of what has always been the history of feminism: passionate disagreement between different schools of thought."[93]

Moira Donegan specifically addressed the problematic and dismissive framing of generational squabbling as a catfight: "The #MeToo moment and its backlash made it clear that there really was a divide among feminists, but analysis of that divide cast it as a mere catfight, or a screaming match between weary mothers and teenage daughters. The implication was that the feminist debate unfolding around #MeToo is a kind of routine domestic drama, something we've seen before."[94] Donegan argued that the disagreement should be explored more deeply for the political and ideological divide it revealed—a divide, in her view, between individualist and social visions of feminism. #MeToo detractors fell within the individualist school of thought, with its focus on personal empowerment, while #MeToo feminists had a more collective vision of the feminist project.

#MeToo feminism was not united on the question of the generational narrative. Some even gestured to the need to better locate #MeToo feminism and its discontents within the history of feminist disagreements—an argument I further develop in the chapters that follow. But, much of this nuance was lost—the preferred narrative being one of a catfight between generations.[95] Headlines like "#MeToo Begins to Show Its Generational Divide," from the much-syndicated Associated Press story,[96] dominated the mainstream media.

Feminism's Generations, Waves, and Tropes

Like all generation gaps, feminism's is not novel but in fact well worn. In the 1990s, disagreements between second- and third-wave feminists were cast as generational conflict. The very discourse of feminism's waves is predicated on generational differences, though not necessarily conflict. In this section, I explore the discourse of waves, gaps, and conflicts within feminism, particularly in terms of their popular representation. I argue that the (mis)representation of generational antagonism, funneled into the narrative of a catfight, was an all-too-handy trope within which to frame the disagreements in #MeToo.

The wave metaphor first appeared in a *New York Times* article in 1968, entitled "The Second Feminist Wave,"[97] which sought to make links between the then-current women's movement demanding social and cultural inequalities and the nineteenth- and early-twentieth-century suffragette movement's activism for the right to vote. "First wave" was coined retrospectively. The metaphor gained traction and took on new resonance with the emergence of the so-called third wave in the early 1990s. On the heels of the Anita Hill hearings, Rebecca Walker announced its arrival in her *Ms. Magazine* article on "Becoming the Third Wave."[98] An outpouring of feminist writing followed, new magazines like *Bust* and *Bitch* featured the work of this generation, and a series of third-wave collections were published.[99] But, from its inception, the third wave was a contested concept. Walker used it to describe her anger and commitment to political activism in the aftermath of Anita Hill's testimony at the Senate Judiciary confirmation hearings of Clarence Thomas:

> I write this as a plea to all women, especially the women of my generation: Let Thomas' confirmation serve to re-mind you, as it did me, that the fight is far from over. Let this dismissal of a woman's experience move you to anger. Turn that outrage into political power. Do not vote for them unless they work for us. Do not have sex with them, do not break bread with them, do not nurture them if they don't prioritize our freedom to control our bodies and our lives. I am not a postfeminism feminist. I am the Third Wave.

Third wave was generational as well as a proclamation of the ongoing importance of feminism—plucking it from the "postfeminist" dust pile. It was a refusal of the claim that feminism was over, declaring it new again. The allegation of its decline had come from older feminists and mainstream culture alike. Some second-wave feminists complained that the younger generation of women was apathetic and depoliticized. Mainstream media declared the death of feminism and the arrival of a postfeminist era. The third wave was born of resistance to all of these narratives.

But, as the term gained traction, its meaning was contested and elusive.[100] Third-wave feminism has been variously described in thematic, generational, and/or issue-based terms. Thematically, it was sometimes said to take its character from poststructural and postcolonial critiques of essentialism in second-wave feminism, with its monolithic notions of sisterhood and the female subject. It was argued that third-wave feminism was inspired by critiques brought by Black and other women of color of second-wave feminism's racial myopia and the failure to integrate an intersectional analysis. Generationally, it was said to apply to younger women—women of Generation X who came of age after the second wave and held a different perspective and set of concerns, in part because "we are the first generation for whom feminism has been entwined in the fabric of our lives." As Baumgardner and Richards wrote, "Feminism is out there, tucked into our daily acts of righteousness and self-respect. . . . For our generation feminism is like fluoride. We scarcely notice that we have it—it's simply in the water."[101] Where the earlier waves of feminism focused on legal and political rights, the third wave broadened its scope to include the everyday—to representation and popular culture, from mainstream media to zines to Riot Grrrl, the underground feminist punk movement. The third wave was said to have eschewed the second wave's sexual negativity in favor of a new sex positivity.[102] From embracing girly culture and femininity to affirming sexual pleasure, the third wave was seen as more inclusive, pluralistic, and nonjudgmental about how individual women negotiate their sexualities.

Then came fourth-wave feminism, which, like its predecessors, is also a contested concept. Even its start date is unclear. In 2009, Jessica Valenti stated, "Maybe the fourth wave is on-line."[103] This wave has been variously described as digital feminism, social media feminism, Internet feminism, and hashtag feminism, and Constance Grady suggests that the "fourth wave's beginnings are often loosely pegged to around 2008, when Facebook, Twitter, and YouTube were firmly entrenched in the cultural fabric and feminist blogs like Jezebel and Feministing were spreading across the web." Kira Cochrane wrote of the fourth wave in the *Guardian* in 2013, "What's happening now feels like something new again. It's defined by technology: tools that are allowing women to build a strong, popular, reactive movement online."[104] The fourth wave seems particularly focused on sexism, rape culture, and sexual harassment, though that does not necessarily distinguish it from what came before. It has been associated with the Slut Walks ignited in 2011 and with London-based Laura Bates's website, Everyday Sexism, an on-line space for women to share their experiences of harassment, sexual assault, workplace discrimination, and other forms of daily sexism.[105] It was popularized by the writing of Jessica Valenti, Roxanne Gay, Rebecca Solnit, and Caitlin Moran and is associated with the viral hashtag #YesAllWomen that got retweeted 1.4 million times in the four days following the mass shooting in Isla Vista, California. A precursor to #MeToo, the hashtag was used by women to share stories of everyday misogyny and sexism.[106] Jennifer Baumgardner, a leading third-wave voice, suggests that the fourth wave evolved to forward the agenda. Much as she described the third wave of feminism as fluoride in the water, so it was with digital fluidity for the fourth wave: "Their experience of the online universe was that it was just part of life." To those who contest the fourth wave she says, "I believe that the Fourth Wave exists because it says that it exists. I believe the Fourth Wave matters, because I remember how sure I was that my generation mattered."[107]

The waves of feminism refer broadly to a chronological sequencing of feminist activism across historical periods. The waves are said to correspond to different generations, with unique issues of focus and distinctive modes of organizing. The wave metaphor has also been the subject of considerable criticism. Many feminist scholars have argued that the idea of successive waves has created an overly monolithic vision of gender activism within any given historical period, as well as a flawed historical narrative about the relationships between the waves.[108] For example, the very idea of a second wave of feminism connected across time to the first generation of the early nineteenth century was created to give the contemporary movement a history. It was not an antagonistic assertion but, rather, served a political purpose. As feminist historian Linda Nicholson has written, "It reminded people that the then current women's rights and women's liberation movements had a venerable past—that these movements were not historical aberrations but part of a long tradition of activism."[109] However, it was a misleading history. Nicholson has argued that the second-wave metaphor created a false connection, suggesting that the gender activism of the past and present could be united around a similar set of feminist ideas, when in fact, the suffragette movement was more divided, and not entirely feminist.[110] It is a reduction that "obfuscates the historical specificity of gender activism." The creation of a connected past and a common identity—what gets called "generationing"—"implies a sort of shared 'reinvention' of the past . . . as a tool to establish or symbolise the belonging to a group."[111] Generationing typically "includes a process of self-definition (of the group) that can be called individuation (of common traits of the members) and a process of differentiation from other groups (members of other generations)."[112] First-wave feminism as a concept was produced by second-wave feminism to serve as its own past.

Other scholars have focused on a similar process of generationing by third-wave feminism that reduced the complex histories and activisms of the second wave. Distinguishing the third wave involved assertions of the collective nature of not only its own identity but also that of the wave that came before. The very process of self-definition and differentiation from the second wave required not only a break from the past but a homogenization of that past. Second-wave feminism was unfairly and inaccurately reduced to a common set of beliefs and sensibilities and often cast, among other things, as white, essentialist, anti-men, anti-sex, anti-agency, and anti-fun. This "popular caricature of second-wave feminism provide[s] a convenient foil against which third-wave feminism can define itself."[113] But as a caricature, it also erased the many contestations within it. From African American and other women of color challenging its racial myopia to the deeply divisive disagreements about sexuality of the sex wars, the political and ideological diversity of the gender activism during this period was rendered invisible.

This reductionist caricaturing was most evident in the popular feminism that emerged in the early 1990s work of Katie Roiphe, Christina Hoff Sommers, Rene Denfeld, and Naomi Wolf. These writers launched an attack on the victim feminism of the second wave. Katie Roiphe's *Morning After: Sex, Fear, and Feminism on Campus* was a scathing critique of the anti-rape movement on college campuses.[114] She disputed the prevalence of date rape and argued that feminism was casting young women as victims who failed to take responsibility for their sexual behavior. Similarly, Christina Hoff Sommers argued that the contemporary feminist movement had been hijacked by radical feminists, whose focus on women as victims of male violence was divorced from the reality of women's lives.[115] She placed the blame squarely on second-generation feminists. Rene Denfeld, in *The New Victorians*, also painted contemporary feminism as a victim feminism, defined by a repressive, prudish ideology reminiscent of the Victorian era.[116] Naomi Wolf, in *Fight Fire with Fire*, took issue with the victim feminism of the second wave and advocated for a power feminism in its place.[117] Second-wave feminists, Wolf said, were "sexually judgmental, even antisexual," and fearful that "to have too much fun poses a threat to the revolution."[118]

These writers received considerable mainstream attention, shaping much of the popular discourse around third-wave feminism and driving many second-wave feminists to push back. In a high-profile quarrel, Susan Faludi dismissed these writers as "pseudo feminists" feeding the patriarchy's backlash against the women's movement's demand for equality.[119] While many self-identified third-wave feminists, as reflected in various edited collections, explicitly rejected Roiphe, Denfeld, and the others as not representative of their movement, these flashpoints had a lingering effect on the popular perception of third-wave feminism, and its conflictual relationship with the second wave. These were, in many respects, the postfeminist writers that Walker and others were reacting against. Although Roiphe and the others did not adopt the third-wave label, they identified as younger women and launched a full-scale assault on the second wave. These writers rejected the alleged victim feminism, Victorian sexuality, and totalizing patriarchal oppression of the second wave.

Despite the disavowal of this narrative by many within the self-identified third wave, the disagreements between older second-wave feminists and these popular feminisms, faux or not, was cast in generational—and conflictual—terms. Not only did the generational paradigm simplify the heterogeneous feminism of both the second and the third wave, but it also became deeply divisive.[120] Waves became synonymous with generations, and differences became evidence of generational conflict. Ideological divides were collapsed into generational ones, through the trope of the generation gap. Many criticized this trope for erasing important questions and nuances in ideological difference, even as it was emerging. Leveen Lois wrote, in 1996, in a critique of Katie Roiphe, "Proclaiming 'my generation is different and therefore better' is a simple answer to the difficult questions raised by discrepancies in ideology and experience but that does not mean it is the correct answer to those questions. Similarly, nostalgizing or demonizing the past serve equally well, depending on the speaker, as a means to avoid the harder work of negotiating the challenges of the present."[121] The assertion of a monolithic past as part of a distinctive generational present may have helped to shore up political subjectivities and agendas by creating an "us versus them," but it did so by running roughshod over the complexities and contradictions of gender activism across different historical periods: "Generational paradigms, then, do not provide an accurate trope for explaining actual differences but rather an easy but inaccurate metaphor invoked by individuals with widely diverging agendas."[122]

This generational narrative was deployed in popular culture and mainstream media, in ways that amplified division and antagonism. Alice Winch, concerned like so many others with the pejorative framing of the "catfight," has observed,

> The media report and foreground moments when feminists disparage each other, honing in on instances of generational hostility in order to amplify them. Using the trope of the catfight between women of different ages is a key way in which feminism is depicted, as it is effective in locating feminism in the past, as no longer relevant, while simultaneously framing differences between activists as insurmountable.[123]

"The generational catfight between feminists became a favorite media handle for discussing feminism."[124] Nothing new, it has been used to frame ideological disagreements from one wave to another through to the current #MeToo moment. Ideological conflict is reduced to generational conflict, which is, in turn, reduced to the catfight: the nasty way that women battle it out over scarce resources, be they men, power, or professional success. Cultural historian Susan Douglas has explored the way the catfight has operated as a "staple of American popular culture."[125] She described the catfight as an "especially sloppy faux combat," characterized by catlike fighting—hair pulling, scratching, and biting—in contrast to a "real" fight by men.[126] Catfights are simultaneously eroticized and belittling. Calling a disagreement a catfight is a highly gendered way of dismissing its seriousness. The emphasis on women's competition with one another implicitly dismisses and ridicules feminism's collaborative objective of improving women's lives. The feminist catfight in popular culture and mainstream media is a kind of mockery of feminism, depicting women as unable to transcend their petty rivalries. It was a trope always at the ready to absorb meaningful feminist disagreement.

The fourth wave as it has emerged was not expressed in particularly oppositional terms. Fourth-wave feminism was talked about as something digital, exciting, and different that engaged younger women on-line. It was generational, insofar as it was expressed as the gender activism of millennials. But it did not exhibit the kind of generational antagonism against the second or third waves that preceded it—not, that is, until the #MeToo conflicts appeared, at which time the trope of generational conflict was again deployed, providing a simple and reductive explanation of the disagreements. Some #MeToo feminists resisted the generational narrative, for many of the same reasons that feminist scholars have resisted the wave/generational metaphor. Sady Doyle, Michelle Dean, and Constance Grady each addressed elements of this critique, rejecting the caricaturing of the second wave as a monolith and suggesting that attention should instead be focused on the history of ideological difference. Donegan flagged both the ease of generation-gap narratives—characterized by "ageism and incuriosity—the reflexive pre-sumptions that the old are too timid and the young are too reckless"—and the tendency to categorize feminism, in contrast to other political movements, in waves.[127] However, she also squarely laid part of the blame for the generational narrative on #MeToo detractors:

> But another reason why #MeToo has been framed as a generational conflict is because the individualist feminists of the anti–#MeToo backlash have framed their own resistance to the movement as grounded in wisdom, realism and, above all, maturity. To them, all this talk of a reimagined, recreated new world sounds hopelessly naive. Daphne Merkin summed up the tenor of the anti–#MeToo assessment in her article in *The New York Times*, when she wrote to the women coming forward: "Grow up, this is real life."[128]

Yet, putting the blame on the #MeToo detractors for restarting the gen-erational war is perhaps to downplay Donegan's first point: that the generational narrative is an easy-to-grab, familiar way to package the feminist conflict. The detractors resorted to the language and sensibilities of generational conflict precisely because it was such a common trope.

CONCLUSION

The generational divide was a well-worn trope deployed to make simple sense of feminist conflict. When feminist disagreement emerged within #MeToo, it was an easy metaphor to invoke. But, as critiques of the femi-nist wave and generational frames have pointed out, it is a metaphor that obscures widely divergent ideological positions. The generation gap is enduring, as much for psychoanalytic as for historical reasons. However, a genealogy of the present requires a break from its totalizing worldview, wherein everything is seen through its lens. The generation metaphor distorts both the historical and the intellectual continuities and discontinuities.

This is not to say that there are no generational differences. Some feminist scholars have explored the specificity of the third wave, recognizing the ways in which the "specific socio-historical context . . . produces new configurations of gender relations," and with it, new subjectivities of gender activism.[129] Just as an overemphasis on generational conflict can flatten the differences within successive waves of feminist activism, so too could a rejection of differences *tout court* between generations flatten the historical specificity of each period. In challenging the narrative, I do not suggest that generational experience and affect are not at play. Younger women—millennials and Generation Yers—have come of age and are negotiating their professional and personal lives in a very different society and sexual landscape than the Baby Boomers of second-wave feminism, or the Generation Xers of the third wave. The history of this present has yet to be written. Digital culture has transformed the everyday world, including the everyday experience of sexism. Scholars have begun to explore the particular ways in which digital cultures are mediating gender and sexuality, across sexual expressions, identities, and practices.[130] Nor can younger women be faulted for imagining that the world was going to be a safer place. Second- and third-wave feminists fought the battles for new laws against sexual assault and sexual harassment. As mothers, they told their millennial daughters they could do or be anything they wanted. It turns out that that was not true. An entirely legitimate frustration and anger erupted with the #MeToo movement.

A reparative reading needs to leave space for generational variances—in experience and affect. But, a generational narrative alone is limiting and obscures so many of the underlying differences and disagreements. As I argue in the chapters that follow, the debates within #MeToo also track those of the sex wars. Illustrating the principled points of disagreement around sexuality, consent, and law can, in my view, elucidate the stakes, beyond the generational impasse and anger. There are significant principled differences in understanding that characterize earlier feminist disagreements—disagreements that continue to play out. Appreciating these differences is a first step in finding ways to negotiate them.

2

FEMINIST SEX WARS

Then and Now

The feminist sex wars of the 1970s and 1980s were highly polarizing and antagonistic debates between feminists. While sexuality, sexual representations, and sexual practices were all contested, no issue was as divisive as pornography. On one side were anti-pornography, or radical, feminists who equated the sexual objectification of women with sexual violence and oppression. On the other side were sex-radical feminists, who rejected this vision and the theory of sexuality on which it was predicated, seeking to create space for the liberatory potential of sexuality for women. The story of the sex wars has been told many times.[1] My objective here is to offer a brief feminist intellectual history of these debates, past and present, and tease out the commonalities. To truly understand where we are right now requires that we return to this feminist past. Through the lens of feminist flashpoints, I tell the story of the sex wars, then and now, and the underlying disagreements around sexuality, agency, and law that continue to plague us.

I pay particular attention to debates about the role of law—less discussed than other aspects of the sex wars. The highly visible radical feminists advocating censorship versus the sex radicals who opposed it is a narrative that only reflects the final stage of these wars, when the two sides lined up over the Civil Rights Ordinance, and law itself became a site of struggle over the meaning of pornography and sexuality. However, radical feminists themselves were divided over the question of legal regulation and censorship. Further, the focus on censorship has left critical questions of law's role in the legal regulation of sexuality unexplored and unresolved. While lawyers and legal academics were not prominent in the sex wars until the final stage, there were nascent and divergent theories of law emerging on both sides—differences that carry forward into the current feminist contestations.

The chapter then turns to what I call "Sex Wars 2.0." While this part of the chapter is no longer focused on pornography, I argue that current feminist debates on sexual harm track the same disagreements as earlier sex wars. Both sides state their opposition to sexual violence, but disagree on how to define and regulate it. On one side, feminists seek stricter enforcement of existing laws, as well as harsher civil and criminal penalties for both sexual harassment and sexual assault, pointing to the pervasive nature of sexual violence against women, the under-enforcement of existing laws, and the lax penalties against even those convicted. On the other side, feminists are critical of the overly broad definitions of sexual harassment and sexual assault, as well as the potential overreach for criminal and civil remedies.[2] Some argue that the definitions of sexual harassment, on campuses and beyond, are too broad, potentially lumping in consensual sexual behavior.[3] Others debate the appropriate definition of consent, questioning the feminist enthusiasm for affirmative consent.[4] By reviewing some of the high-profile flashpoints of Sex Wars 2.0, particularly in relation to campus sexual violence, I argue that these debates fracture along the same axes of disagreement about sexuality, consent, and law that figured in the early sex wars.

PART ONE: THE SEX WARS THEN

The Beginning

The 1970s witnessed the emergence of a feminist critique of male sexual violence and heterosexuality as an oppressive institution for women. Groundbreaking books—Susan Brownmiller's *Against Our Will*, Andrea Dworkin's *Women Hating*, and Dianne Russell's *Politics of Rape* focused feminist attention on the link between sexual violence against women and women's oppression. While initially the critique of pornography

was subsumed within this more general critique of sexual violence, pornography was increasingly being named as a culprit. As early as 1974,
Robin Morgan proclaimed that "pornography is the theory, rape is the
practice."[5] Brownmiller identified pornography as part of the problem:
"Pornography, like rape, is a male intervention, designed to dehumanize
women, to reduce the female to an object of sexual access."[6] Dworkin
focused in on pornography in *Women Hating* as a practice of women's
oppression.

Anti–violence-against-women activists began to take a keen interest in the representations of sexual violence. In 1976, Women against
Violence Against Women (WAVAW) was founded in Los Angeles, focusing on sexual violence in mainstream media and arguing that these
images demean and dehumanize women and reinforce their oppression.
WAVAW did not focus on pornography, but on violence against women
more generally.[7] Yet, the group's genesis lay in protests against a horror
film entitled *Snuff*. The film had a violent murder scene spliced onto the
end, seemingly committed by the film crew. It was intended to look like
an unplanned and authentic murder. The film opened in New York to
much publicity and controversy, with protests leading to an investigation by the New York district attorney, who concluded that the scene
was simulated. In Los Angeles, WAVAW sought to prevent the film's
release, then protested its screenings. While demanding boycotts of the
theater chain, they also turned to law, persuading a municipal judge and
local police to view the film. The court found that the film violated the
state obscenity law. More protests ensued, and within a week of opening,
the theater chain withdrew the film, prompting the ad hoc WAVAW to
come together as a formal organization.

But, WAVAW strategies were subsequently focused on consumer boycotts, letter-writing campaigns, and public protests. The organization
rejected government censorship, demanding instead "that companies
exercise 'corporate responsibility.'"[8] "We oppose censorship from simple
self-interest: we want to protect our own freedom to speak publicly, however limited it may be in practical terms."[9] The underlying sentiment

was one that would find resonance with other anti-censorship feminists, regardless of their positions on pornography, namely, that state censorship would likely result in the censorship of feminist voices.[10] WAVAW organized a national boycott against Warner Communications, in relation to the advertising campaign of the Rolling Stones' album *Black and Blue*: "I'm Black and Blue with Rolling Stones." WAVAW distinguished the boycott from censorship: "We are not advocating censorship but rather encouraging people to realize that as consumers we have the right to make an economic vote in regards to the policies of industry."[11] The distinction between demanding corporate responsibility and government action, one subsequently lost in the narratives of the sex wars, is important to keep in view, as decades later the #MeToo movement would make reminiscent demands. WAVAW activists wanted change; but they did not turn to the state for it. Despite an early success in using the courts and obscenity law, WAVAW steered away from censorship.

The first feminist organization to specifically target pornography, Women against Violence in Pornography and Media (WAVPM), was founded in San Francisco in 1977. Some of its founding members, Dianne Russell, Kathleen Barry, Laura Lederer, and Susan Griffin, would each author key anti-pornography texts. WAVPM not only targeted pornography; it often focused on S/M pornography. In what would come to be a common trope of anti-porn feminism, Dianne Russell in her 1977 *Chrysalis* article, deployed images of S/M to exemplify pornography as violence against women: "Women are portrayed as enjoying being raped, spanked, or beaten, tied up, mutilated and enslaved." Consensual sexual practices were conflated with rape; S/M imagery as the stand-in for all pornography equated with violence against women. One of their first protests was a local theater with live sex acts that WAVPM identified as S/M-themed.

WAVPM's position came to the attention of the local lesbian S/M community, who in 1978 founded Samois. Two of its founding members, Pat Califia and Gayle Rubin, would go on to publish key sex-radical texts and become leading voices in the sex wars. They were disturbed by the conflation of S/M sexuality and violence against women. Their written requests of WAVPM to discuss their position on S/M were repeatedly rebuffed.[12] The escalation of conflict between WAVPM and Samois represents the beginning of the sex wars. WAVPM would refuse to allow members of Samois to attend their conferences, buy their slide shows, or otherwise engage with them.[13] This early framing of anti-pornography feminism and sadomasochism as ideological opponents would be deployed throughout much of the sex wars.[14]

In 1978, WAVPM organized the first ever national anti-pornography feminism conference, which culminated with the first Take Back the Night March. Much of the conference focused on the emerging critique of pornography, its link to violence against women, and the opposition to S/M. But, the conference also gestured to internal divisions on the use of law. Whereas WAVAW had clearly eschewed any resort to law or censorship, WAVPM was divided. Speakers at a panel on legal restrictions on pornography and the First Amendment were equally divided. Susan Brownmiller and Jill Lippitt, a lawyer and board member of WAVPM, favored using law, while Susan Griffin and Camille LeGrand argued against it. Lippitt argued that the next generation of feminist lawyers could draft laws "to eliminate violent porn while protecting artistic expression."[15] She supported prohibiting "the mass distribution of for-profit films and periodicals which visually and explicitly depict women and children in a violent, degrading and brutal manner." In contrast, LeGrand claimed that any such legislation would be used against women; the selective and political enforcement would result in censoring feminist, gay, and lesbian materials. LeGrand reminded the audience of the history of the Comstock legislation, which had been used against dissemination of birth control information.[16] At the closing speech of the conference, Dianne Russell unequivocally threw her support behind the use of law: "Portraying women . . . bound, raped, beaten. . . . for sexual stimulation . . . should be banned."[17] The schisms ascribed to the feminist sex wars were in fact dividing anti-pornography feminists themselves. The speakers agreed on the analysis of pornography and sexual violence, but they disagreed on the question of law.

In 1979 Women Against Pornography (WAP) was set up in New York City and included Susan Brownmiller, Laura Lederer, Andrea Dworkin, Robin Morgan, and Gloria Steinem. The organization's mandate was to eliminate hard-core pornography. The same year, Andrea Dworkin published *Pornography: Men Possessing Women*, a foundational text of anti-pornography feminism. Dworkin argued that pornography was a system of domination and submission, eroticizing the abuse, humiliation, and subordination of women: "Pornography is a celebration of rape and injury to women."[18] The feminist critique as articulated by WAP feminists now saw pornography not only as a causal factor of sexual violence but as a site of harm and violence toward women.

It was during the same period that some anti-pornography feminists began to articulate a distinction between erotica and pornography. Gloria Steinem argued that there was a "clear and present difference" between the two—that feminist objections to pornography were not wholesale rejections of sexual representations or, indeed, of sex.[19] Erotica was "a mutually pleasurable, sexual expression between two people who have enough power to be there by positive choice," whereas in pornography, "its message is violence, dominance and conquest. It is sex being used to reinforce some inequality, or to create one, or to tell us that pain and humiliation are really the same as pleasure."[20] Steinem recognized that the religious Right made no distinction, supporting instead the "indiscriminate repression of all non-procreative sex."[21] The distinction would come under heavy criticism from sex radicals as unsustainably subjective. But, given that the anti-pornography feminists would also come to be criticized as "anti-sex prudes," it is important to recognize that some radical feminists were seeking to carve out a sex-positive space, albeit a limited one. And it was one that implicitly recognized some limited possibilities for women's sexual agency; as Steinem described the erotic, it represented sexual encounters where women had "enough power to be there by choice." As the sex wars escalated, this recognition of the possibility of agency would get overshadowed by the radical feminist emphasis on women as victims of sexual violence.

WAP did not initially endorse censorship. Wendy Kaminer, at the time a member of WAP, drafted its position paper on the First Amendment: "We do not advocate censorship. We respect First Amendment strictures against prior restraint on any form of expression."[22] The position paper stated that WAP did not seek to close any "businesses that deal in pornography" or advocate for "any general prohibitions on the publication or production of pornographic material." WAP vowed to respect the privacy of individuals in their homes: "We have not put forward any repressive legislative proposals and we are not carving out any new exceptions to the First Amendment." But, it did not eschew law entirely. Rather, it endorsed a change in the definition of obscenity, so that "it focuses on violence, not sex." The statement emphasized that this would be done within the existing procedural requirements of obscenity law, which held that obscenity is not protected speech. The statement also hinted toward future proposals: "We are working hard . . . to develop strategies for effective private action against the pornography industry." The nature of such action was not elaborated; however, it seemed like a harbinger of the civil rights ordinances that were to come a few years later.

While WAP did not endorse censorship, many of WAP's leaders became increasingly outspoken supporters of legislative action. Brownmiller continued to argue that pornography did not deserve First Amendment protection—that the degrading and dehumazing images of women should be restricted. In an opinion piece in a local newspaper, and then, in front of a national audience on the *Phil Donahue Show*, Brownmiller argued that legislative action was needed to address the problem of pornography.[23] While other anti-pornography feminists who appeared alongside Brownmiller on the show endorsed WAVAW-like consumer boycotts, it was increasingly the voices of those in favor of legal restrictions that were at the forefront of the movement.

As the anti-pornography movement picked up steam, dissenting feminist voices began to emerge. After running a workshop at WAP's 1979 East Coast conference, Ellen Willis challenged WAP's analysis of pornography in a highly influential article in the *Village Voice* that set out many of the themes of the sex-radical critique.[24] She challenged WAP's sweeping condemnation of pornography, by suggesting that women could enjoy and be empowered by it. WAP's attempt to redefine pornography as violence, not sex, fell apart since not all pornography depicts violence. Nor did WAP's attempt to distinguish pornography from erotica hold up: "What turns me on is erotic; what turns you on is pornographic."[25] Willis insisted on the possibility of women's sexual agency in viewing pornography:

> A woman who is raped is a victim; a woman who enjoys pornography (even if that means enjoying a rape fantasy) is in a sense a rebel, insisting on an aspect of her sexuality that has been defined as a male preserve. Insofar as pornography glorifies male supremacy and sexual alienation, it is deeply reactionary. But in rejecting sexual repression and hypocrisy—which have inflicted even more damage on women than on men—it expresses a radical impulse.[26]

Willis identified an anti-sex sentiment in the anti-pornography critique. WAP's focus on erotica as "beautiful, romantic, soft, nice, and devoid of messiness, vulgarity, impulses to power, or indeed aggression" was feminine, not feminist, their repulsion by heterosexuality "the thinnest of covers for disgust with sex itself." Willis also took on WAP's positions on legal interventions. She observed that although Brownmiller and others claimed not to advocate censorship, they had endorsed the Supreme Court's position that obscenity is not protected speech. She set out an anti-censorship argument that would become a sex-radical staple: obscenity law—even one redefined to focus on violence, not sex—would only be used against dissenting sexualities: "In a male supremacist society the only obscenity law that will not be used against women is no law at all." The core of what would emerge as the sex-radical position— sexuality as a site of pleasure, an insistence on the possibility of women's agency, and a critique of the use of law—were all present in Willis's article

In 1980, the National Organization of Women (NOW) passed its Resolution on Lesbian Rights, a resolution that included a denunciation of pornography, prostitution, S/M, and pederasty. The resolution indicated that anti-pornography feminists were now center stage in the national women's movement. But the resolution also spawned further dissent and mobilized opposition. In one letter published in the feminist magazine *Plexus* following the resolution, over 190 activists and academics denounced the resolution as "advancing an oversimplified and puritanical ideology."[27] Another letter drafted by emerging feminist leaders of the sex-radical position, including Ellen Willis, condemned the "tone and substance of the resolution [as] offensively moralistic. . . . We believe that all people . . . have an inalienable right to freedom of sexual association with a consenting partner, regardless of whether others approve of their behavior."[28]

Califia and Rubin's work would continue to insist on S/M as a consensual sexual practice and take anti-pornography feminism to task for its narrow conception of women's sexuality, sexual variance, and consent.[29] The emerging sex-radical position focused on the negative and conservative sexual ideology that embodied the critique of pornography and S/M sexuality, as well as on the importance of consent. These voices were amplified in the Sex Issue of *Heresies* in 1981, the first collection of feminists concerned with anti-pornography advocates' negative approach to sexuality. While the editorial collective noted the lack of consensus on any issues, they wrote that a common theme was exploring sexual desire. The collection included poems, drawings, cartoons, short stories and nonfiction essays. Pat Califia once again defended S/M sexuality as consensual. Paula Webster's 1992 essay "Pornography and Pleasure" not only condemned anti-pornography feminism's narrow conception of sexuality but argued for a more positive vision in which feminism should include "an active pursuit of our gratification." Webster argued that envisioning women "only as victims of sex" would continue to undermine women's "sexual autonomy and subjectivity." She insisted, "It is time to organize for our pleasure as well as protection."[30]

The sex-radical feminist position was coalescing, articulating the need for a more positive vision of sexuality that affirmed pleasure and agency.

The debates over the use of law escalated in the early 1980s, as some anti-pornography feminists became alarmed with the rise of the new Right and the highly conservative, anti-sex climate that it was ushering in. Jill Lippitt, lawyer and WAVPM member, who at the 1978 conference had argued in favor of using law, rejected the use of law in 1980: "I simply do not trust what the patriarchal, racist and elitist state would do with the expanded powers of suppression which we feminists might give to them," she wrote in *NewsPage*. WAVPM formally rejected the pursuit of new legislation or government action against pornography in 1981.[31] Wendy Kaminer, a lawyer who had previously written WAP's position paper on censorship, resigned her membership in 1980 because of First Amendment concerns. Kaminer, who went on to become an anti-censorship advocate and eventually a #MeToo feminist detractor, wrote in WAVPM's newsletter that anti-pornography should stay focused on education, not censorship.[32] Giving the state the power to ban pornography would be "far more dangerous to us all than the 'power' of pornography."[33]

The Middle: The Barnard Conference

By 1982, many battle lines had already been drawn. Dissident feminist voices expressed concern over the narrow conception of sexuality espoused by anti-pornography feminism. Censorship was becoming a site of contestation, although it divided the anti-pornography feminists as well. Then came the "Barnard—The Scholar and the Feminist IX: Towards a Politics of Sexuality" conference, held at Barnard College. The explosive conference came to be described as a defining moment of the sex wars. But the stage had already been set.

In her letter of invitation, Carole Vance expressed hope that the conference's focus on sexuality would advance the current debate. Vance noted that growing feminist interest in the issue as represented in journals, magazines, and "recent activism on pornography and sexual violence" did not exhaust the range of women's experiences. The conference would seek to expand the conversation, beginning with the question, "How do women get sexual pleasure in patriarchy?"[34] Although the conference was not intended to focus solely on pornography but rather to raise a broad range of sexuality issues, from the rise of the New Right to the significance of racial and class differences in women's experiences of sexuality, organizers were nonetheless cognizant of the "potential explosiveness of a conference on sexuality, given the current polarization in the feminist community on the issue of pornography."[35] Vance's concept paper opened by stating, "The conference will address women's sexual pleasure, choice and autonomy, acknowledging that sexuality is simultaneously a domain of restriction, repression and danger as well as a domain of exploration, pleasure and agency."[36] It argued that it would be wrong to focus only on pleasure without addressing patriarchy, sexual violence, and agency. From its inception, the conference was designed to explore sexuality as a site of both pleasure and danger.

Despite the broad agenda, in a controversial decision, anti-pornography feminists were not invited.[37] The week before the conference, women who identified themselves as members of anti-pornography groups denounced "the conference organizers for inviting proponents of 'anti-feminist' sexuality to participate. They criticized the conference for promoting patriarchal values antithetical to the basic tenets of feminism, and they objected to particular participants by name, reportedly portraying them as sexual deviants."[38] Two days before the conference, in a decision made by Barnard president Ellen Futter, college administration seized fifteen hundred copies of *The Diary of a Conference on Sexuality*, intended for participants.[39]

The day of the conference, anti-pornography feminists arrived to protest. They distributed a leaflet entitled "We Protest," signed by the Coalition for a Feminist Sexuality and against Sadomasochism,[40] which accused the conference of "silencing the views of a major portion of the women's movement." The leaflet stated that not only had feminists opposed to pornography been excluded but also the conference included "organizations that support and produce pornography, that promote sex roles and sadomasochism, and that have joined the straight and gay pedophile organizations in lobbying for an end to laws that protect children from sexual abuse by adults." Organizations and individuals were named, including No More Nice Girls and Ellen Willis, Samois and Gayle Rubin, and the Lesbian Sex Mafia and Dorothy Allison. In endorsing "pornography, sex roles, and sadomasochism and equating it with liberation for women," the conference was promoting the very values and institutions that oppress women.

The leaflet became a lightning rod of controversy, "outing" individual women associated with marginal sexual practices, containing inaccurate allegations, and garnering media attention. Extensive quotations were published in *Off Our Backs* and the leaflet in its entirety was published in *Feminist Studies*, without the names redacted. Some of the organizations and women named were not associated with S/M sexual practices. No More Nice Girls, for example, was primarily associated with abortion rights, and had endorsed neither pornography nor S/M. As a petition objecting to the leaflet stated, "The effect was to stigmatize those individuals identified with controversial sexual views or practices."[41] In a letter to *Feminist Studies*, Carole Vance wrote, "You don't seem to understand that the sexual margin is a very dangerous place, peopled by employers who fire you, landlords who evict you, and police who arrest you. If you are not on, or accused of being on, a sexual margin, you need to educate yourself about the situation of women who are, be aware of the very real threats they face, and act responsibly in protecting them."[42]

The tactics were denounced by conference participants and others: "Feminist discussion about sexuality cannot be carried on if one segment of the feminist movement uses McCarthyite tactics to silence other voices."[43] Joan Nestle—one of the "unnamed women" accused of "championing butch/femme sex roles"—said, "They use guilt by association, distortion, and censorship," tactics she described as "familiar to the McCarthy era in which if you went to a Pete Seeger concert, you were subpoenaed because he had been subpoenaed."[44] Ellen Willis wrote, "This

is nothing less than a demand for a blacklist, which no radical movement worthy of the name can countenance."[45] The editors of *Feminist
Studies* subsequently issued an apology for reproducing the leaflet, and
invited the women named in it to respond.[46] For many, the damage had
been done.

Vance argued that the leaflet, with its focus on the so-called big
three—pornography, S/M, and butch/femme—as well as subsequent
media coverage, "gave birth to a phantom conference" that bore little
relationship to the actual one.[47] A glance at the program—and the
Diary—shows the broad range of sexuality issues, including those three
topics, on the agenda: anti-abortion activism; teenage romance novels;
age, weight, and disability discrimination; sexual purity; and the maintaining of class and racial boundaries.

The Barnard protest further mobilized the sex-radical movement.
From public petitions to private conversations, sex-radical feminists articulated their positions and garnered broad support for an alternative
discussion of sexuality. As Lynn Comella argued, "Barnard helped mo-
bilize, in a much more concerted way, feminist opposition to the anti-
pornography position. . . . It helped to create what we might think of as
a social formation, a coalition of sex radicals and pro-sex feminists committed to sexual freedom, autonomy and anti-censorship."[48] It not only
"crystallized opposing viewpoints and political stances" but simultaneously created an oppositional discourse that entrenched reductionist
views of each side. The ensuing "ideological turf war over who defines
feminism's relationship to sexuality" saw each side's perception of the
other feature almost as prominently as their actual views.[49] Nuance was
lost, as feminist disagreement took a decidedly nasty turn, with ad ho-
minem attacks, denunciations of intellectual opponents as anti-feminist,
and reductionist misrepresentations of interlocutors. The polarization
would deepen post-Barnard.

The conference aftermath saw a clear articulation of the sex-radical
vision of sexuality—one that emphasized sexual pleasure and brought
women's sexual agency into view, while not rejecting the premise that

sexuality was also a site of danger. The sex radicals sought to affirm the neglected side of the danger/pleasure, victim/agent binaries; but their express purpose was to reduce sexual danger and increase the possibilities of sexual pleasure in women's lives. The fundamentally different understandings of sexuality and agency that characterized the sex wars were coming into focus, despite the often reductionist account. The question of law, in contrast, was largely absent or at best marginal in the discussions. The Comstock laws made an appearance in Dubois and Gordon's analysis of nineteenth-century feminism. Gayle Rubin explored the role of sex laws in criminalizing consensual but marginal sexuality. But law had not yet emerged as a major preoccupation of the anti-pornography feminists, and thus was not a concern of the sex radicals. That would change in the final stage of the sex wars, where the two would face off again, but this time, directly on the terrain of law.

The End: Civil Rights Ordinance and FACT

The final major battle of the sex wars revolved around an attempt to regulate pornography, spearheaded by Catharine MacKinnon and Andrea Dworkin through municipal civil rights. This phase is seen to epitomize the sex wars, and its divides. It marked a distinctive phase—and a continued narrowing of the focus of the sexuality debates. MacKinnon, not a player in the earlier sex wars, only arrived on the scene as a young lawyer in the post-Barnard moment and would come to exert enormous influence over legal feminism and beyond, including over the Sex Wars 2.0.[50]

The role of law had been a source of discord among anti-pornography feminists, and none of the organizations took an unequivocal position in favor of it—at least, not until the arrival of MacKinnon and the Civil Rights Ordinance. Many anti-pornography feminists supported legal action, but none had been actively pursued. Others, who shared the anti-pornography analysis, strongly opposed the use of law. The sex radical feminists had not focused their critique on law; while some had expressed concern over censorship strategies, their focus tended to be on articulating alternative visions of women's sexuality and sexual autonomy. But, in the ordinance phase, law became the site of conflict.

The ordinance battles began in 1983. Post-Barnard debates were still raging in the pages of the feminist press, with letters to the editors in *Off Our Backs* and *Feminist Review*. MacKinnon and Dworkin, who had been coteaching a course on pornography at the University of Minnesota law school, were asked to testify at a Minneapolis public hearing about restructuring adult-business zoning laws. They argued against the zoning ordinance, and instead in favor of a civil rights approach to pornography. They were subsequently hired to draft revisions to the city's Civil Rights Ordinance that would define pornography as sex discrimination.[51]

The ordinance stated the anti-pornography feminist position in unequivocal terms: "Pornography is central in creating and maintaining the civil inequality of the sexes. Pornography is a systematic practice of exploitation and subordination based on sex which differentially harms women." The ordinance defined pornography as

the sexually explicit subordination of women, whether in pictures or in words, that also includes one or more of the following: (i) women are presented dehumanized as sexual objects, things or commodities; or (ii) women are presented as sexual objects who enjoy pain or humiliation; or (iii) women are presented as sexual objects who experience sexual pleasure in being raped; or (iv) women are presented as sexual objects tied up or cut up or mutilated or bruised or physically hurt; or (v) women are presented in postures or positions of sexual submission, servility, or display; or (vi) women's body parts—including but not limited to vaginas, breasts, or buttocks—are exhibited such that women are reduced to those parts; or (vii) women are presented as whores by nature; or (viii) women are presented being penetrated by objects or animals; or (ix) woman are presented in scenarios of degradation, injury, torture, shown as filthy or inferior, bleeding, bruised, or hurt in a context that makes these conditions sexual.[52]

The ordinance created four unlawful discriminatory practices: trafficking (the production, sale, exhibition, or distribution of pornography), coercion into performing for pornography, forced exposure to pornography, and assault caused by pornography. Individuals could bring a civil rights action on the basis of any of these practices. The remedy included damages, but also the removal and banning of offending materials.[53] It was this power that moved the proposed ordinance into the censorship domain.

MacKinnon and Dworkin mobilized an outpouring of local feminist support in favor of the ordinance.[54] WAP supported the Minneapolis initiative, and many of its leading members, including Robin Morgan, Gloria Steinem, and Phyllis Chester, sent letters of support to the Minneapolis City Council. Dorchen Leidholdt went to Minneapolis from New York to help the campaign.[55] While WAVPM had rejected the pursuit of new legislation, some of its leaders stepped up to support it. Diana Russell, a WAVPM founder, went on record in the *New York Times* in 1984 as favoring legal prohibitions.[56] Leidholdt would go on to defend the ordinance from its critics, and WAP would throw its support behind promoting similar ordinance initiatives across the country.

While the ordinance was twice passed by the Minneapolis City Council, it was twice vetoed by the mayor. In the midst of the Minneapolis campaign, the City of Indianapolis hired MacKinnon as a consultant to draft a similar ordinance, which was passed by the City Council and signed into law by Mayor William Hudnut III on May 1, 1984.[57] The politics in Indianapolis were very different from those in Minneapolis. Whereas the Minneapolis ordinance had garnered the support of local feminists, as well as neighborhood organizations, the Indianapolis ordinance was overwhelmingly a religious conservative initiative.[58] The mayor recruited councilwoman Beulah Coughenour, a Republican activist who had been involved in the "Stop the ERA" movement, to introduce the law. Coughenour then hired MacKinnon (and not Dworkin) to draft the law. No local feminist organizations were consulted or mobilized. At City Council, in a vote of twenty-four to five, Republicans all voted in favor while Democrats voted against. Unlike the more progressive if divisive politics behind the Minneapolis ordinance, the political dynamics in Indianapolis evidenced the New Right's enthusiasm for anti-pornography politics and, as many observed, the unlikely alliance of feminism and conservatism.[59]

The Indianapolis ordinance was challenged by the American Booksellers Association, as violating the First Amendment. In November 1984, the US District Court for the Southern District of Indiana found the ordinance unconstitutional.[60] The challenge and judgment were cast in classic First Amendment terms. District judge Sarah Barker held that the definition of pornography in the ordinance was much broader than the category of obscenity (which the Supreme Court has held is not protected speech), and therefore was a restriction on speech traditionally protected by the First Amendment. The court held that the state's interest in prohibiting sex discrimination was not so compelling as to outweigh the interest of free speech. "Adult women generally have the capacity to protect themselves from participating in and being personally victimized by pornography." Accordingly, it held that the state's interest in protecting women's well-being by prohibiting "the sexually explicit subordination of women" was not sufficiently compelling to outweigh the First Amendment.[61] Even if the interest was compelling and did outweigh the interest in free speech, the failure to define the "subordination of women" was unconstitutionally vague. Finally, it held that the provisions related to coercion and forcing pornography failed to meet requirements for prior restraint, and therefore the ordinance as a whole failed for imposing unconstitutional prior restraint on First Amendment expression. The City of Indianapolis appealed.

By this time the ordinance movement faced newly organized *feminist* opposition. In 1984, New York–area feminists formed the Feminist Anti-Censorship Taskforce (FACT) to educate about the dangers of the ordinance. An ordinance modeled on that of MacKinnon/Dworkin had been introduced by Republican Michael D'Andre in Suffolk County, New York. It took a far more conservative turn, stating that pornography causes "sodomy" and "destruction of the family unit," as well as crimes and immorality "inimical to the public good."[62] Several women associated with the sex-radical critique attended the hearings and were disturbed by the significant turnout of religious conservatives supporting the ordinance. As Vance describes, "FACT formed quite spontaneously and coincidentally at the time of the Suffolk Hearings; we formed what we thought would be a temporary group to educate other feminists about this development. We also wanted to educate the general public that within the feminist movement there are divergent views about pornography and about the Ordinance."[63] FACT's original members included Carol Vance, Ellen Willis, Kate Willis, and Ann Snitow, all attendees at the Barnard conference and vocal critics of anti-pornography feminism. Nan Hunter emerged as a leading voice. Lisa Duggan was also a member. FACT went to women's conferences and concerts distributing leaflets about what was happening in Suffolk. According to Vance, "We found that people who were very sympathetic to the anti-porn analysis still drew the line at this law." FACT would expand, as chapters were established to fight local ordinance initiatives.

When the City of Indianapolis filed an appeal to the district court ruling, FACT filed an amicus brief, seeking to bring a specifically feminist objection to the ordinance.[64] The FACT brief, authored by Nan Hunter and Sylvia Law, sought to demonstrate that there were competing feminist understandings of pornography and to advocate for a different understanding of sexuality. FACT argued that censoring sexually explicit images would be damaging to women's sexuality. It was against censorship, but it was also for a more expansive vision of women's sexuality and sexual agency. Hunter and Law were explicit about the objective of the FACT brief: it was about putting forward a legally legible and persuasive First Amendment argument, but it was also about mobilizing feminist opposition to state suppression of sexually explicit material.[6] They understood that this was not only a legal struggle against censorship but a broader political one that included a contestation over the very meaning of pornography and women's sexuality.

As the legal battle proceeded through the courts, the feminist battles intensified. The anti-pornography feminists supporting the ordinance repeatedly denounced their FACT critics. Robin Morgan and Kathleen Barry pronounced, "FACT and its supporters . . . degrade and caricature the word feminism by using it to describe their defense of pornography."[66] MacKinnon stated, "The FACT brief is a crime against women."[67] She also condemned FACT as traitors to the movement: "The Black movement had its Uncle Toms, the labor movement has its scabs, Feminism has FACT."[68] MacKinnon would repeatedly insist that there was only one feminist position on pornography. Following a debate with Nan Hunter, she expressed her regret at even participating: "I did not want to do the debate at all because by its structure, it furthered the fraudulent notion that there are two feminist positions on this issue."[69] It was a double obscuring of feminist disagreement: it not only rejected the feminism of FACT but also refused to acknowledge the division within radical feminism itself about the use of law. In a definitional struggle for feminism, anti-pornography activists claimed to be the only true representatives, denouncing disagreement as not feminist.

Shadows of the earlier debates were cast over the anti-pornography feminist critique of FACT. S/M still figured prominently. Dorchen Leidholdt, in explaining why she refused to debate FACT, told a television producer, "FACT is a small group of lesbians that defend pornography and sadomasochism in the name of feminism."[70] S/M was a recurring motif in the anti-pornography defense of the ordinance, providing an easy visual connection between pornography and violence. Linking FACT with S/M created guilt by association. Claims like Leidholdt's that FACT "fronts for the ACLU, which in turn fronts for and is partially funded by the pornographers"[71] delegitimized their feminist credentials.

Law became the site of feminist debates on the meaning of sexuality and sexual autonomy. MacKinnon, Dworkin, and their supporters saw pornography as a microcosm of the danger that sexuality presented to women. They argued that it was the site of women's subordination—that women were victims of male sexual aggression in and through pornography. The ordinance sought to embed this vision of pornography in law. FACT sought rather to argue that sexuality was a complex site of danger and pleasure for women, and that women exercise sexual agency. As Duggan argued,

> The proposed ordinances are dangerous because they seek to embody in law an analysis of the role of sexuality and sexual images in the oppression of women with which even all feminists do not agree. Underlying virtually every section of the proposed laws there is an assumption that sexuality is a realm of unremitting, unequaled victimization for women. Pornography appears as the monster that made this so.

Closely connected to the critique of the radical feminist vision of sexuality was the question of women's agency: "Women are agents, and not merely victims, who make decisions and act on them, and who desire, seek out and enjoy sexuality."[72] FACT pointed to the history of the legal regulation of women's sexuality, and the ways in which protectionist laws had often been deployed against women by religious conservatives. They saw this as a cautionary tale of how the ordinance could be used, especially given the contemporary rise of the New Right. They saw in the ordinance a vision of sexuality—women's in particular—that was aligned closely with that of the Right.

While these divisions over sexuality and agency were readily apparent by the time of the Barnard conference, the ordinance had the effect of further narrowing the debate to pornography and law. Although FACT remained animated by the broader sex-positive analyses of sexuality, such as those on the Barnard conference agenda, the ordinances forced FACT to focus their response on pornography. Similarly, sex-radical visions of sexuality were turning to the law. Early on, while they had expressed anxiety over the censorious potential of anti-pornography feminism, the question of legal regulation was not a central concern. As soon as anti-pornography feminists made their move to law, so did they

The question of whether law in general and the civil rights remedy in particular should be used to regulate pornography became the focus of debate. Law was not only the site for broader disagreements over women's sexuality; the use of law itself became part of the disagreement.

This narrowing of debate led to a reconfiguration of support and opposition. The FACT brief was signed by more than two hundred prominent feminists—many now familiar: Carole Vance, Gayle Rubin, Joan Nestle, and Ellen Willis. But significantly, the list also included feminists who had once sympathized with the radical feminist critique of pornography. Adrienne Rich, Kate Millett, and Betty Friedan were among the signatories. Many feminists who were sympathetic to the radical feminist critique of sexuality more generally and pornography in particular were alienated by the turn to law. No matter how hard MacKinnon and Dworkin tried to argue to the contrary, the ordinance was viewed as a form of censorship. MacKinnon and others would repeatedly argue that FACT and its sympathizers misunderstood or misrepresented the ordinance. It was not criminal law giving the state the power to bring prosecutions, but rather it gave individual victims the power to do so. But FACT was able to frame the ordinance through the powerful lens of the First Amendment. Seeing the ordinance as a form of censorship, many once supportive feminists became wary. Adrienne Rich captured much of this sentiment in her explanation of why she signed the FACT brief, despite her support of many of the premises of the anti-pornography critique. She worried that any legislation banning pornography would be used by the Right against women and would lead to "a loss of images, words, and information empowering to women, the loss of our counter statements, the burial of the very dialogues we need to be having among our communities, in order to organize and act instead of collapsing in fragments."[73] Law became a site for the realignment of feminist attachments.

In August 1985, Judge Easterbrook, writing for the court of appeals, upheld the district court ruling.[74] The court held that the definition of pornography in the ordinance discriminated on the basis of the content of speech. Under the First Amendment, the state may not choose one viewpoint over another; but the ordinance did just that. It prohibited speech that subordinates women, but allowed speech that portrays women as equal: "This is thought control. It establishes an 'approved' view of women, of how they may react to sexual encounters, of how the sexes may relate to each other. Those who espouse the approved view may use sexual images; those who do not, may not."[75] In a nod to anti-pornography feminism's analysis, the court accepted "the premises of this legislation. Depictions of subordination tend to perpetuate subordination."[76] But in the court's view, "This simply demonstrates the power of pornography as speech." In relatively straightforward First Amendment terms, the court held that because pornography is speech, there was no basis to justify government restriction, and concluded that the definition of pornography was therefore unconstitutional.

* * *

Legal and political battles continued. The City of Indianapolis again appealed. In the summer and fall of 1985, while the Supreme Court appeal was pending, a new local ordinance initiative was underway. MacKinnon and Dworkin succeeded in getting the ordinance to a referendum in Cambridge, Massachusetts, but in November 1985, the proposal was defeated. All the while, debates raged on in the feminist press. In 1986, the Supreme Court summarily dismissed the appeal.[77] The legal battle was over, and the anti-pornography feminists had lost. But, in the broader struggles over the meaning of women's sexuality and agency, it is harder to assess the relative wins and losses. Anti-pornography feminism, in its final phase, had mobilized many supporters in a high-prolife political campaign, bringing significant media attention to their cause. At the same time, their legal strategy and denunciatory politics had alienated many within the feminist community who had once sympathized with the anti-pornography analysis but recoiled at the idea of turning to law. Pornography, as a feminist issue, receded. Yet, MacKinnon's version of radical feminism—renamed "dominance feminism"—would become the "ascendant feminist legal theory," and its influence would be felt for decades to come.[78]

SEXUALITY, AGENCY, AND LAW

Anti-pornography feminists' critique of heterosexuality led them to oppose pornography as well as other practices like S/M and prostitution seen as intimately linked to the oppression of women. Sexuality was a site of danger, pornography a key place for its perpetuation. The link between pornography and violence shifted. In its earliest days, violent sexual images were framed as symptomatic of broader sexual violence. Over time, pornography came to be seen as a cause of sexual violence. In its final ordinance stage, pornography itself became a form of violence against women. But, the focus on pornography was part of a broader critique of sexuality under conditions of patriarchy. The idea of women being oppressed through sexuality informed even the earliest debates. MacKinnon would later articulate a theory of dominance and subordination: women's inequality was produced through heterosexuality itself, which represented an institutionalization of "male sexual dominance and female sexual submission." From the early anti-pornography activism to the later articulation of MacKinnon's dominance feminism, her understanding of sexuality focused on women as victims of male sexual violence. This vision made the idea of women's agency and consent elusive. As MacKinnon wrote, "If sex is normally something men do to women, the issue is less whether there was force and more whether consent is a meaningful concept."[79] MacKinnon and the anti-pornography feminists before her challenged liberal ideas of consent as a simple dividing line. While the sex radicals accused the anti-pornography feminists of being anti-sex, it is also worth highlighting that some anti-pornography feminists also sought to articulate a more positive sexuality through the albeit much-maligned category of the erotic. It was an attempt to create a limited space for women's sexual desire and agency.

There was not consensus among anti-pornography feminists regarding the role of law. In the early days, radical feminists focused on the sexism they saw in advertisements and sexually explicit images. Strategies included consumer boycotts and protests to raise awareness. The early organizations—WAVAW and WAVPM—did not seek legal solutions to the problem of pornography, although individual feminists of WAVPM and WAP who came to focus more exclusively on pornography were increasingly divided on the issue. The equivocation of the anti-pornography movement changed with the intervention of MacKinnon and Dworkin and the civil rights ordinances. This turn to law has often come to be seen as "the" radical feminist position on pornography, and MacKinnon and Dworkin as "a stand-in for the anti-pornography movement as a whole."[80] This was not always the case. Dworkin's views were influential from the earlier days of the anti-pornography movement. MacKinnon's influence would cast a long shadow over the subsequent development of feminist legal theory and activism. But the instrumentalist turn to law only occurred in the final phase of the sex wars.

The sex radicals' more complex vision of sexuality as a site of danger and pleasure for women, in which women could be agents, developed dialogically, in opposition to the vision of radical feminism. They acknowledged the potential harms associated with sexuality, but resisted the exclusivity of that vision. The sex radicals recognized that much of mainstream pornography was deeply sexist, but argued that sexism was neither inherent nor exclusive to pornography. In their writings and activism, they focused more on the pleasure side of the equation, seeking to create more space for women to articulate desire and agency. From the initial interventions of the S/M feminists who defended S/M as a consensual practice through the Barnard conference to the FACT brief, sex-radical feminists emphasized women's sexual agency, in contrast to anti-pornography feminism, which focused on women's sexual victimization.

Judith Butler offers a slightly different telling of the sex-radical movement, but one that fits with the story being told here. She has argued that pro-sexuality feminism actually took the insights of radical/dominance feminism as its starting point, recognizing that "sexuality is culturally constructed within existing power relations."[81] As a result, there is nowhere "outside" or "beyond" but rather, for Butler, the critical question was whether and how to operate within these power relations in ways that disrupt them. Sex-radical feminists were effectively seeking ways to disrupt patriarchal sexualities from within, in and through subversive acts of identification. In other words, feminist pornography or BDSM or the many other sexual practices promoted by the sex radicals were acts of performing sexuality within the matrix of power in ways that did not disavow the matrix, but sought modest subversions from within. Butler's narrative suggests, again, that the two sides of the sex wars were not as far apart on power and sexuality as the dominant narrative would have us believe. It is not that they entirely agreed, but neither did they entirely disagree about sexuality and power.

From the beginning, the sex radicals seemed to share an antipathy towards legal intervention. Early critiques by Willis opposed censorship; however, it was not their main focus. As the strength of the anti-pornography movement grew alongside its increasing support for legal restrictions, so did the sex-radical critique of the censorship of pornography. By the mid-1980s, the sex-radical position was focused on opposing legal restrictions, particularly in and through the intervention of FACT in the constitutional challenge to the anti-pornography Civil Rights Ordinance. There was an anti-interventionist spirit to the sex-radical feminists, captured by their discourse of *anti*-censorship. Opposing the ordinance did not require sex-radical feminists to develop a broader position on engagement with law. They were against the ordinance, and they were against the censorship of sexually explicit images. The anti-censorship work would continue, as attention was diverted to the increasing censorship of the Right. By the 1990s, anti-pornography feminists were no longer the enemy; the enemy was the state, with the infamous censorship battles around Mapplethorpe, the NEA Four, and others. The sex radicals found common cause with an emerging queer critique. Together they took issue with the Right's attempt to regulate and repress sexual representations. For sex radicals, the feminist sex wars gave way to the Right's war on sex.[82]

The sex-radical critique and underlying vision of law went beyond anti-censorship. Repeated emphasis on consent gestured toward future theorizations and interventions. The emerging queer/sex-radical critique would take aim at the regulation of consensual sexual practices of the type identified by Rubin in "Thinking Sex," from sex work to LGBT sexuality. The anti-regulatory impulse was one that would increasingly be directed to the consensual side of the consent/nonconsent equation. As Duggan and Hunter argued, "Although we recognized that 'consent' is socially constructed, we nonetheless argued that it remains a centrally important concept in relation to sex law."[83] As the war on sex from the Right increasingly targeted nonnormative sexualities and practices, the queer/sex-radical critique pushed back at the surveillance and criminalization of consensual practices, gesturing toward some of the anti-carceral critiques that would emerge in the next round of the sex wars.

The sex-radical critique of law was not only a negative, anti-regulatory one. Kathryn Abrams suggested that the FACT brief in particular hinted towards a social-constructionist vision of law.[84] FACT argued that the sexual double standard and the image of women as victims of dangerous male sexuality embedded in protectionist legislation would only serve to reinforce this deeply problematic vision of women's sexuality and agency. While it may not have been foregrounded,[85] it is a vision of law made legible as a socially constitutive discourse, which produced meaning in the world. FACT, not unlike the anti-pornography feminists, engaged with law as a site of discursive struggle over the meaning of women's sexuality and sexual agency. This vision of law, as socially constitutive of legal subjects, plays an important role moving forward.

The story of the sex wars is often remembered in the popular imagination (read Wikipedia) in starkly oppositional terms, with radical feminists and sex-radical feminists lining up along a series of axes: danger/pleasure, victim/choice, censorship/anti-censorship. There is some truth in this framing—it was sometimes the way that each side characterized the other, and the axes capture the relative emphasis of each side of the debate. But neither side of the sex wars was as one-dimensional or homogeneous as this story suggests. Despite their divisions, both sides were *feminist*, concerned with gender and power and improving social justice for women, however different their diagnoses and prosciptions may have been. Radical feminists were against what they understood as violent sexual practices; but they also sought to articulate a more positive sexuality through the erotic. Sex radicals affirmed the importance of sexual pleasure and agency for women, but they also recognized the reality of sexual danger in women's lives. While the sex wars were characterized by deep divisions on questions of sexuality, agency, and law—and a hostile and antagonistic rhetoric that reinforced this framing—the divisions were slightly more complicated than the axes suggest. It is, I think, helpful, in reflecting back on this history, to keep these nuances and tensions in mind; a reading of the sex wars attentive to the more nuanced claims and their metamorphosis over time may be productive in both analyzing the contemporary feminist debates and finding ways to break the enduring hold of the binary antagonisms.

PART TWO: THE SEX WARS 2.0

In 1995, Lisa Duggan and Nan Hunter wrote that, although the porn wars had largely subsided, "they have consequences that are with us still."[86] Indeed, over twenty years later, the sex wars are with us still. While the two camps continued to hold similarly opposing views, they turned to new issues. Many on the radical feminist side moved to anti-trafficking work. Others migrated to anti–sexual violence work. The sex radicals shifted attention to newer threats to nonnormative sexualities, in anti-censorship battles of the culture wars. While the understandings of sexuality remained divergent, they developed to a large extent in two solitudes. The dominance feminists focused on sexual violence, the sex radicals on the regulation of consensual sexual identities and practices.

There would be occasional dust-ups, but nothing like the intensity of the 1970s and 1980s.

In the 1990s, sexual violence on campus became a lightning rod that seemed to reignite the debate once more. Kathryn Abrams, for example, argued in 1995 that both a popular and an academic feminism were challenging the growing influence of dominance feminism, and replaying many of the same debates of the earlier sex wars.[87] The popular feminism, like that espoused by Katie Roiphe and Naomi Wolfe, provocatively challenged victim feminism, with arguments that echoed earlier sex-positive feminists. Academic feminism insisted on a more complex subjectivity for women, including but not limited to questions of sexuality. Abrams noted that while the sex-positive critique of the sex wars had only a negligible impact on law and legal theory, a more complex vision of law was emerging. The popular debates around sexuality were largely eclipsed by the generational frame discussed in chapter 1, and the sex wars did not fully erupt. But Abrams pointed out important continuities—and discontinuities—in feminist debates around sexuality, agency, and law. These underlying disagreements would continue to simmer beneath the surface.

Sex Wars 2.0—this current iteration—does not have a clear beginning, middle, or end. While the 1990s conflicts faded, a range of feminist sexuality debates continued in the 2000s. Feminists still disagreed on the regulation of sex work, from decriminalization to asymmetrical criminalization. On-line sexual speech and harassment, and how to appropriately respond to so-called revenge porn—the nonconsensual distribution of intimate sexual representations—became hot topics. Discussions continued to revolve around sexuality as a site of danger, women as sexual agents versus victims, and the role of the law in redressing sexual harm, and in the 2010s they again boiled over into the public sphere, largely in relation to campus sexual violence.

In 2011, the Office for Civil Rights (OCR) of the Department of Education issued a Dear Colleague Letter (DCL) providing new guidelines for colleges and universities receiving federal funding.[88] Title IX of the Education Amendments of 1972 prohibits sex discrimination in education.[89] The letter stated that sexual harassment and sexual violence are forms of sex discrimination and called for universities and colleges to take "immediate and effective steps to end sexual harassment and sexual violence." The DCL built on the *Sexual Harassment Guidance* previously issued providing that sexual harassment was a form of sex discrimination under Title IX.[90] The DCL stated that "the requirements of Title IX pertaining to sexual harassment also cover sexual violence" and made clear that student sexual misconduct complaints were to be governed by Title IX. The letter stated that schools must ensure that "grievance procedures provide for prompt and equitable resolution of sexual harassment complaints" and set out the parameters for those procedural requirements. The standard of proof to be used was the preponderance of evidence standard as typically used in civil litigation under Title IX.[91] The letter also set out obligations to establish preventative education programs and comprehensive survivor resources.

Complaints started coming. A group of students, including Alexandra Brodsky, who would become an outspoken anti–sexual violence activist, filed a Title IX complaint against Yale University in 2011.[92] Students from other campuses began organizing. At Amherst, following the publication of a first-person account of sexual violence and the college's failure to respond that went viral,[93] Dana Bolger would emerge as an anti–sexual violence leader. In 2012, she cofounded an on-line publication called *It Happens Here*, where survivors could post stories of both their sexual assaults and the inadequate institutional responses.[94] Informal networks of student activists emerged across campuses. Bolger and Brodsky would meet to share strategies and stories, as they, along with others, were mobilizing against sexual violence.[95] This campus anti-violence organizing became particularly visible in 2013. Andrea Pino and Annie Clarke filed a Title IX complaint against the University of North Carolina for the university's handling of sexual assault complaints.

Their case and the emerging movement received national attention in the *New York Times* in March 2013.[96] In April, three dozen students and alumni at Occidental College filed a federal complaint alleging violations of their civil rights following reports of sexual assault. Students from Dartmouth and Swarthmore colleges, the University of California at Berkeley, and the University of Southern California followed suit, bringing Title IX complaints against their schools. By the summer of 2013, informal networks were formalizing. Pino and Clarke founded End Rape on Campus to support and assist students in holding their universities responsible for sexual violence. Brodsky and Bolger founded Know Your IX, an on-line educational campaign focused on student rights under Title IX and equipping them to file complaints. Momentum grew alongside mainstream media attention.

Sexual violence once again gained national attention when in 2014, Emma Sulkowicz began carrying a mattress around Columbia University, vowing to continue until her assailant was expelled from campus. In April 2013, Sulkowicz had filed a complaint of sexual assault against another student, asking that he be expelled. In November, Columbia found the student not responsible, and Sulkowicz's request for an appeal was turned down by the dean. In the spring of 2014, Sulkowicz appeared with US senator Kirsten Gillibrand at a press conference about sexual violence on campus, telling her story about having been sexually assaulted. A few weeks later, she and two dozen other students filed a Title IX complaint against Columbia University and Barnard College for mishandling their sexual-assault complaints. In May, Sulkowicz was featured on the front page of the *New York Times* in an article about the anti–sexual violence movements on campuses.[97] The same month, *Time* magazine published her essay "My Rapist Is Still on Campus."[9] Sulkowicz was becoming a poster child for the anti–sexual-violence on-campus movement, but she would reach new heights in the fall of 2014, as she began to carry the dorm mattress with her everywhere on campus. Sulkowicz devised *Mattress Performance: Carry That Weight* as part of her senior thesis;[99] she carried a dorm mattress throughou the academic year, right up to Convocation in the spring of 2015.[100] The protest/performance received tremendous attention, with stories in the *New York Times*, the *Washington Post*,[101] network news shows,[102] and no less than twenty-two stories in *New York Magazine*. In January 2015, she attended the State of the Union address as the guest of Senator Gillibrand.

This period also marked the beginning of a visible feminist critique of the anti-rape movement and the expansion of Title IX.[103] In July 2014, Harvard University announced its new sexual- and gender-based harassment policy and procedures.[104] Since the Dear Colleague Letter in 2011, the OCR had initiated several Title IX investigations across the university, including one at the law school.[105] The new policies were intended to bring Harvard University into compliance with federal requirements. But law professor Janet Halley was disturbed by both the substance and the procedure of these new policies.[106] She drafted a detailed memo outlining her concerns.[107] Halley insisted on the importance of the current moment for colleges and universities to correct their "slipshod, dismissive and actively malign handling of sexual harassment claims, and to offer genuine remedies for victims." She insisted that things could be done better, in ways that reflected the principles of fairness, equal protection of minority students, free speech, and academic freedom. Halley was the driving force behind a letter sharply criticizing the new policies that would appear in the *Boston Globe*, signed by twenty-eight Harvard Law School professors: "As teachers responsible for educating our students about due process of law, the substantive law governing discrimination and violence, appropriate administrative decision-making, and the rule of law generally, we find the new sexual harassment policy inconsistent with many of the most basic principles we teach."[108] Their objections mirrored those in Halley's memo. Substantively, they argued that the policies expanded prohibited conduct, by adopting a definition of sexual harassment that went beyond what was required by Title IX. They also objected to the expansion of prohibited conduct regarding the sexual actions of students who were impaired or incapacitated, in ways that they said were one-sided. Procedurally, they objected to the policy's failure to provide an opportunity to discover the facts, examine witnesses, and mount a defense. They opposed the combination of investigation, prosecution, fact finding, and appellate review functions in one office, as well as the failure to provide adequate representation for the accused. In effect, the professors argued that the policies were substantively too broad and procedurally unfair. Their objections received national attention.[109] Harvard University ultimately allowed the law school to develop its own policies and procedures, subsequently approved by the OCR.[110]

Nancy Gertner, one of the signatories, published an article in the *American Prospect*[111] explaining why, from a feminist perspective, she opposed the Harvard policies. She argued that although attention to campus sexual violence was long overdue, there were difficult questions that needed to be addressed: "Where should the Title IX violation line be? What was a reasonable adjudication process?" Further, how should Title IX complaint procedures balance the rights of the complainants with those of the accused? Gertner highlighted her experience as a women's rights advocate, a criminal defense attorney, and a federal judge to defend the importance of fair process, and she outlined the deficiencies of the Harvard sexual-violence policy. She offered a counterexample, citing Oberlin College's Title IX disciplinary process as a "symmetrical due process" that better balanced the rights of the parties. She concluded, "Feminists should be concerned about fair process, even in private institutions where the law does not require it, because we should be concerned about reliable findings of responsibility."[112] Gertner was not alone. Halley, Jeannie Suk Gersen, and Elizabeth Bartholet would also continue to bring a feminist voice to their mainstream and scholarly articles critiquing the expansion of Title IX surveillance of campus sexual conduct.[113]

In February 2015, Laura Kipnis entered the fray, publishing an article in the *Chronicle of Higher Education* highly critical of new campus codes governing faculty-student relationships, provocatively titled "Sexual Paranoia Strikes Academe."[114] It focused on a Title IX complaint at Northwestern, for failing to punish a professor (Peter Ludlow) accused of "unwelcome and inappropriate sexual advances." Kipnis, a self-described feminist, wrote in her polemical style, denouncing what she called the sex panic that was overtaking campuses, arguing that "sexual paranoia reigns." She was critical of how policies were framing women as incapable of consent: "What becomes of students so committed to their own vulnerability, conditioned to imagine they have no agency?" She specifically referenced the feminist debates that had come before on these questions of women's agency: "A 21 year old incapable of consent? A certain brand of radical feminism—the late Andrea Dworkin for one—held that women's consent was meaningless in the context of patriarchy."

One of Ludlow's complainants (unnamed in the article) and another graduate student took issue with the article and initiated a Title IX complaint against Kipnis. One said that the essay was retaliatory and created a hostile environment, the other that it created a chilling effect on student ability to bring sexual misconduct complaints. Northwestern launched a formal Title IX investigation against Kipnis. In a second article in the *Chronicle*, published while the investigation was ongoing, she described it as an "inquisition."[115] She denounced the ways in which Title IX was being used to allow "intellectual disagreement to be redefined as retaliation." The day the article went on-line, Kipnis received notice that Northwestern had cleared her of the charges.

Kipnis would become the subject of a second Title IX investigation, following the publication of her book *Unwanted Advances: Sexual Paranoia Comes to Campus* in April 2017. An elaboration on her initial *Chronicle* article, the book delved more deeply into the Title IX investigations, particularly the one against Peter Ludlow. Her explicitly feminist perspective diverged from what was driving the Title IX complaints, calling for a "grown up feminism" promoting women's agency rather than reinforcing the conservative narratives of female passivity and feminine deference. Kipnis is a feminist in the sex-positive tradition, and her critique of Title IX is located in the concern about a vision of sexuality as dangerous, of women as victims, and of legal regulation as potentially reactionary. Shortly after her book's publication, four Northwestern faculty members and six graduate students initiated another Title IX complaint, claiming that she had violated the sexual harassment policy by engaging in retaliatory behavior. Northwestern would ultimately find her not responsible.[116] Several days later, the graduate student who had been involved in both of the Title IX complaints launched a civil lawsuit against Kipnis and HarperCollins, the publisher of her book, claiming invasion of privacy, defamation, and the intentional infliction of emotional distress. Jeannie Suk Gersen, one of the Harvard law professors who opposed the Harvard policies, wrote about Kipnis's "endless trials" in the *New Yorker*, just weeks before the explosion of #MeToo.

At roughly the same time Laura Kipnis wrote her first polemic against Title IX, *The Hunting Grounds*, a documentary by director Kirby Dick and producer Amy Ziering about sexual violence on campuses, was released (February 2015). The film featured the stories of Pino and Clark, alongside other sexual assault survivor/activists on campuses across the United States. It examined the failure of college administrators to take complaints seriously as well as the fraternity system, and included an interview with Caitlan Flanagan of the *Atlantic*— the same #MeToo feminist detractor who would take the Aziz Ansari story in Babe.net to task—speaking about the ways colleges might protect fraternities, whose members become a source of future donations. Senator Kirsten Gillibrand makes a brief appearance. *The Hunting Grounds* premiered at the Sundance film festival to considerable critical acclaim,[117] went into theatrical release (ironically, by Radius-TWC, a division of the Weinstein Company), and eventually was aired on CNN. It was nominated for multiple awards, including an Oscar in both the best documentary category and best song for Lady Gaga's "Until It Happens to You."

The Hunting Ground would become a lightning rod of feminist controversy. At the time of its release, Emily Yoffe—another of the eventual #MeToo feminist detractors—challenged the accuracy of the film, questioning some of the statistics along with its failure to explore the increasingly significant role of the Office of Civil Rights in investigating colleges.[118] Yoffe returned to the film in a hard-hitting article in Slate focusing on allegations made against Brandon Winston by Kamilah Willingham, accusing him of sexually assaulting her friend and classmate at Harvard Law School.[119] Yoffe looked at the transcripts of both the criminal proceedings and Harvard's investigation. She told a very different story than the one presented in The Hunting Ground. She argued that Willingham's accusations were taken seriously first by Harvard, and then by the district attorney. Winston was found responsible for sexual harassment and put on "dismission," a form of expulsion that would allow him to reapply for admission. While he appealed, he missed the 2011–2012 academic year. In the spring of 2012, the faculty voted to dismiss the charges against Winston and allow his return that fall. It did not end there. In October 2012, Winston was indicted by a grand jury on two felony counts. With criminal charges pending against him, Harvard placed him on an involuntary leave of absence. The jury ultimately did not find him guilty of sexual offenses, but instead of a misdemeanor of a "nonsexual nature." Yoffe points out multiple inconsistencies of testimony, and the extent to which Willington's credibility was called into question, and concludes that the filmmakers did not tell a balanced, objective story, but rather let their "politics color . . . their presentation of the facts."

Yoffe was not alone in her critique. In November 2015, the Harvard law professors were back at it, with nineteen of them releasing an open letter criticizing The Hunting Ground.[120] Building on Yoffe's investigation, the professors denounced the film as "a seriously false picture both of the general sexual assault phenomenon at universities and of our student Brandon Winston."[121] The film, they point out, suggests the use of force and drugs on the victims—suggestions not supported by any of the evidence. They noted that no final decision maker found him responsible for sexual assault; even the Office of Civil Rights, which found Harvard responsible for several Title IX violations, did not fault the vindication of Winston by the law school faculty. The law professors pulled no punches:

> We believe that Brandon Winston was subjected to a long, harmful ordeal for no good reason. Justice has been served in the end, but at enormous costs to this young man. We denounce this film as prolonging his ordeal with its unfair and misleading portrayal of the facts of his case. Mr. Winston was finally vindicated by the Law School and by the judicial proceedings, and allowed to continue his career at the Law School and beyond. Propaganda should not be allowed to erase this just outcome.[122]

The filmmakers struck back. First, in a statement e-mailed to the *Harvard Crimson*, Dick and Ziering denounced the law professors' letter, saying it was "irresponsible and raises an important question about whether the very public bias these professors have shown in favor of an assailant contributes to a hostile climate at Harvard Law."[123] In an opinion piece in the *Huffington Post*, they again denounced the professors: "These aggressive actions send a very chilling message to all current and future students at Harvard and Harvard Law: if you report a sexual assault, your professors may come after you publicly."[124] Jeannie Suk Gersen responded in the *New Yorker*, noting the seriousness of the allegation of hostile climate and arguing the critical importance of a distinction between disagreement and sexual harassment.[125] She referred to the Laura Kipnis sexual harassment complaints as a dangerous precedent in collapsing the two.

In September 2015, Emily Bazelon published "The Return of the Sex Wars" in the *New York Times Magazine*.[126] Her story of the emerging debates between the anti-rape movement on campuses and the feminist critics was told in large part through the role of two protagonists, Catharine MacKinnon and Janet Halley. From the rise in Title IX complaints to Sulkowicz's *Carry That Weight* to the Battle of Cambridge[127] to the Kipnis controversy, Bazelon hit the major touchpoints, interviewing many key players, as she attempted to map the terrain of the new sex wars. She linked the legacies of anti-pornography radical feminism and the sex-positive feminism of the early sex wars with the anti–rape survivor movement and feminist critics, respectively. Bazelon describes MacKinnon, doyenne of radical-into-dominance feminism and lawyer activist behind the anti-pornography ordinances, as "an intellectual touchstone" of the anti–rape survivor movement. She quotes leading activist Alexandra Brodsky: "She resonates with us for recognizing the way sexual violence holds back individuals and classes of marginalized people from flourishing." Like MacKinnon, Bazelon observes that these activists view the law as a tool to resist women's oppression in general and sexual violence in particular.

Halley, who arrived on the scene after the sex wars, was cast as a modern-day version of sex-positive feminism. Halley took on MacKinnon's vision of sexual harassment in the Joseph Oncale case, involving an allegation of sexual harassment by a man against his all-male co-workers. Halley argued that simply analogizing Oncale with a woman for the purposes of sex discrimination was a mistake that carried with it a host of dangers for sexual minorities. Halley's critique of sexual harassment law and dominance feminism was based largely on its characterization of women as victims of sexual violence, devoid of agency. As Bazelon described Halley, "Throughout her legal career, she has cautioned against treating sex exclusively as a danger from which women should seek the authorities' protection." Her critique of Harvard's sexual misconduct policies was in line with this legacy, but also reverberated

more broadly "as the latest salvo in a long-running war, with deep intellectual roots, over how to grapple with rape and sex as a feminist."

These popular flashpoint critiques were reflected in academic scholarship. Jeannie Suk Gersen and Janet Halley were deeply critical of the
dominance-feminist approach to sexual violence and the creeping expansion of Title IX. Suk and Gersen argued against the expansion of
federal prohibitions against sex discrimination and sexual violence to
include the oversight of sex itself within educational institutions.[128] In
what they call "bureaucratic sex creep," they argued that the policies and
procedures colleges and universities have been required to adopt have
begun to conflate sexual violence and harassment with "ordinary sex,"
and are counterproductive to the objective of addressing the serious
harms of rape, sexual assault, and sexual harassment.[129] They argued
that the concept of "crime" alongside the broad definitions of sexual
assault used in the federal reporting requirements went well beyond
the criminal definitions of rape and sexual assault. These overreaching
definitions, including the definition of sexual harassment as "conduct of
an unwelcome nature," were not accompanied by protections for the accused. In other words, definitions are broad, and procedural protections
weak, and in operation had the potential to spill over into the regulation
of "ordinary sex."

Janet Halley was similarly critical of Title IX policies and procedures in her scholarly writing, reflecting on the the need for feminists
to think harder about hard cases.[130] She argues that the prototypical
cases of young women being drugged and assaulted, intoxicated and
raped, or of those who consented to some sex but were forced into
having more, are cases where feminist advocacy for the rights of the
survivors—or "the use of the megaphone"—is justified. But these pro-
totypes do not exhaust the range of cases that are being brought under
Title IX. Halley begins with a high-profile case at Hobart and William
Smith College where a young woman reported being raped at a party
at the beginning of her freshman year. The case, as reported in the
New York Times, became a rallying cry for anti-rape activists.[131] Halley

suggests that the facts of the case were ambiguous: while it seemed clear that the young woman had been raped, there was no certainty as to the identity of the particular student(s) responsible. Halley argues, in her provocative style, "The furor over Anna's case amounts to pressure on schools to hold students responsible for serious harm even when—precisely when—there can be no certainty about who is to blame for it. Such calls are core to every witch hunt. Speaking as a feminist governor to other feminist governors, I have this simple message: we have to pull back from this brink." Halley identifies what she considers to be different types of hard cases and complaints, including those involving racial and sexual minorities, and those involving voluntary intoxication. She worries about the asymmetrical relevance of impairment on complainants and respondents, coupled with the problems of memory loss associated with intoxication. She argues that policies like Harvard's that consider intoxication relevant for the complainant's ability to consent but irrelevant to the respondent's conduct create a problematic double standard that puts women's agency at risk: "It entails a commitment to the idea that women should not and do not bear any responsibility for the bad things that happen to them when they are voluntarily drunk, stoned, or both. This commitment cuts women off—in theory and in application—from assuming agency over their own lives. Since when was that a feminist idea?" Consistent with her advocacy on Harvard's sexual harassment policies and procedures, Halley argues for a more measured approach that asks hard questions.

Elsewhere, Halley takes on the standard of affirmative consent for sexual assault as debated by the American Law Institute, and as adopted by several states for the purposes of Title IX complaints.[132] While the precise definitions of affirmative consent vary, the standard is typically one that requires conscious and voluntary agreement.[133] The laws typically articulate the circumstances that do not constitute a valid excuse for the accused's belief that the complainant consented, including if that belief arose from intoxication or recklessness of the accused, the accused failed to take reasonable steps to ascertain whether the complainant was consenting, or the accused knew or should have known that the complainant was incapacitated due to intoxication. Halley sees in these definitions, celebrated by anti-rape activists, an overly broad, repressive, and deeply conservative vision of sexuality. These "affirmative consent requirements—in part because of their origin in a carceral project that is overcommitted to social control through punishment in a way that seems to me to be social-conservative, not emancipatory— . . . . will foster a new, randomly applied moral order that will often be intensely repressive and sex-negative."[134] Halley explicitly takes on MacKinnon's critique of consent and her proposal to move toward a standard of "unwanted" sex.[135] She sees in this legacy of dominance feminism a deep conservatism predicated on women's helplessness and lack of agency. In this vision, "women often—in some versions, always or almost always— consent to sex with men under pervasively coercive conditions of male domination that render their consent descriptively and morally meaningless."[136] Halley argues that it is a standard that can capture a broad range of desired but later regretted sexual encounters.[137]

SEXUALITY, AGENCY, AND LAW REDUX

The feminist debates around sexual violence on campus and Title IX fracture along the axes of disagreement about sexuality, agency, and law that figured in the early sex wars.[138] Anti-rape activists are the intellectual inheritors of anti-pornography radical feminism of the early sex wars and the dominance feminism of its later years. Indeed, the influence of MacKinnon was often made explicit. Anti-rape feminism has focused on the ongoing danger that sexuality presents to women and the difficulties of consent in unequal social conditions. While they point to the failure of law to prevent and redress sexual violence, they nevertheless see the law as an instrument for change. They support broader definitions of sexual violence and sexual harassment, and a more expansive vision of affirmative consent.

The feminist critics, on the other hand, are the intellectual inheritors of the sex radicals, with their concerns over sexual negativity, women as victims, and the potentially repressive role of law. They do not contest whether sexual assault, sexual violence, and sexual harassment are harmful, but rather how broadly sexual harm should be defined and how narrowly consent should be defined, for the purposes of making that conduct legally actionable. Like that of the sex radicals of the earlier sex wars, it is a critique concerned with how regulating sex can conflate the distinction between consensual and nonconsensual sexual conduct and the construction of women's sexuality exclusively in terms of victimization. Echoing the earlier sex radicals, it insists on sexuality as a site of both danger and pleasure, but leans towards the pleasure side, pushing back at the regulatory creep.

Neither the anti-rape activists nor their feminist critics are *exactly* like the feminists that came before. Anti-rape activists, for example, did not stake their claims against pornography, nor sexual minorities. While their focus is on sexual violence, and thereby the danger part of the danger/pleasure equation, they do not eschew the pleasure side. Indeed, these feminists are in many respects post–third wave, tending to embrace their right to a positive sexuality, straight, gay, or beyond. But, in their focus on sexual violence, their vision of agency and consent leans more to the victimization side of the spectrum. They see coercion where their feminist critics see agency. Yet, also unlike their radical feminist predecessors, many anti-rape activists affirm consent, albeit while seeking to expand its legal meaning. The "consent is sexy" campaigns that have become popular on college and university campuses seek to educate and change sexual behavior through sex-positive messages and a celebration of consent.[139] Finally, while they have turned to legal instruments, their vision of the law is not entirely uncritical. From Sulkowicz's mattress performance to their savvy deployment of social media, the anti-rape activists do not place all hope exclusively in legal institutions and remedies.

Similarly, the feminist critics have evolved from their sex-radical roots, particularly in relation to the law, which was not a major concern until the ordinance stage of the sex wars, and then the focus was exclusively on anti-censorship. Currently, feminist critics are drilling down on legal regulation, both substantively and procedurally. Like that of the early sex radicals, this critique, developed in the wake of increasing reliance on criminal law and incarceration, questions the role of law in regulating sexuality, and fears its repressive and conservative potential. The feminist critics are informed by an understanding of the disproportionate impact of violent policing and carceral politics on disadvantaged communities—African American, immigrant, poor, Indigenous, mentally challenged. This anti-carceral sensibility extends beyond the study of criminal law, as carceral logics of punishment themselves extend beyond the criminal realm. A sharp focus on how the expansion of Title IX impacts disadvantaged communities is a recurring theme. While the sex-radical critique was concerned with the impact on sexual minorities, the current iteration includes a broader range of racial and socioeconomic inequality.

Despite their turn to law, many anti-rape activists agree, at least partially, with this critique of the carceral state. Alexandra Brodsky's *New York Times* opinion piece, for example, was critical of the controversial sentencing of Brock Turner, but also opposed mandatory minimums and the criminal justice system more generally: "Although mandatory minimums were meant to reduce disparities, in practice they hurt the populations some reformers sought to protect.[140] Minorities and people with lower incomes are more likely to be arrested, and then more likely to be charged with crimes that carry higher mandatory minimums than others who commit the same act."[141] Brodsky's critique echoed carceral feminism, arguing that criminal law is not the only legal option:

We also have to look outside criminal law. The high visibility of the Turner case obscures the extreme rarity of rape prosecutions. Justice and accountability, then, will require increased access to the civil legal system where victims, not prosecutors, can decide whether and how to bring a case. The law in California makes it easier to take sexual abusers to court than it is in most other states, but legal representation is often prohibitively expensive. We need better state and private funding for legal services for survivors.

Like the feminist critics, Brodsky embraces a more complex vision of law, attentive to the different modalities of legal regulation. This is a contested issue within anti-rape activism. MacKinnon has argued for a radical redefinition of the criminal law of sexual assault that would extend to "unwanted sex,"[142] and many advocate for a more affirmative consent standard within the criminal law. It is worth recalling that in the early days of the sex wars, the anti-pornography feminists were similarly divided about resorting to law. While anti-rape activists today continue to turn towards law, the particular way in which they do so is not monolithic. Some, like Brodsky, explicitly adopt the discourse of the anti-carceral feminist critique, a critique directed to the legacy of radical and dominance feminism.

Despite differences between then and now, there are common threads in the underlying feminist investments and contestations. Disagreements over definitions of sexual harm, consent, and the potential role of law continue to be characterized by antagonism, with opponents caricaturing and denouncing the other side. Clashes are often met with excommunication from a feminist community; dissenters are cast as traitors, pornographers, conservatives, harassers, McCarthyites. But hopefully this brief history has highlighted the principled arguments at stake. Although the extent of the disagreements can get exaggerated in fiery rhetoric, legitimate competing visions of sexuality, gender, and law are implicated, raising important questions—what constitutes sexual harm, and how broadly those sexual harms should be defined; the relative degree of women's autonomy under conditions of sexual inequality; how consent should be legally defined; legal regulation of sexual harm; whether law can be a source of betterment and empowerment for women or is so deeply embedded in social inequalities of race, sexuality, and gender that it is destined to reproduce them. Feminists across sides and time have disagreed on the answers and strategies for activism and reform. Their opposing views, I will argue in the next chapter, are precisely what underlay feminist polarization around #MeToo.

3

#METOO AS SEX WARS

Chapter 1 reviewed the way in which the feminist disagreements within #MeToo were cast as generational. In this chapter, I return to these debates through the lens of the sex wars, arguing that the #MeToo feminist contestations are part of an intellectual history that reproduces the same disagreements over sexuality and its regulation. I argue that contemporary #MeToo feminists are the intellectual inheritors of both the radical feminists of the 1970s and 1980s and the dominance feminists of Sex Wars 2.0. The #MeToo feminist detractors, in contrast, are direct descendants of the feminist sex radicals of the sex wars, then and now. Reflecting these broader sex wars, the #MeToo movement has produced similar fractures around sexuality, agency, and the role of law in regulating sexual harm.

I am particularly interested in the controversies around the role of law in the #MeToo movement, and the extent to which the feminist contestations echo the debates of the sex wars, past and present. While the disagreements around sexuality and agency are easily tracked to the divisions of the sex wars, the role of law is more complicated. #MeToo feminism does not have a clearly articulated theory of law. Indeed, one of the notable features of the #MeToo movement to date has been the extent to which it has played out in nonlegal forums, from social media to board rooms, bypassing courts and legal actions. Yet, this speaks volumes about law: the sheer exposure of the pervasiveness of sexual violence in women's lives is a performance of law's spectacular failure. While they are slightly harder to discern, I argue that the feminist disagreements swirling around #MeToo reflect underlying conflicts and tensions about the role of law in addressing sexual harm. #MeToo feminism challenges the exclusive power of law as the arbiter of sexual violence. Yet, as radical/dominance feminisms did, #MeToo feminism at times gestures towards more law, which paradoxically only reinforces law's power.

The feminist detractors express concern about #MeToo going too far: substantively, in terms of the range of conduct being included, and procedurally, in terms of the absence of due process. There are two versions of this critique of #MeToo. The first is built on the assumption that law alone has the authority to determine the existence of sexual harm; there can be no sexual harm unless the law says so, and the law cannot say so without due process. The second, broader critique directly challenges the power of law, particularly criminal law. Robust procedural protections and more restrictive definitions of sexual harm are required as a bulwark against the carceral state, but this critique seeks to displace the carceral approach with alternatives. Both versions critique the absence of due process and the lumping of sexual practices, but they do so for very different reasons, from different intellectual traditions, and with different implications. The specter of the sex wars can be seen in each.

Drawing parallels runs the risk of reproducing a starkly oppositional picture; however, just as the earlier sex wars were more nuanced than is often remembered, a close—and slightly reparative—reading of the feminist #MeToo disagreements suggests that they are not as binary as often presented. By avoiding oversimplifying, looking at the more subtle gradations and potentially overlooked commonalities, I will explore continuities and echoes between feminist arguments today and those of the past, through two basic questions. What are feminists actually arguing about in #MeToo, and how do these arguments relate to past ones?

SEXUALITY

#MeToo is a movement about sexual harm. Feminist disagreement revolves around what constitutes that harm—how broadly or narrowly it should be defined. The understanding of sexual harm relates to an underlying understanding of sexuality. To what extent is sexuality a site of danger and oppression for women? The answer is relatively straightforward when it involves archetypical cases of sexual assault and sexual harassment, aka, the Weinstein monster. But where there is more ambiguity, as in the case of Aziz Ansari, disagreements—sometimes generational—about the nature of sexual misconduct arise.

Here is where applying the sex-wars lens is interesting. #MeToo feminists and #MeToo feminist detractors line up along the axes of the sex wars of danger versus pleasure. On one side, the #MeToo feminists, like the radical feminists before them, approach sexuality as a site of danger. The very power of #MeToo has been its performative revelation of sexual assault and sexual harassment as a daily reality in women's lives. #MeToo feminists, like the radical feminists who struggled to make rape and harassment visible in the 1970s and 1980s, have revealed the extent to which sexual harm and danger remain ubiquitous for women. Sexuality continues to be a site of danger for women. Sexual misconduct, in turn, is seen on a spectrum of sexual violence, where some of the harms women experience fall short of sexual assault or sexual harassment.

On the other side, the #MeToo feminist detractors can be viewed as the intellectual inheritors of the sex radicals, emphasizing the importance of sexuality as a site of pleasure for women. Daphne Merkin, for example, wants to retain space for sexual desire, for flirting and the ambivalences of sexual attraction.[1] Deneuve et al. defend sexual freedom for women, including what they describe as "a freedom to *bother* as indispensable to sexual freedom."[2] Their position emerges, much like the earlier sex radicals', dialogically: #MeToo feminist detractors argue against what they see as the excesses and dangers of the #MeToo movement that goes too far when it extends beyond the Weinstein archetype:

"Rape is a crime. But trying to pick up someone, however persistently or clumsily, is not—nor is gallantry an attack of machismo."

These #MeToo debates track the earlier sex wars, as each side frames the other in ways that border on caricature. Bracketing the intergenerational epithets, the feminist contestants also reproduced some of the common tropes of the sex wars. #MeToo feminist detractors like Deneuve and Weiss seek to defend sexual pleasure, casting #MeToo feminists as anti-sex Puritans. In response, #MeToo feminists seek to protect women from sexual danger and denounce their critics as not feminist. #MeToo detractors called #MeToo a sex panic and a witch hunt. #MeToo feminists called the detractors part of the backlash by the forces of the patriarchy. As with the sex wars that came before, each side framed the other in starkly oppositional terms, with a bitter affect and more than a little name calling.

But as with the earlier feminist sex wars, a simplified danger/pleasure axis complete with caricatures does not do justice to the arguments at play in feminist disagreements over #MeToo. A slightly less paranoid reading suggests ways in which the more nuanced arguments around sexuality of the earlier sex wars show up in the #MeToo contestations. It is not that the danger/pleasure axis is not relevant; it is that it is not absolute. Disagreements, then and now, have always been around the relative *emphasis* to be placed on sexuality as a site of danger versus sexuality as a site of pleasure.

Radical feminists of the first sex wars, their dominance feminist successors of 2.0, and #MeToo feminists emphasize sexuality as oppressive and dangerous for women. Sexual harms are broadly defined and pervasive. In the shift from sexual harassment and sexual assault to the more contested terrain of sexual misconduct, #MeToo feminists have tried to illustrate the ways in which sexuality remains treacherous for women, as they negotiate unspoken inequalities and subtle coercions. However, just as the earlier radical feminists sought to carve out a space for women's sexuality within the much-maligned realm of erotica, #MeToo feminists seek to affirm the possibility of a positive sexuality for women.

These feminists have sought to create a safe space where women can negotiate sexuality and sexual freedom on a more equal footing. In so doing, many of the #MeToo feminists articulate a vision of sexuality for women that sounds remarkably similar to that of the *sex radicals* of the first sex wars. Van Badham, for example, writing in response to the allegation that #MeToo feminism is puritanical about sex, says, "That's why we are angry. . . . Not because we are puritanical, as the letter claims, but because we are seeking joy from sexual contact on our own terms."[3] In language that echoes that of Carol Vance and the sex radicals, Van Badham argues that #MeToo feminism is all about increasing sexual pleasure by reducing sexual danger: "'Sexual liberty' is the right to determine your own sexual behavior, without coercion."[4]

Conversely, the #MeToo feminist detractors are not only about sexual pleasure. Much like their sex-radical predecessors, they begin with an insistence on their opposition to violence against women. Just as the sex radicals made it clear that they opposed rape and domestic violence, the #MeToo feminist detractors denounce sexual assault and sexual harassment. "Rape is a crime," begins the Deneuve letter. Feminist detractors recognize that sexuality is a site of danger for women, and they want that danger reduced. However, just as with the sex radicals, there is a "but" that follows. "Rape is a crime but . . ." begins the Deneuve letter. In the earlier sex wars, sex radicals saw the radical feminist emphasis on sexuality as dangerously overbroad, reductionist, and monolithic. In the #MeToo context, this manifests as a continuing anxiety over the breadth of sexual harm, where harm comes to take up all the oxygen in the room, leaving no space for the potential pleasures and ambivalences of sexual desires. On the danger/pleasure continuum, is there an overemphasis on danger that spills into sexual negativity? Emily Yoffe, for example, specifically citing the feminist critiques of Sex Wars 2.0, expresses concern over the ways in which sex is constituted as an ever-present danger for women: "As Laura Kipnis, a feminist professor at Northwestern, writes in her book, *Unwanted Advances*, 'I can think of no better way to subjugate women than to convince us that assault is around every corner.'"[5]

Back to the question of where to place the emphasis: #MeToo feminists and their feminist detractors disagree over which forms of sexual conduct are harmful enough to be included within the ambit of #MeToo. In the early sex wars, feminists explicitly disagreed over pornography, S/M, and sex work. Similarly to Sex Wars 2.0, for the #MeToo contestors, it is less about specific practices and more about how broadly sexual harm should be defined. Is Al Franken's behavior a sexual harm? Is Aziz Ansari's? #MeToo feminists say "yes." #MeToo feminist detractors say "maybe not." Many feminist critics worry about diluting the power of the movement by lumping together the trivial and the serious. It is not that Franken's and Ansari's behavior is good; it is that it is not bad enough—it is not a "real" harm. As I explore below, this disagreement is partially a line-drawing exercise about sexual harms and the law. But, beyond the question of law, some #MeToo detractors do not see sexual harm where #MeToo feminists do. Flanagan and Weiss do not view the sexual interaction between Grace and Aziz Ansari as a sexual harm. Deneuve and Merkin do not think flirtation at work is a sexual harm.

The feminist disagreements over sexuality and the relative emphasis on the danger/pleasure axis lead to a different set of anxieties that swirl around the #MeToo movement. These disagreements and their echoes of the sex wars are visible in the debates around #MeToo as witch hunt and sex panic. The witch hunt claim was made in large part by nonfeminist critics. From Woody Allen to Liam Neeson, luminaries of the entertainment industry weighed in. Austrian filmmaker Michael Haneke, for example, stated, "This new puritanism coloured by a hatred of men, arriving on the heels of the #MeToo movement, worries me. . . . As artists, we're starting to be fearful since we're faced with this crusade against any form of eroticism."[6] But, the critique was also made by feminists. Beginning with Masha Gessen, many detractors have expressed concern that #MeToo represents another in a historical series of sex panics in America.[7] Gessen writes that "it is particularly troubling that the frenzied sequence of accusations and punishments is focussed on sex

Locating herself as a person who self-identified as #MeToo, she worries that the movement is playing into what David Halperin has called "America's War on Sex." Drawing on the insights of sex radicals and queer theorists, she observes how American society has "invented new ways and reasons to police sex."[8] The expansive approach to sexual violence on college campuses and the lumping together of the trivial and the serious lead her to suggest that #MeToo runs the risk of becoming a sex panic built on exaggerated dangers. "Sex panics in the past have begun with actual crimes but led to outsize penalties and, more importantly, to a generalized sense of danger."

Judith Levine picked up on Gessen's concerns: "The last couple of months also echo a troublesome history, however, whose legacy persists in the law and the Zeitgeist. 'When does a watershed become a sex panic?' Masha Gessen asked recently in the New Yorker. The answer: what we are witnessing are not the omens of a looming sex panic; they are the symptoms of the one we are already in, and have been in for forty years."[9]

Levine connected the current #MeToo movement with the moral panic around child sexual abuse of the 1980s, as a warning of the potential abuses of overreach. Similarly, Joann Wypijewski in the Nation delved deep into the idea of #MeToo as a sex panic, citing some of the academic literature, and seeking to bring clarity to the way the term was being used. "A sex panic, or moral panic, is a social eruption fanned by the media and characterized by alarm over innocence (stereotypically, white women and children) imperiled. The predator is a lurking, shape-shifting social presence, a menace against which the populace must be mobilized—and has been since at least the 'white slavery' panic of the 1880s–1910s, but almost continuously since the mid-20th century."[10] She argues that the current #MeToo movement fits much of the definition. For Wypijewski, when "ambiguous sexual interactions and harassment are put in the same box,"[11] as they have been with #MeToo, it creates a sex panic that risks reinforcing the racism of the carceral state. Those flagging the sex-panic anxiety, much like the sex radicals before, fear that sexuality is being represented as singularly and omnipotently dangerous.

Deneuve called the movement a witch hunt, specifically addressing the ways in which men were becoming random targets of #MeToo allegations. The term became a more idiomatic way to refer to the ideas underlying a sex panic. Claire Berlinski, admittedly of dubious feminist credentials, cleverly shifted the label to "Warlock Hunt," since it was men who were being hunted: "Mass hysteria has set in. It has become a classic moral panic, one that is ultimately as dangerous to women as to men."[12] Like other detractors, she begins by denouncing the "real" harms: "Do not mistake me for a rape apologist. Harvey Weinstein stands credibly accused of rape." Berlinski takes aim at sexual misconduct, citing the academic literature on moral panics. Underlying the sex-panic critique is the notion of ever-present danger, with sexual predators around every corner. Moral panics overstate the danger; sex panics overstate the danger about sex in particular.

Many #MeToo feminists denied the allegations of sex panics and denounced the discourse of witch hunts.[13] Early on in #MeToo, none other than Caitlin Flanagan wrote "To Hell with the Witch Hunt Debate" in response to Gessen and others raising the specter of a sex panic.[14] Following the Deneuve letter, many feminists wrote that Gessen was wrong.[15] In the *Guardian*, Van Badham pointedly wrote, "Catherine Deneuve: Let Me Explain Why MeToo Is Nothing like a Witch Hunt."[16] Sophie Gilbert similarly declared, "No, #MeToo Isn't McCarthyism."[17] These #MeToo feminists defended the necessity and reasonableness of #MeToo's exposure of pervasive sexual violence against women. It was neither a witch hunt nor a moral panic—the harm was real, not fabricated, the allegations appropriate, not excessive. A few feminist commentators even suggested that categorizing #MeToo as a witch hunt represented its own sex panic.[18]

The debate emerging in academic commentary rather than mainstream media helps reveal how the sex panic/witch hunt debate sets up its own yes/no binary that precludes a deeper look at sexualit as a site of both danger and pleasure for women. It builds on earlier insights around moral panics but redirects attention to how Berlinski and others are engaged in their own sexual hysteria. Katie Gentile argues, "Morality is the trope designed to hide the vulnerability and shame of heterosexual masculinity when it faces any challenge."[19] Gentile recognizes the potential for #MeToo to "swing towards increasing puritanism" precisely because of the patriarchal systems that produce women as sexually vulnerable: "Projecting the morality onto women reinforces their supposed vulnerable victimization, elevates sex as the site of this traumatic humiliation, and liberates men from their accountability."[20] It is a critique that begins to break out of the binary of the sex-panic debate, and the pleasure/danger axis. As with sex radicals before, an exclusive focus on sex as danger for women risks reinforcing the very patriarchal discourses that have constituted women as sexual objects.

Each side was hurling the accusation of sex panic or moral panic at the other. What if, instead of choosing sides and playing into the antagonistic structure of the sex wars, we recognized that each has characteristics reminiscent of sex panics? What if both sides are partially right? The history of exceptionalizing sex continues to make it ripe for moral panics. That both #MeToo and "the witch hunt" can be framed as sex panics speaks volumes about the myriad ways sex and sexuality are understood, and may point to commonalities between the antagonists. Sex is susceptible to sex panics. And once it becomes a panic, the controversy spins out of feminist control. Sexuality is contested, subject to deep anxieties and a history of surveillance, neither of which have been particularly beneficial to women.

We need to recognize the multiple and contradictory ways women have been subject to surveillance, control, and oppression in and through sexuality. The very articulation of women's sexual subordination and the associated harms runs the risk of reinforcing the sexualization. Women are harmed and controlled through sexual violence. But articulating that harm threatens to reinforce dominant sexual discourses about women's victimization, weakness, and need for protection. The sex wars, then and now, have circled these paradoxes, each side trying to address the harms of controlled or uncontrolled sexuality. A way out might be to recognize that both sides might be right.

Some feminists have sought to bridge this divide. Rebecca Traister envisions #MeToo as not only about sex but fundamentally about power.[21] She shares Gessen's concern "that this moment will end with a recommitment to patrolling women's virtue and undermining their sexual agency." The problem, she argues, might be mitigated if we recognized "that this is not, at its heart, about sex at all—or at least not wholly. What it's really about is work, and women's equality in the workplace, and more broadly, about the rot at the core of our power structures that makes it harder for women to do work because the whole thing is tipped toward men."[22] The problem lies not in the fact of sexuality but in the constitution of women as sexualized objects.

> What makes women vulnerable is not their carnal violability, but rather the way that their worth has been understood as fundamentally erotic, ornamental; that they have not been taken seriously as equals; that they have been treated as some ancillary reward that comes with the kinds of power men are taught to reach for and are valued for achieving. How to make clear that the trauma of the smaller trespasses—the boob grabs and unwanted kisses or come-ons from bosses—is not necessarily even *about* the sexualized act in question.

Traister further tries to disarticulate sexual acts from women's identities, and reorient the discussion to one of inequalities of power in the workplace. It is an analysis informed by the insights of sex radicals and their contemporaries that seeks to break the traditional sexualization of women and the exceptionalization of sexual harm—to challenge how women are constituted in and through the discourses of sexual harm and vulnerability. Traister's more nuanced analysis can then share the concern about sex panics, while also taking seriously the need for "addressing and beginning to dismantle men's unjustly disproportionate claim to every kind of power in the public and professional world."[23] Traister's intervention is an important one that refuses the simplistic divides that have plagued the sex wars and might help extricate #MeToo feminist contestations from the antagonistic binaries of the earlier sex wars. But, it is at risk of being drowned out by the catfights—a favorite of mainstream media, to which both feminist supporters and feminist critics alike fall prey.

#MeToo feminist contestations hold much in common with the sex wars on the question of sexuality, both in substance and in caricature, threatening to reinforce the danger/pleasure axis. But, just as in the earlier sex wars, #MeToo feminists and feminist detractors have more in common than first meets the eye. #MeToo feminists strongly affirm women's right to say yes to sex, while feminist detractors affirm their right to say no to sex. Both sides worry that the controversies around sexuality can quickly get coopted to maintain the status quo and its deeply problematic discourse around sexuality (although their emphases on which parts are most problematic differ). The loud message remains one of polarized antagonisms, where #MeToo feminists are framed as anti-sex puritanical victims who want protections from male sexuality, while #MeToo feminist detractors are characterized as callously indifferent to the reality of sexual violence against women.

Agency and Victimization

Alongside the danger-versus-pleasure disagreements is a second set related to victimization, agency, and consent. #MeToo, as a movement against sexual violence, is about women (and some men) as victims of this sexual violence. #MeToo feminists and #MeToo feminist detractors line up along the sex-wars axis of victims versus agents. The millions of women who said "me too" identified themselves as having been subjected to sexual assault and/or sexual harassment. They identified themselves as the victims—or, in a shift in language, the survivors—of sexual violence.

#MeToo feminist detractors repeatedly point to the movement's characterization of women as victims, devoid of sexual agency. Framing her remarks in generational language, Merkin wrote, "We seem to be returning to a victimology paradigm for young women, in particular, in which they are perceived to be—and perceive themselves to be—as frail as Victorian housewives."[24] The Deneuve letter opined that, instead of liberating women, the #MeToo movement was at risk of "enslav[ing] them to a status of eternal victim and reducing them to defenseless preys of male chauvinist demons."[25] Gessen argued that "women are increasingly treated like children: defenseless, incapable of consent, always on the verge of being victimized."[26]

These concerns reached a fever pitch in the aftermath of the Ansari story. The detractors were quick to criticize Grace for failing to exercise agency. Flanagan lambasted her: "Apparently there is a whole country full of young women who don't know how to call a cab."[27] Weiss expressed a similar concern that #MeToo was "transform[ing] what ought to be a movement for women's empowerment into an emblem for female helplessness." She observed, "The single most distressing thing to me about this story is that the only person with any agency in the story seems to be Aziz Ansari. The woman is merely acted upon." This obliteration of agency is another example of #MeToo going "too far." The feminist detractors with their often inflammatory language—intellectual inheritors of the sex radicals—reject the status of women as exclusively sexual victims, seek to preserve agency, and refuse an all-encompassing predatory male sexuality.

The debate often zeroed in on the question of consent, and the contested terrain of affirmative consent. While many #MeToo feminists argue in favor of an affirmative consent standard, the #MeToo detractors liked to mock and caricature it. Weiss, for example, calls out "digital hosannas by young feminists, who insisted that consent is only consent if it is affirmative, active, continuous and . . . enthusiastic."[2]

Merkin sarcastically wrote, "Asking for oral consent before proceeding with a sexual advance seems both innately clumsy and retrograde, like going back to the childhood game of 'Mother, May I?'"[29]

Once again the sex wars of old—with radical feminists insisting that women did not and could not consent to prostitution or pornography, sex radicals arguing that women's sexual agency needed to be recognized and affirmed—get performed. In the campus sexual assault debates of the 1990s, activists seeking to make the prevalence of date rape visible were met with the likes of Katie Roiphe, who insisted that women take responsibility for their sexual choices. Even before #MeToo erupted, the most current round of the sex wars, particularly on university campuses, replayed this victimization/agency debate. While activists again sought to reveal the prevalence of sexual violence on campuses, others pushed back against what they saw as draconian sexual-violence policies that undermined women's sexual agency.[30]

#MeToo feminists focus on problematic sexual encounters and the absence of robust consent, while detractors focus on the overemphasis on women's sexual victimization and the absence of agency. MacKinnon's ghost—the impossibility of consent in a sexuality constituted in and through women's oppression—haunts the discussion. Many #MeToo feminists post-Ansari have sought to promote a discussion of sexual interactions that are "dubiously consensual."[31] But there are also clear echoes of the sex radicals' emphasis on the importance of recognizing sexual agency in women's lives, of not overly determining women as victims of predatory male heterosexuality. Indeed, Gessen even invoked the earlier feminist sex wars in her critique of #MeToo: 'The battles . . . concerned a lot of the issues directly relevant to the current moment of sexual renegotiation. One such issue is consent. One side argued that no consensual act should be punishable by either law or social sanction. The other side focussed on the limits of consent, arguing that consent was sometimes—or even most often—not entirely freely given, and that some things, like injury sustained during S & M sex, could not be the object of consent." Gessen then weighed in, unapologetically, on the side of consent and agency.

In response to this victimization critique, #MeToo feminists, trying to complicate the dichotomy, argued that they were attempting to shift the conversation on consent and sexual harm. Osita Nwanevu argued that "these young feminists don't want to criminalize all dubiously consensual encounters, as Weiss argues, but rather subject them to criticism."[32] Emma Gray wrote of the "gray area" of sexuality, where the problem is not the absence of consent from a legal standard, but the ways in which sex may still be experienced as harmful; where, in Traister's words, sex may still be "bad in ways that are worth talking about."[33] Traister had earlier written about sex that could be consensual but neither wanted nor desired. #MeToo feminists, particularly in the aftermath of the Ansari story, were trying to broaden the conversation to include the many problematic ways in which women may have unwanted sex and negotiate their sexual lives in less than ideal or equal conditions. Anna Silman similarly argued that it was not about consent: "As critics of the Ansari story have pointed out, these aren't stories where women firmly vocalize a lack of consent; rather, these are stories about how young women—having internalized society's messages about how it is their responsibility to please men, to be compliant, to be down for anything—end up acquiescing to something that makes them feel rotten inside."[34]

Many of the #MeToo feminists were not simply refusing the possibility of consent in a MacKinnonesque fashion but were arguing that the conversation needed to move to a more robust version of consent, and in fact beyond consent. The more subtle responses where sexuality is a site of ambivalence—often lost in the preferred catfight narrative—are from #MeToo feminists who have tried to promote a more nuanced discussion. Emma Gray writes of the need "to renegotiate the sexual narratives we've long accepted. And that involves having complicated conversations about sex that is violating but not criminal."[35] Inheritors of the more complicated vision of the sex radicals, these feminist voices seek to disrupt and nuance sexuality and consent.

As with sexuality, #MeToo feminist contestations share much in common with the sex wars then and now, on questions of victimization versus agency. They disagree on the relative emphasis on women as victims of sexual violence (tracking danger) versus women as sexual agents (tracking pleasure). They caricature each other's positions on the victim/agency axis in ways that obscure nuance. The debates threaten to reproduce this simplified axis and as in the earlier sex wars, the commonalities get missed. While much of the nuance is lost in the more individualistic iterations of their arguments, #MeToo feminist detractors do offer an important reminder of the paternalistic ways in which women have been historically constituted as victims in need of protection. In a manner reminiscent of sex radicals' opposition to radical feminism's focus on victimization, feminist detractors recognize sexuality as socially and historically constituted in ways that oppress women. All agree that women have been victims of male sexual violence. They just disagree on the implications of that history for the present.

While #MeToo feminists came out of the gate with messages of women's pervasive victimization by male sexual violence, they are adamant about creating space for their sexual agency. As Badham declared, "We are seeking joy from sexual contact on our terms." Echoing the demands of sex radicals, #MeToo feminists seek to renegotiate the terms of sexuality. They seek to reveal the multiple ways that agency is constrained and falls short of illegal coercion within contemporary heterosexuality. #MeToo feminists may sound like radical and dominance feminists in their denunciation of widespread sexual violence, but they also echo the sex-radical message that women do exercise sexual agency, albeit in limited ways, and the goal should be to expand that agency.

The message that comes through loud and clear is one of #MeToo feminists highlighting a culture of victimization, and #MeToo feminist detractors saying, "Pull yourself up by your bootstraps and call a cab." However, once again, both sides of the #MeToo debate echo Carol Vance's powerful assertion of sexuality as a domain both of "restriction" and of "agency."[36] To focus on the former "ignores women's experience with sexual agency and choice," while focusing only on the latter "ignores the patriarchal structure in which women act."[37] #MeToo feminists and #MeToo feminist detractors both seek, in Vance's words, to "envision a world which makes possible women's sexual autonomy and sexual choice." The differences are real; the antagonists do not agree on the extent of women's sexual agency.[38] Highlighting points of similitude is not intended to gloss over disagreement in favor of a utopian feminist consensus; rather, it shines a more complex light on the conflict, and offers glimpses of potential synergies. Feminist disagreement might be put to productive use, in rethinking the victim/agency paradox.

Law

#MeToo did not emerge as a movement about law. It was in fact a protest against law's failure. Law has repeatedly refused to recognize harm, from police not laying charges to prosecutors not pursuing them to acquittals and dismissals of "allegations" of sexual violence against women. Exposing the ubiquity of sexual violence underscored the failure of law to adequately redress or prevent it. #MeToo initially played out in nonlegal forums—powerful men were felled through media reports and corporate firings, bypassing courts and litigation. #MeToo feminism not only points out law's failure; it challenges the centrality of law as the arbiter of sexual violence. #MeToo's feminist critics, in contrast, worry about the potential abuses of this challenge.

In this section, I tease out these underlying feminist disagreements about law and how they track earlier conflicts. However, I also argue that there are deep tensions regarding the role of law, both within #MeToo feminism and among the feminist detractors—tensions that reside in the underlying power of law as the exclusive arbiter of sexual violence. Both #MeToo feminism and #MeToo feminist critics challenge the power of the law while also reinforcing it. This complicated relationship with the law is reminiscent of the feminist disagreements that have come before.

#MeToo emerged as both a critique of law's failure and a challenge to law's exclusive power to define and adjudicate sexual harm. The millions of public iterations of #MeToo were a powerful performance of regulatory failure—the sheer pervasiveness of sexual violence underscoring the colossal failure of law to adequately redress or prevent it. Laura Hudson observed, in response to the growing backlash,

> If the environment created by #MeToo is less than ideal in its standards of proof, that is a direct product of a deeply broken justice system where only an estimated seven out of a thousand rapes will result in a felony conviction. There's a reason why cases of rape and harassment have increasingly been tried in the court of public opinion: it is the only court where most victims have a chance in hell of experiencing anything close to justice.[39]

#MeToo was criticizing a "broken justice system," while presenting a challenge to it. As Hudson infers, since the justice system, criminal and civil, fails to address sexual harm, women have taken their stories of sexual injury elsewhere. They have shared them with mainstream and social media.

In taking their stories outside of law—outside of criminal and civil prosecutions— #MeToo presents a direct challenge to the law's exclusive power to define sexual harms. Law has long been the arbiter of sexual violence, both defining harm and deciding case by case whether it has occurred. It functions as the metric of the truth of the claim. In the days of the early radical feminists, sexual harm was barely cognizable in law. But, in the intervening years, and in large part due to feminist law reform, sexual harm has become entrenched in law. Feminists recognized this discursive and constitutive power of law, seeking to make a range of harms against women legible and legitimate in and through their recognition in law. Recognizing sexual assault, domestic violence, and sexual harassment as criminal and/or civilly actionable has been a crucial feminist strategy that has made the harms legible. Indeed, this was part of the thinking behind the failed attempt by radical feminists to make pornography legally actionable. To make a practice legally action-able is to make it cognizable as a harm. It is part of the symbolic power of law reform. But, paradoxically, this feminist strategy also reinforced law's power as the arbiter of the truth claim. As adjudicator, it reinforced law's power to determine whether the harm has occurred.

#MeToo represents a fundamental challenge to law's exclusive power to define and adjudicate sexual violence. #MeToo feminists refuse to allow the law—its failure—to determine the existence of sexual harms. They have not only taken their stories outside the legal realms of pros-ecutions and courtrooms; they are refusing to allow law to define the harms. As Jessica Valenti has argued, "#MeToo is not about what's legal, it's about what's right."[40] Women, she says, are more focused on "shifting norms than enforcing the ones we already have." #MeToo is about rec-ognizing sexual injury beyond what the law delineates and challenging the normalization of those injuries. Anna Silman similarly observes that #MeToo is not about law but about changing the conversation to "one in which women are eager to discuss and change expectations around sexual manners more generally, *not just to litigate right and wrong*. It's a more complicated conversation, because the boundaries transgressed are less clear, the villains less outsized, the causes less concrete."[41]

#MeToo feminism seems to have much in common with early radical feminist activism—seeking to expose sexual violence, without advocat-ing legal intervention. #MeToo emerged as a kind of collective con-sciousness raising, a revelation of the pervasiveness of sexual violence in women's lives. In its first iterations, #MeToo was not a demand for legal changes. As with radical feminism in the early part of the sex wars, law was not the terrain where the conversation was taking place. Radical feminists initially eschewed the role of law but eventually became di vided over it. Early radical feminists—through Women Against Violence Against Women and even Women Against Violence in Pornography and Media—rather saw consumer boycotts as the tools to bring about change in the representation of women in media. Similarly, the early days of #MeToo focused on the companies that Weinstein, Lauer, Rose, Spacey, and others worked for or ran: Weinstein Company, NBC, ABC, Netflix. The hashtag blew up with no concerted strategy driving it—but the response to accusations was all about corporate responsibility. This evokes the early strategies of radical feminists—an overlooked parallel that was one of their most successful engagements (pre-ordinance struggles). RCA records did in fact change its advertising policies.

#MeToo feminism can be seen as a call to bypass the law. It both points out the failure of law through the sheer ubiquity of women's articulations of sexual assault and sexual harassment, and challenges its exclusivity as the arbiter of sexual harm. The power of law has fueled the fire of some of the feminist detractors of the #MeToo movement. Indeed, the first inklings of feminist disagreement about #MeToo were related to the underlying role of law. In late October 2017, Wendy Kaminer—a feminist who has featured centrally in the sex wars, then and now—warned of the perils of "vigilante feminism." Following the #MeToo allegations against senior journalist Mark Halperin[42] and Leon Wieseltier from the *New Republic*, Kaminer expressed concern about the impossibility of balancing the mandate to believe all women with fairness towards the accused: "Categorically believing accusers turns a mere accusation of wrongdoing into proof that it occurred. Women who cheer this virtually irrebuttable presumption of guilt, considering due process for alleged harassers a component of rape culture, are cheering a thoughtless, treacherous form of vigilante feminism."[43] Similar criticisms took root following the allegations against Al Franken, when #MeToo detractors expressed two sets of concerns—a substantive concern that #MeToo had gone too far, lumping more trivial behaviors with serious sexual misconduct, and a procedural one, that #MeToo was violating the due process of alleged perpetrators.[44]

Both the procedural issue of the relevance of due process and the substantive issue over the scope of the behavior that is appropriately captured by #MeToo are related to underlying disagreements about the relationship between law and sexual harm. There are two versions of this critique of #MeToo. The first is one that is produced by the power of law. Underlying the procedural and substantive critique is the understated assumption that law (and often criminal law) has the authority to determine the existence of sexual harm. The second, broader critique is one that more directly challenges the power of law (and often criminal law). Robust procedural protections and more restrictive definitions of sexual harm are required as a bulwark against the carceral state. Both versions critique the absence of due process and the lumping of sexual practices, but they do so for very different reasons, from different intellectual traditions, and with different implications.

Due Process

The most common, and narrower, due process critique of #MeToo is intertwined with the power of criminal law as the sole arbiter of sexual harm. At a basic level, due process is only invoked in the face of state action. If, as in the early #MeToo allegations against Weinstein, Lauer, Rose, et al., there is no state action, then there is no requirement of due process. But law's power to define and arbitrate the truth of sexual violence is cast over each iteration of #MeToo. There can be no sexual harm unless the criminal law says so. There can be no criminal law without due process, which necessarily includes the presumption of innocence. Accordingly, in the absence of a criminal trial establishing that sexual harm occurred, there is no harm deserving of consequence. Because if there is no trial, there is no harm. By this logic, if law alone has the power to define sexual harm, there can be no sexual harm without law, and accordingly without due process. Individual men being fired for alleged sexual harms is transformed into a violation of due process where no such requirement exists, precisely because of the very discursive power of law over sexual harm.

Some #MeToo feminists added fuel to the fire of this critique. Emily Linden famously tweeted, "I'm actually not at all concerned about innocent men losing their jobs over false sexual assault/harassmen allegations. Sorry if some innocent men's reputations have to take a hit in the process of undoing the patriarchy, that is a price I am absolutely willing to pay."[45] Feminist (and many nonfeminist) critics jumped on statements like these, and expressed concern about the demise of individual men in the absence of the presumption of innocence. As Daphne Merkin opined in the *New York Times*, "I don't believe that scattershot, life-destroying denunciations are the way to upend [sexism and the abusive power of the patriarchy]. In our current climate, to be accused is to be convicted. Due process is nowhere to be found."[46]

Yet, the principles of due process are not strictly speaking relevant. It is generally accepted that due process is a protection against arbitrary government action. Procedural due process requires that government follow fair procedures before depriving an individual of life, liberty, or property. It applies to criminal proceedings, but also to civil and administrative proceedings that involve individual claims against the government. The presumption of innocence has an even narrower scope—it is a basic principle that applies to individuals who have been accused of crimes. Neither media reports nor corporate firings implicate due process or the presumption of innocence. Media reporting is governed by journalistic standards of verification and the potential of defamation claims. Corporate firings are governed by employment standards, contract law, and potential of wrongful dismissal claims. Due process is not among the standards or principles.

Yet, due process *sounds* relevant. As some legal commentators have observed, the allegations of the violation of due process and the presumption of innocence are being deployed colloquially: "Due process as a cultural matter is influenced by legal ideas but is really a cluster of fluid notions that arise when people in different social and political contexts react to what they perceive as unfairness, abuse, and oppression."[47] The concerns underlying the due process objections are not about the constitutional requirements of due process. Rather, the concepts of due process and the presumption of innocence have become discursive stand-ins for the idea of fairness. To say that there is no due process is the equivalent of saying, "It's not fair." And that is precisely the way the due process objection has been used in the wake of the #MeToo allegations. To be accused of sexual misconduct in the absence of a criminal trial, with its due process protections, is said to be unfair. And the perceived unfairness comes back to the power of law: there can be no sexual harm unless the law has said so. The power of law to exclusively define and arbitrate sexual violence makes due process sound relevant, even where it is not.[48] This narrower feminist critique of the absence of due process can then be seen to be produced by and reinforcing of the power of law over sexual harm. There can be no sexual violence unless law says so, and there can be no law without due process. Law—and law alone—should be the arbiter; otherwise, it is not fair.

But, there is also a broader feminist critique of due process that challenges the role of law in addressing sexual violence. Emily Yoffe, discussing the Al Franken case, makes connections with the campus sexual violence policies and its feminist critics. She quotes from Elizabeth Bartholet, Nancy Gertner, Janet Halley, and Jeannie Suk Gersen's *Fairness for All under Title IX* paper[49] that the procedures on campus today "'are frequently so unfair as to be truly shocking." For example, "'Some colleges and universities fail even to give students the complaint against them, or notice of the factual basis of the charges, the evidence gathered, or the identities of witnesses.'"[50]

Judith Levine made even more explicit connections between #MeToo and the critique of carceral feminism. She warns of the perils of #MeToo following a carceral approach, with its emphasis on retribution and state punishment. She points out that this approach is one that results in the disproportionate incarceration of African American men, while simultaneously leaving behind "poor women of color, single mothers, sex workers, undocumented immigrants, transwomen, and the incarcerated."[5] Levine makes a plea for #MeToo to avoid these past mistakes—to "resist the thrill of Jacobin purges"—and points out that "the *longue durée* of mass incarceration and punitive surveillance teaches us that state violence is no answer to interpersonal violence."[52] She argues that #MeToo should instead follow a path of restorative justice: "#MeToo is a kind of spontaneous truth and reconciliation commission. Its greatest power is political—the revelation of systematic oppression."

The underlying defense of due process is here related to a challenge to the carceral inclinations of law in addressing sexual violence. Like the inchoate vision of the sex radicals and the overt critique of anti-carceral feminists in Sex Wars 2.0, the #MeToo critics challenge the expansion of the criminal law to address sexual harms. While the defense of due process can be seen to reinforce the normative power of law, these #MeToo feminist critics also seek to displace the criminal justice system in favor of alternative visions of justice. The position is paradoxical, yet logical: as long as there *is* criminal law, due process is essential, since otherwise innocent and disproportionally marginalized men run the risk of being incarcerated. While the goal may be to displace the carceral approach, the critique of the carceral renders due process and the presumption of innocence in the context of sexual violence all the more important.

Sexual Misconduct

The debates about the relationship between law and sexual violence resonate with the controversies surrounding "sexual misconduct." Well before the Ansari story broke, many of the #MeToo allegations were denounced as going too far. Andrea Peyser, for example, wrote of "lumping" the trivial with the serious, following the allegations against Al Franken and George Bush.[53] It was a critique repeated many times in the aftermath of the Ansari story.[54] Many critics (again, feminist and nonfeminist alike) were quick to note that sexual misconduct is not a legally actionable harm.

Yet #MeToo feminists were not here pointing to the failure of law to address criminal sexual conduct. Rather, in the outpouring of feminist writings in the days following the Ansari story, they were advocating for a broader conversation that rejected the idea that law alone should define sexual injury. In the wake of the Ansari story, many said conduct that falls short of criminally or civilly actionable conduct can still be experienced as harm and is worthy of discussion. Admittedly, in the Babe.net story, Grace ultimately articulated the harm she had suffered as sexual assault. Yet, many other feminists approached her story with a more nuanced view. Jessica Valenti, for example, tweeted, "Our standard for sexual behavior has to be more than what's legal or illegal."[55] Emma Gray similarly observed, "The sexual encounter Grace described falls into what I see as a gray area of violating, noncriminal sex—the kind of sex that Rebecca Traister described in 2015 as 'bad in ways that are worth talking about,' what Jessica Valenti described on Twitter as an interaction that the 'culture considers "normal," but is "oftentimes harmful." Behavior need not fall under the legal definition of sexual assault or rape to be wrong or violating or upsetting."[56]

Again, #MeToo feminism seems to resemble early radical feminist positions on sexual violence that did not make demands for law; rather, the earlier movement was a consciousness-raising movement that put various forms of sexual misconduct—including sexist representations—on a spectrum of male sexual violence. So too are #MeToo feminists engaged in consciousness-raising exercises—telling stories of sexual conduct that have left women feeling injured in ways that are hard to articulate.

Yet, this is not what the critics heard—or accepted. Feminist critics argued that including these forms of sexual misconduct trivialized and diluted the "real" power of #MeToo. And this critique was embedded in the power of law to define sexual harm, that is, in the implicit acceptance that a sexual harm is only a real harm if it is illegal. The critique focused on the idea that the conduct of Al Franken or Aziz Ansari was not sexual harassment or sexual assault, and therefore not legally actionable. The critique seems to imply that those alleging the misconduct are advocating that this action *become* legally actionable.

Given law's power to define and arbitrate sexual violence, the idea of sexual harm that is not actionable is not legible; it makes no sense. As a result, the objection of "going too far" is pervasive. Yet, it is unclear that the feminists of #MeToo are necessarily calling for sexual misconduct to be legally actionable. Rather, they are arguing that it needs to be part of a collective conversation about the terms of consensual and ethical sex. But the law's power to define sexual harm makes this claim almost impossible to hear. If there is no legally actionable harm, then there must not be a harm.

The allegations are only trivializing or diluting if sexual harms are viewed as an either/or: either sexual conduct is illegal and harmful, or it is legal and not harmful. Law here is the dividing line. There is no doubt that much of the power of #MeToo was in its revelation of the pervasiveness of illegal sexual misconduct. But, if sexual conduct is seen on a spectrum, rather than simply as an either/or for legal purposes, broader conversations become possible. Questions of consensual and therefore legal but unwanted or ambivalent sex can come into view. This is the conversation that many women want to have in the wake of #MeToo. But the legal binary, and law's power to exclusively define the existence of sexual harm, precludes this very conversation. It is, by virtue of the power of law, reduced to the incommensurable and/or the absurd.

But there was also a broader feminist critique of sexual misconduct related to the critique of the carceral. Some #MeToo feminist critics expressed concern about broadening definitions of sexual harm, which could serve to reinforce broader *legal* definitions. A few feminist writers specifically referred to the work of Janet Halley, Jeannie Suk Gerson, Laura Kipnis—the inheritors of the sex radicals in Sex Wars 2.0—and echoed their concerns. Emily Yoffe, for example, quoted the *Fairness for All* report on the substantive overreach of these policies: "Definitions of sexual wrongdoing on college campuses are now seriously overbroad," the feminist Harvard Law professors wrote. They continued, "They are so broad as to put students engaged in behavior that is overwhelmingly common in the context of romantic relationships to be accused of sexual misconduct." Also citing Halley et al., Judith Levine expressed concern that #MeToo was "conflating a wide range of behaviors as equally harmful, broadening the definitions of illegal acts and hardening their punishment, when the laws we already have are good—they just need to be enforced" and that #MeToo was "yielding to the desire for retribution."[57]

The underlying critique of lumping together a range of bad sexual conduct is related to a challenge to the carceral inclinations of law in addressing sexual violence. As with their critique of due process, these feminist critics are worried about the expansion of the criminal law in addressing sexual harms. It is not that these critics are defending the sexual behaviors as good (although as discussed in the section above, there are differences of opinion on the normativity of the conduct). Rather, it is that in the carceral moment, any articulation of sexual harm is likely to be construed as supporting an expansion of the criminal, as supporting the desire for the retributive, and as reinforcing all of the structural inequalities that haunt the carceral state.

The lumping-together-of-sexual-misconduct critique, then, like the due-process critique, can be seen to have two distinct versions. For some, the problem of lumping is that it trivializes real sexual harm, which must be determined by the law. In this vision, it is incommensurable that there is a harm that is not legally actionable. For others, the problem is connected to overly broad definitions of sexual violence—in criminal, civil, and campus sexual violence policies—and the ties to the carceral. The first reinforces the power of law; the second worries about it.

Viewed in this way, it is also possible to see some parallels across #MeToo and its feminist critics. Both #MeToo narratives and the broader feminist critique of sexual misconduct challenge the power of law as the exclusive arbiter of sexual violence, although they do so in different ways. Regarding due process, where #MeToo and its critics seem so diametrically opposed, both #MeToo feminists and the broader feminist critique see value in moving to alternative registers. If the problem is law—for #MeToo feminists, in its utter regulatory failure, and for the broader critiques, in its carceral modality—then there is a shared inclination to consider turns away from it. Explorations of the potential of restorative and transformative justice are popping up across some of the #MeToo divides

It remains unclear what #MeToo feminism wants from law. Is there a gesture towards more law that would reinforce the power of law? Certainly, discussions about reforms to sexual harassment law are afoot. But demands for further reforms to the criminal law of sexual assault are less evident. Does #MeToo feminism want more law? More criminal law? Or is it simply the societal echo emanating from the power of law? It is too soon to answer these questions, since it remains to be seen how the debates will play out in the aftermath of #MeToo. While much of #MeToo has played out on nonlegal terrains, legal prosecutions are currently underway, and the outcomes are unknowable.

In the past, and in current debates in the context of Title IX and sexual violence on campuses, radical feminists and their contemporary inheritors have argued for more law. These feminists have had no problem turning to the state—or in the context of campus sexual violence, university administrative institutions. They have promoted broader definitions of sexual harm, have advocated for affirmative standards of consent, and are less concerned with procedural protections for the accused. Sex radicals were more skeptical of the turn to the state well before carceral feminism was named, although as some feminist scholars have pointed out, they never developed much of a theory of law.[58] In the current iteration, the feminist inheritors of the sex radicals have a far more developed theory of law. The critiques of carceral and governance feminisms have given rise to a concern with procedural protections, narrower definitions of sexual harms and consent, and a more thorough critique of a punitive penal state.

#MeToo inherits this contested feminist terrain, and its future course remains to be written. It could simply reinforce these antagonisms or look for a way out. Both #MeToo and its feminist detractors are tied up in a feminist Gordian knot—both, in different ways, risk reinforcing the very power of criminal law while seeking to challenge it. The damning critique of law and the overtures towards more law, real or imagined, operate to reinforce the normative power of law around sexual violence. The critics, conversely, in defending due process and narrower definitions of sexual harm, also reinforce the normative power of the criminal law as the exclusive arbiter of sexual violence, while some challenge the carceral state. It is a current instantiation of an enduring dilemma—how to address the harms without reinforcing the deeply problematic discourses of sexual difference.

Ann Pellegrini has written eloquently of the power of #MeToo and the limitations of the legal language that flows from it: "The capacity to represent sexual violence, to give words to one's experience, is important; it may even be mutative. But these narratives take shape through already existing linguistic conventions and conceptual frames. 'The law' is a powerful conceptual frame, which offers an alluring promise of truth and nothing but the truth. It may overtake other ways of thinking about, talking about, and addressing sexual violence."[59] Pellegrini observes the ways in which legal definitions of sexual harm demand that "individuals narrate their experience in terms legible to the state or other empowered arbiters of the claim a victim is bringing."[60] But, these legal definitions may well obscure "what happened, even as they come to capture and, potentially, distort what can be said or known." She returns to the gray of sexuality, and the need to move outside of law's exclusive frame: "We need to provide and cultivate in an ongoing way other discursive and institutional sites where the gray, the messiness of what can go wrong in sex and in human relating, can be discussed, and conduct those discussions outside the frame of 'the law.'" Pellegrini has no concrete answers, but she asks crucial questions: "How do we push back against the legal and bureaucratic 'capture' of the ways we frame, talk about, and seek remedy for sexual violence? How do we talk about sexual errors, bad sex, sex that disappoints without going to court in actual fact or in our imaginations?" How, in other words, can we talk about sexual harms in ways that are not already defined by law?

CONCLUSION—HISTORY IN THE PRESENT

Just like the Sex Wars 2.0, the feminist contestations within #MeToo are at risk of becoming antagonistic and inflammatory. They do not need to do so. We can bring our history into the present. We need to listen to voices of the past in complexity rather than caricature. The debates and failed projects of feminism past are, I believe, crucial in developing more composite approaches to the regulation of sexuality in general, and sexual harm in particular.

History warns us that sexuality debates are easily hijacked by those without feminist sensibilities. Both sides of the historical and current feminist sex wars have found themselves in uncomfortable alliances— radical feminists with social conservatives and a puritanical anti-sex position; sex radicals with sexual libertarians and anti-feminists who deny the very existence of sexual harms. Each side decries the other for its nonfeminist alliances and implications, paying less attention to its own. Yet, a truth lies in the historical appropriation of feminist narratives, by all sides.

Our history warns us that contestation is easily reduced to caricature. Just as the earlier sex wars are often seen through the simplified lens of how each side painted the other, so too do the current sex wars, and their manifestation in the debates over #MeToo, run that risk. We need to find ways to read disagreement that are not reductive, dismissive, or insolent. There is a long and unproductive legacy of feminists denouncing each other as not feminist. To state the obvious, this simply needs to stop. However, the affects of contestation need to be taken seriously, as feminists and others search for better ways to negotiate the difficulties of disagreement. History also warns us that feminist contestation is easily reduced to "either/or," rather than ambivalence, partialities, and humility. #MeToo feminists could fall into the trap of reifying the "either/or" of sexuality by denouncing their critics, not only as not feminists but as having little or no contribution to make to the debate.

How then might we reconsider sexual harms and modalities of legal regulation? The conversations initiated through #MeToo—despite their popular appropriation into binary thinking—create the possibility for a rethinking of sexual harms, women's agency, and the role of law. If we move beyond the either/or of legally recognized sexual harms, which either does or does not bring the full force of the state to bear on the conduct, the accused, and the victim, we might be able to open a different conversation about sexuality—one that recognizes sexuality as a site of both danger and pleasure; that recognizes women's agency and the pervasiveness of sexual violence; and that even acknowledges that law need not occupy the field of definition of sexual harms. Recognizing the potential harm of sexual misconduct need not be equated with recognizing the harms of sexual assault or sexual harassment. Sexual misconduct does not have to be understood as criminally or civilly actionable. It could be reframed in more ethical terms— in the language of respect and desire. The misunderstanding around sexual encounters could be a place to begin a discussion about sexuality rather than a legal truth claim seeking to vindicate one party or the other.

Loosening law's hold—and, particularly, criminal law's hold—on the definition of sexual harms could lead to deeper feminist conversations, allowing for an affirmation of sexual harm, without endorsing a carceral state. Nor does this suggestion need to be seen in binary terms as entirely rejecting the role of law in the regulation of sexual harm. Might the critique of the carceral lead to more fulsome engagement with civil claims rather than criminal ones? And might it also trigger a rethinking, in terms of not only definitions of harm but also remedial responses? These debates and their underlying antagonisms and hostilities need to be broken open if #MeToo is to contribute to a new and transformative sexual politics. These are the questions to which I now turn.

4

READING BESIDE THE QUEER/ FEMINIST DIVIDE

Avital Ronell, a professor of German and comparative literature at New York University, was accused of sexual harassment by her former male graduate student, Nimrod Reitman. An eleven-month Title IX investigation found that Ronell had engaged in physical and verbal sexual harassment that was "sufficiently pervasive to alter the terms and conditions of Mr. Reitman's learning environment."[1] NYU suspended her for the 2018–2019 academic year without pay. The media initially framed the incident as a kind of #MeToo reversal; as the *New York Times* headline asked, "What Happens to #MeToo When a Feminist Is Accused?"[2] But, there were many more twists and turns. Not only was Ronell a woman and her accuser a man; she was the professor and he was the student; she was a lesbian and her accuser, a gay man. The details that emerged in the press made for salacious he said/she said reading. Ronell sent intimate and flirtatious e-mails. According to Reitman, the e-mails were part of a pattern of ongoing sexual harassment. According to Ronell, "Our communications—which Reitman now claims constituted sexual harassment—were between two adults, a gay man and a queer woman, who share an Israeli heritage, as well as a penchant for florid and campy communications arising from our common academic backgrounds and sensibilities."[3] According to Reitman's Title IX complaint, the conduct went further than unwanted e-mails: Ronell, on many occasions, demanded he sleep in her bed; she touched and kissed him. Ronell denied all allegations of sexual contact. She sought to discredit the complaint—and the complainant—as a less than competent graduate student: "His main dilemma was the incoherency in his writing, and lack of a recognizable argument."[4]

The case first became public through a letter of support leaked by a philosophy blog. The letter, written to the president and provost of NYU, was signed by fifty-one academics, including prominent feminist and queer academics such as Judith Butler, Joan Scott, and Gayatri Spivak.[5] The letter became its own cause célèbre. The signatories admitted that they had little information about the case—"we have no access to the confidential dossier"—but expressed their admiration for Ronell. They stressed Ronell's fame and influence: "We wish to communicate first in the clearest terms our profound and enduring admiration for Professor Ronell whose mentorship of students has been no less than remarkable over many years."[6] The letter detailed her professional accomplishments and influence in the fields of German studies, comparative literature, and literary studies: "Her intellectual influence is felt throughout the humanities. . . . There is arguably no more important figure in literary studies at NYU than Avital Ronell whose intellectual power and fierce commitment to students and colleagues has [sic]established her as an exemplary intellectual and mentor in the academy."[7] As if such proclamations were not already worrisome (for important intellectuals have been among the leading harassers of our time), then came the kicker: Ronell's intellectual status was presented as the reason to not discipline her: "We testify to the grace, the keen wit, and the intellectual commitment of Professor Ronell and ask that she be accorded the dignity rightly deserved by someone of her international standing and reputation." Apparently, those with less status are somehow less deserving of dignity. The letter continued, arguing that terminating Ronell's employment would, according to the signatories, be a loss for the "humanities, for NYU and for intellectual life during these times [that] would be no less than enormous." The very last sentence of the letter, though—"she deserves a fair hearing"—might have been the only reasonable one, although, by implication, it suggested she had not been given one.

The letter produced an outcry within the halls of academia,[8] but the scandal and the letter went viral when the *New York Times* published an article on August 13, 2018.[9] The Twitterverse and blogosphere lit up with a broad range of condemnations, feminist and anti-feminist alike.[10] Ronell supporters were cast variously as anti-feminists, powerful status quo defenders, hypocrites. Within a few days of the *New York Times* article, Reitman filed a lawsuit against Ronell and NYU.[11] The statement of claim brought to light more details of the allegations against Ronell. Shortly thereafter, Judith Butler expressed her regret at signing the letter. In a letter to the *Chronicle of Higher Education*, Butler acknowledged that the letter writers should have been more fully informed, should not have attributed negative motives to Reitman, and should not have implied "that Ronell's status and reputation earn her differential treatment of any kind."[12]

The Ronell controversy emerged alongside allegations against Asia Argento. Argento had been one of the first actresses to come forward against Harvey Weinstein and had been a strong voice in the #MeToo movement. But in August 2018, the *New York Times* reported that she had paid $380,000 to a young actor named Jimmy Bennett, who had accused her of sexual assault.[13] The allegations were, predictably, used to attack the legitimacy of the #MeToo movement and to label its leaders "hypocrites."[14] #MeToo detractor and self-described feminist Bari Weiss, of the *New York Times*, joined in the fray: "Women are hypocrites. Women are abusers. Women are liars. Just like men."[15] Weiss went on to connect the Argento allegations with those against Ronell, noting in particular the letter signed by "academia's biggest feminist luminaries." Weiss described the defense of Ronell, and by implication, any defense of Argento, as "a repeat of the sexual harassment stories we've spent the past year reading about, only with the genders flipped."[16]

Weiss was setting up a straw horse, at least on the Argento front, because feminists did not come running to her defense. Tarana Burke, #MeToo founder, tweeted, "I've said repeatedly that the #metooMVMT is for all of us, including these brave young men who are now coming forward."[17] For Burke, the central issue of #MeToo is power, not gender: "Sexual violence is about power and privilege. That doesn't change if the perpetrator is your favorite actress, activist or professor of any gender." Rose McGowan, a close ally of Argento's in the #MeToo movement, initially expressed sympathy for Argento, tweeting, "None of us know the truth of the situation and I'm sure that more will be revealed." However, after considerable on-line backlash, McGowan deleted the tweet, stating that she was not defending Argento,[18] and proceeded to distance herself. The Argento case fueled the media framing of the Ronell case and its implications for #MeToo: What happens when a woman is charged with sexual misconduct? The inference, sometimes made explicit, was that these "reverse" allegations would undermine the legitimacy of the movement, because feminists were hypocritically defending their own. However, the debates between feminists were different, as some did seek to articulate anxieties around the role of sex and sexuality in the Ronell/Reitman case.

The controversy reveals a queer twist in the sex wars. In this chapter, I unpack the positions taken in the Ronell debate, noting that among them was a uniquely *queer* one. I argue that while the Sex Wars 2.0 lens is helpful in explaining the Ronell controversy, it demands a broader analysis. I return to the discussion of the sex wars from chapter 2 and highlight a related but different set of divisions, not contesting feminisms but rather feminist versus queer frameworks. Indeed, the Ronell controversy picks up where the sex wars left off: the Title IX debates on campus sexual violence. Unlike the high-profile cases of #MeToo discussed in chapter 3, the Ronell case was first and foremost a Title IX claim, and the reactions echoed much of what the Title IX critiques have been saying since before #MeToo. But, they did so queerly.

This chapter dips into queer theory, focusing in particular on its anxieties around sexual regulation. I examine how queer critiques of sexuality and sexual regulation build on the sex-positive side of the sex wars but break with a feminist gender-based analysis, adding a distinctive flavor. Starting with a queer lens on the debates over sexuality raised by the Ronell case, I then turn to theory more proscriptively as a way to break from the sex wars. Those familiar with queer theory, which tends towards the anti-normative and anti-regulatory, will understand that this is a *queer* place for it. However, I take it in a different and hopefully productive direction, using Eve Sedgwick's later work on reparative reading to bridge the chasms between feminist and queer interpretations. Her strategy of "reading beside" provides a means of reading the contesting claims of the sex wars and #MeToo together. The chapter moves from a reparative reading of the Ronell controversy back to Senator Al Franken, discussed earlier. Nothing may seem obviously queer in the Franken case, but queer readings offer a way to reconceive of the ordinary, the heterosexual, the paradigmatic forms of harassment. And a reparative reading, of reading the multiple claims beside each other, offers a promising reconstruction of the conflicts.

REREADING AVITAL RONELL AND THE TWISTING #METOO NARRATIVES

The first public stone in the Ronell controversy was thrown by Brian Leiter, a law professor at the University of Chicago, in a post about the letter on his widely read philosophy blog entitled "Blaming the victim is apparently OK when the accused in a Title IX proceeding is a feminist literary theorist."[19] It went viral.[20] Leiter noted that the details of the Title IX complaint against Ronell were unknown to him but that they were, more remarkably, irrelevant to the letter. He quoted some of its more outrageous passages and linked to the original, letting it speak for itself. The opening salvo—the "hypocrisy and entitlement of these precious 'theorists'"[21]—was an accusation of feminist hypocrisy.

The letter produced a flurry of criticism and condemnation in the hallways of academia and the Twittersphere. As Neil Gluckman first reported in the *Chronicle of Higher Education* two days after the Leiter post, "In short order, the letter drew condemnation from scholars on Twitter, some of whom called it 'appalling' and 'embarrassing.'"[22] A few signatories stood by their decision. Prominent feminist scholar Joan Scott told the *Chronicle*, "This is an example of a kind of misuse or abuse of Title IX" insofar as the allegations against Ronell did not, as she understood it, involve quid pro quo sexual harassment or unwanted physical contact.[23] The article noted that Scott was a coauthor of a 2016 report from the American Association of University Professors on the *History, Uses, and Abuses of Title IX*.[24] Catherine Simpson, another prominent feminist scholar and former dean of graduate studies at NYU, similarly stood by her decision to sign, noting that although she believed in due process, the timing of the letter was in response to a fear that Ronell's tenure was about to be revoked. But, their remarks did little to temper criticism.

A second article in the *Chronicle* a week later reflected similar sentiments, criticizing the letter for its appeal to status and reputation.[25] The article drew parallels with a sexual assault claim brought against Dragan Kujundzic, a professor of Russian studies at the University of California, Irvine in 2004, where Jacques Derrida weighed in, writing a scathing letter to the university, threatening to withhold the remainder of his promised scholarly papers: "[W]here does [the complainant] find the grounds, how can she claim to have the right to initiate such a serious procedure and to put in motion such a weighty juridico-academic bureaucracy against a respectable and universally respected professor?"[26] The article noted that Judith Butler, the lead author of the Ronell letter, had also written a letter at the time criticizing the sexual harassment policies that had been deployed against Kujundzic. Leiter again weighed in, noting the parallels and arguing that out of the public eye, the academics did "not hesitate 'to pull rank' as a defense to allegations of sexual harassment and misconduct." In Leiter's view, what was so shocking about the Ronell letter was that "so many of those involved profess to be feminists, but at the same time are doing exactly what every 'high status male has tried to do when facing accusations of misconduct."[27]

Butler was also quoted in the article; in an e-mail to the *Chronicle*, she attempted to clarify her position that reputation should not be a defense but expressed her concern that "allegations are quickly accepted as proo of guilt prior to any process that allows for evidence to be presented and considered":[28] "Sexual harassment is real and pervasive, and so it is all the more important that we know what we mean by that term, and that we have fair ways to adjudicate allegations and guarantee due process so that we can all have confidence in the procedures."[29] Butler was expressing a well-established, indeed increasingly mainstream, position about the potential pitfalls of Title IX allegations in particular and #MeToo in general, reviewed in previous chapters. However, the tone of the letter itself would continue to overshadow any attempt to complicate the concerns of those who signed it.

The controversy spread within academia, but became a public sensation with the publication of the *New York Times* article "What Happens to #MeToo When a Feminist Is Accused?" on August 13, 2018.[30] The letter and its "grace, the keen wit, and the intellectual commitment" defense again featured prominently in the reporting. But so did, for the first time, the details of the alleged behavior set out in the Title IX report that had been obtained by the *New York Times*.[31] The article reported that Reitman said Ronell "had sexually harassed him for three years, and shared dozens of emails in which she referred to him as 'my most adored one,' 'Sweet cuddly Baby,' 'cock-er spaniel,' and 'my astounding and beautiful Nimrod.'"[32] The article further detailed Reitman's allegations: "Professor Ronell kissed and touched him repeatedly, slept in his bed with him, required him to lie in her bed, held his hand, texted, emailed and called him constantly, and refused to work with him if he did not reciprocate."[33] It described repeated sexual harassment and sexual touching, beginning in 2012 in Paris and continuing in New York, where she allegedly showed up at his apartment, asking to stay because the power had gone out. Each time, Reitman alleged, Ronell engaged in nonconsensual sexual touching. The article also described the ongoing e-mail exchanges between Reitman and Ronell, which detailed "her affection and longing for him."

Ronell had remained quiet during the early stages of the controversy, allegedly because of a confidentiality agreement, but she eventually spoke out. The *New York Times* article included her statement categorically denying any and all accusations of sexual harassment and sexual assault. The relationship was not sexual and their exchanges simply reflected a "penchant for florid and campy communications."[34] In a press release issued a few days later on behalf of Ronell, the e-mails were described "as largely gay-coded, with literary allusions, poetic runs and obviously exaggerated expressions of tenderness."[35] In an interview with the *Chronicle*, Ronell again denied the allegations of inappropriate sexual conduct and described the e-mails as "freely reciprocated."[36] Ronell stated that she would not impose her "zany, affectionate, over-the-top kind of sheltering gestures on people who don't seem to require or ask for that from me."[37] She described the banter as simply how she talks with her gay friends in Manhattan's West Village.[38] But, Ronell also went on the offensive, suggesting that she was the one who had been manipulated: "I'm heartbroken that my fast and loose and exuberant and stupid and childish use of language can somehow be gathered up to be a viable weapon against me."[39] The real victim, according to Ronell, was Ronell herself. She was critical of what she described as a rush to judgment that reflected a veering off to "sexual paranoia" and at the same time operated to let other harassers off the hook. According to Ronell, the focus on her "allows for patriarchy to say, 'See, there's a predator woman—they have libidos, too—so now leave us alone so we can go around and have our encounters with 18-year-old girls.'"[40]

The high-profile exposé produced an outpouring of writing, deeply critical of the letter and of Ronell's behavior, from across the political spectrum. A number of commentators picked up on the theme of feminist hypocrisy. Scott Greenfield, a defense attorney and close friend of Reitman's attorney, went on the offensive: "It was an extortion letter." His ire was focused on the feminists who signed it: "Forget the jargonized rhetoric about power dynamics and oppression. To these feminist scholars, Title IX is just a bludgeon to beat men into submission, and they fought to protect one of their own from facing the consequences of her sexual abuse."[41] Christina Hoff Sommers, of 1990s anti-feminist sex-wars fame, tweeted repeatedly about the letter, calling it "astonishing," to the point that it almost seemed like a hoax. Echoing the hypocrisy sentiment, Sommers wrote, "Some leading feminist scholars have supported [Ronell] in ways that echo the defenses of male harassers."[42]

Many feminist and progressive voices joined in on the critique, although they were categorical that neither Ronell nor the letter undermined #MeToo, with varying positions on why this was the case. "Feminists aren't a monolith," tweeted Dana Bolger, a founder of Know Your IX. The views of those who signed the letter, she said, "shouldn't be attributed to every feminist everywhere, many of whom vehemently disagree with them."[43] Beatrice Louis, in a trope all too common to the sex wars, denounced the signatories of the letter as "not feminist": "No single individual today can make a stand-alone claim to be the arbiter of feminism, or what is feminist. But this is not only anti-feminist, it is an alarming and condemnable abuse of intellectual stature and standing."[44]

A second theme in the feminist response was that gender should be irrelevant in sexual abuse. Olivia Goldhill, in an article deeply critical of the letter, insisted that all accusations must be taken seriously: "There should be no exception to these rules, even when the professor under investigation is a woman."[45] Beatrice Louis wrote that there was nothing any less serious about the female harassment of male victims.[46] This insistence on gender neutrality in sexual violence emerged as a response not simply to the allegations of feminist hypocrisy from more mainstream and conservative critics but also to the subsequent interventions of some of the letter writers. Joan Scott, for example, told the *Chronicle of Higher Education* that she stood by her signature, arguing that "this is an example of a kind of misuse or abuse of Title IX." Scott coauthored a report by the American Association of University Professors on "The History, Uses, and Abuses of Title IX."[47] Another signatory, Dianne Davis, in an e-mail to the *New York Times*, noted her support for #MeToo and went on to say, "But it's for that very reason that it's so disappointing when this incredible energy for justice is twisted and turned against itself, which is what many of us believe is happening in this case."

Scott and Davis expressed concern about Title IX's shift away from its more feminist roots of addressing discrimination against women. But attempts to situate Title IX within its feminist history were often simply framed as Greenfield-type denunciations of feminists seeing Title IX as "a bludgeon to beat men." The feminist response insisting on the gender neutrality of Title IX, #MeToo, and approaches to sexual violence was an attempt to beat back this accusation of feminist hypocrisy or, worse, of feminists as bloodthirsty man haters. Yet, in so doing, it represented a liberal feminist elision of structural inequities, focusing on a formal-equality approach to sexual violence.[48]

A fresh take on the Ronell controversy arrived with a post by NYU professor Lisa Duggan (of the sex wars fame) on *Bully Bloggers* entitled "The Full Catastrophe."[49] Duggan, in a queer take on the Ronell case and #MeToo, described "a shift from neo-liberal carceral feminism to the privatization of feminism, a reliance on corporate boards to dole out consequences," and an accounting of the ways queer faculty have been accused of sexual harassment precisely because of their hypersexualization in the public mind.[50] Duggan touched on the e-mail exchanges between Ronell and Reitman: "The nature of the email exchange resonates with many queer academics, whose practices of queer intimacy are often baffling to outsiders," noting alternative forms of intimacy "amongst queers."[51] Duggan asked many hard questions while offering no direct defense of Ronell. But, much of her textured analysis got lost in what followed. Jack Halberstam tweeted Duggan's piece, adding, "This is a clear, politically savvy take on the Ronell case by Lisa Duggan. Enough of the he said/she said, let's move to the analysis. Enough Twitter outrage and Facebook high horse, read this, circulate and get real!!"[52] Masha Gessen, in the *New Yorker*, applauded Duggan's effort to complicate the narrative and to think beyond the current Title IX structure.[53] Gesturing towards a more restorative model, she wrote, "Perhaps justice can be found neither in the closed investigations nor in open court but in a different sort of public forum."[54] The social media outrage, however, continued, as Duggan and Halberstam were cast as Ronell defenders. Real or perceived these defenses provoked yet another explosion on social media. Duggan's commentary, coupled with the "queer credentials" of some of the signatories of the letter—most notably Judith Butler—produced a reaction to these queer theory "defenders." While by August 20, Judith Butler had expressed regret for the letter,[55] the discursive damage seemed to have been done, and she remained, for the critics, part of the problem.

Taking yet another distinctive, if predictable, turn, the Ronell controversy became framed as a generational issue of power, with the academic establishment defending its own. While this critique began to emerge before Duggan's intervention,[56] the latter became a focal point. Josephine Livingstone, for example, argued that Ronell's case was not about the hypocrisy of #MeToo but rather proved #MeToo's point about the nature of power. The reaction of the academics—the letter writers, Duggan, Halberstam—she argued, was effectively a consolidation of established power. They acted as if they were outsiders, "without awareness that they are now the tenured, the published, the well-off, the powerful; precisely the demographic that #MeToo proposed to investigate."[57] Andrea Long Chu, a former teaching assistant to Ronell, made similar arguments in an influential article for the *Chronicle of Higher Education* entitled "I Worked with Avital Ronell. I Believe Her Accuser."[58] Chu not only shared her stories of Ronell's abusive and narcissistic conduct but denounced those like Duggan and Halberstam as "left wing academics" who, in allegedly coming to Ronell's defense, were doing the work of the academy: "Make them successful, give them awards, power, enormous salaries. That way, when the next scandal comes along—and it will— they will have a vested interest in playing defense."[59] Unlike the earlier instantiations of the #MeToo debate, this was not simply a matter of a generation gap; it was a gap of generational power within the academy— senior academics, oblivious to their influence and authority, versus the academic precariate: current and former graduate students, teaching assistants, part-time lecturers.

Along similar lines, Corey Robin argued that the problem was power, not sex: "Depending on whom you believe, Ronell's claims on Reitman may or may not have been for sex, but the sex was only one part of the harassment. Ronell's largest claims were on his time, on his life, on his attention and energy, well beyond the legitimate demands of an adviser on an advisee."[60] Sex, he argued, often clouds the issue, and he alluded to the sex-wars nature of these debates: "One side focuses on the special violation that is supposed to be sexual harassment; the other side (including many feminists) accuses the first of puritanism and sex panic. Try as they might, neither side ever gets beyond the sex."[61] Robin then focused on the exchanges between Ronell and Reitman as exchanges of unequal power between a professor/supervisor and a graduate student.

While the case faded from public view, the conflict continued. With Ronell set to return to the classroom in the fall of 2019, the NYU Graduate Student Union continued pressuring the administration, demanding her termination and calling for broad institutional change.[62] Student leaders denounced NYU's decision: "[NYU is] literally permitting harassment. . . . This is a permissive environment for harassment; there aren't consequences."[63] While Ronell was suspended without pay for a year, from the students' perspective, the penalty was insufficient. Nothing short of termination, it would seem, would suffice. This demand went hand in hand with calls for reform that would implement restorative justice, a point I return to below. In February 2020, NYU announced that Ronell was on a leave of absence, and would not be teaching in the spring term, though the university stated that her leave had nothing to do with the complaint.[64]

#Sex Wars 2.0, with a Queer Twist

The generational power narrative of the Ronell case evokes the generational war narrative of #MeToo. Instead of millennials versus second-wave feminists, we have senior, tenured academics versus graduate students and precariously employed academics. There is a degree of affect, coupled with acute power differentials, that gives the debate a markedly generational flavor. But, as I have argued in relation to

#MeToo broadly, the generational debate supplemented with the power analysis does not tell the full story of the underlying disagreements at play. The Sex Wars 2.0 lens can offer a powerful counternarrative that better explains the principled conflicts that have erupted in the wake of #MeToo. A few commentators alluded to the sex wars in their discussion of the Ronell controversy. Corey Robin indirectly invoked them in his argument that sex tends to cloud rather than illuminate discussions.[65] Lisa Duggan, somewhat more obliquely, referred to the debates within different strains of contemporary feminism on questions of sexual harassment. In my view, the sex-wars frame helps to better explain what is at stake in the underlying disagreements over sexuality. But, to consider the disagreements in relation to the Ronell controversy, we need a supplemental retelling of the sex wars.

To this point my Sex Wars 2.0 narrative has focused on divisions between feminists: radical/dominance feminists versus sex-positive feminists. Enter a queer/feminist divide. While early sex-positive feminism, particularly the work of Gayle Rubin, heavily influenced the emergence of queer theory,[66] it represented a break from feminism and emerged as a lens through which to focus on sex and sexuality independent from gender. Rubin challenged feminism's claim on the sexuality field, and argued that it was essential "to separate gender and sexuality analytically to more accurately reflect their separate social existence."[67] It was time, she claimed in 1984, to develop an "autonomous theory and politics specific to sexuality."[68] In *Epistemology of the Closet*, Sedgwick argued in her famous Axiom 2 that "the study of sexuality is not coextensive with the study of gender; correspondingly antihomophobic inquiry is not coextensive with feminist inquiry."[69] For Sedgwick, sexuality and gender represent two distinct analytic axes. The emerging body of queer theory demarcated the study of sex and sexuality, without gender or feminism, producing a sophisticated body of work that troubled heteronormativity, independent of feminism's focus on male/female relationships. Queer theoretical work investigates sex and sexuality hierarchies irreducible to gender as the axis of power.

Queer theory represented a break from gay and lesbian studies. While the term "queer" has been appropriated to refer to things LGBT—queer marriage, queer community, queer parenting—this is not the meaning here. Rather, I invoke the intellectual history of queer theory that rejects these very identity categories, seeking to deconstruct the homosexual/ heterosexual opposition. Queer theory is admittedly tough to pin down. From its inception, its deconstructive nature has refused the definitional.[70] As Lauren Berlant and Michael Warner have written, "Queer theory is not the theory *of* anything in particular."[71] However, if we go back to its roots in the foundational writings of Eve Sedgwick, Gayle Rubin, and Judith Butler, among others, it is possible and useful to identify several basic themes or critical predispositions.[72] Foucault's argument that sexuality is a discursive production rather than a natural condition[73] also lies at its core. Queer theory has developed as an interrogation and deconstruction of the multiple discursive productions of sexuality, seeking to denaturalize the assumed connections among sex, gender, and desire. The year 1990 was a big one, with the publications of Judith Butler's *Gender Trouble*, Eve Sedgwick's *Epistemology of the Closet*, and Teresa de Lauretis's coining of the term "queer theory," describing it as "a refusal of heterosexuality as the benchmark for all sexual formations."[74]

While queer theory, as articulated by Butler and Sedgwick, was very much about critical reading practices, located within theory and literary studies, it was the product of a deeply political moment—the AIDS crisis of the 1980s. It had an urgent political impulse, with activist organizations like ActUp and Queer Nation challenging the intense homophobia fueled by the AIDS crisis. Rallying around slogans like "Silence = Death," it was an anti-assimilationist, in-your-face politics of survival. Douglas Crimp states that it was "within this new political conjuncture that the word queer has been reclaimed to designate new political identities."[75] I emphasize the political origins of queer theory because although known they are often forgotten. Queer politics was a call for things to be otherwise—a call for life, for a sexual life in the face of the devastation of the AIDS crisis and stigma of a "gay" disease. Just as the sex wars of the

1970s and 1980s were the product of a particular political moment, so too was the emergence of queer politics, and the theory inspired by it.

Early queer theorists, like Butler and Sedgwick, took aim at essentialist constructions of homosexuality, gender, and sexuality. Butler argued that sex, gender, and desire are discursively produced and performed. Sedgwick explored the homosexual/heterosexual dichotomy. Through these works, queer theory took aim at the dichotomy between gay and straight, homosexual and heterosexual, suggesting that these dichotomies were themselves part of the problem. The homo/hetero distinction normalized heterosexuality and reinforced the very static and essentialist conceptions of sex, sexuality, gender, and desire. It was similarly a critique of identity—specifically, gay and lesbian identity claims—problematizing the essentialization of gay identity against a heterosexual norm. Queer theory was also positioned as a critique of the normal, and by extension, of normative sexuality. David Halperin defined "queer" as whatever is "at odds with the normal, the legitimate, the dominant."[76] He elaborated, "Queer demarcates not a positivity but a positionality vis-à-vis the normative—a positionality that is not restricted to lesbians and gay men but is in fact available to anyone who is or who feels marginalized because of her or his sexual practices."[77] Or as Kathryn Stockton Bond puts it, "It's the strange that we like, if we're for the queer."[78] Queer theory emerged as a critic of and resistance to sexual regimes of normalization.[79]

This description is of a very 1990s queer theory as it first emerged in some of the foundational texts. It has traveled far afield since that time, on no singular path. Queer of-color critique exploded the whiteness of queer theory. While Roderick Ferguson coined the term "queer of-color critique" in *Aberrations in Black* as a method for challenging the discourses that conceal the intersections of race, class, gender, sexuality, and nation, he was in part giving name to a critique that emerged in earlier work by Barbara Smith, Cathy Cohen, and José Esteban Muñoz, among others. Not unlike queer theory's initial rejection of the singular axis of gender, scholars of color rejected the exclusive focus on sexuality. Some queer theory took a decidedly temporal turn, exploring questions of queer time and queer futures.[80] Some turned to affect, exploring precognitive feelings, often with a focus on the more negative ones. Building, again, from Sedgwick's focus on shame,[81] queer theory has explored feelings associated with social exclusion, from shame to despair to regret.[82] Some questioned the anti-normativity of queer theory and whether it was always positioned against. Robyn Weigman and Elizabeth Wilson argued, "Queer theory has maintained an attachment to the politics of oppositionality (against, against, against)."[83] Lisa Duggan and Jack Halberstam argued back, stating that the claim was based on overgeneralizations, flattened the complexities of queer studies, and was predicated largely on pre-2000 queer theory, and defended the importance of the critique of norms.[84] Each of these queer theory instantiations overlapped, with multiple encounters, engagements, and disagreements. Indeed, many of the very same scholars were the interlocutors across these strands, weaving an increasingly complex web of things queer.

The deconstructive, oppositional, anti-normative character—or perhaps caricature, thereby sidestepping the question of whether it really is or really is not—of queer theory has lent it an anti-regulatory character. To the extent that queer theory *has* considered law, it explored the ways in which sex and sexualities are discursively constituted and (over) regulated. Its impulse is anti-regulatory. David Halperin and Trevor Hoppe's book, *The War on Sex*, which explores the overcriminalization of nonnormative sex and sexual minorities, is a great example. From the criminalization of HIV to the punitive measures against sex work, the queer critique argues against the continued surveillance and criminalization of sex, tending to bracket, rather than explore, the sexual harms of nonconsensual sex. Halperin briefly discusses the regulation of sexual violence:

> The war on sex should not be confused with the heightened
> awareness of sexual violence, rape and the sexual abuse of

READING BESIDE THE QUEER/FEMINIST DIVIDE > 133

children along with a greater determination to do something
about them by means of law and social policy. There is nothing wrong with using legal and moral pressure to reduce the
incidence of sexual assault, forced prostitution and child pornography featuring real children. . . . [T]hose are all instances of
grievous bodily harm.[85]

He insists that preventing sexual harm is an important objective: "It is
not only legitimate but indeed imperative to stop people from using sex
to harm one another. Sexual freedom is not a license to abuse others for
one's own pleasure."[86] Halperin then shifts, noting that preventing this
kind of sexual harm "should not furnish a pretext for an all-out war on
sex that permanently identifies sex itself with danger."[87] This is the full
extent of their engagement with the regulation of "real" sexual harm. We
are left to draw the lines ourselves between "grievous bodily harm" that
the law should address, and all of the sex that it should not.[88]

* * *

The War on Sex then turns to focus, exclusively and incisively, on this
war on nonnormative sex and the idea that sex itself is dangerous. The
authors document the many ways in which sexual freedom is currently
under siege. There are strong overtones of the feminist sex-wars debates
opposing sexual danger and sexual freedom. The borders between feminism and queer theory are not strictly policed in this volume. Halperin
notes that contributors share the view that there is "no fundamental,
substantive, irreconcilable opposition between feminism and sexual
freedom,"[89] meaning that feminism aligned with the side of the sex wars
that emphasizes the importance of sexual freedom and sexual agency.
Judith Levine, the outspoken feminist #MeToo detractor discussed in
chapter 3, contributed an essay to the collection locating the emergence
of a sex panic around sexual offenders within the history of the feminist sex wars. In language more than a little reminiscent of sex-positive
feminism, she wrote, "If we are to end sexual violence by cracking down

on sexual freedom, we are trading one oppression for another."[90] The language is echoed by Halperin, who wrote that readers will need to ask themselves which is worse, "rare, horrific crimes committed by deranged individuals or a systematic, increasing, massive, generalized encroachment on civil liberties by the state? At the moment, the balance between sexual freedom and the need for protection from sexual danger has shifted to the advantage of the latter. Can we redress the balance in a responsible way?"[91] Despite the call for balance, the sexual danger part remains unexplored. Indeed, the dichotomy set up is itself rhetorical: "rare, horrific crimes committed by deranged individuals" brackets, and perhaps inadvertently obscures, the not-rare sexual harms committed by nonderanged individuals on a daily basis—the very phenomenon performed by #MeToo.

Much of *The War on Sex* provides an incisive critique of criminal law's overregulation of nonnormative sexuality. It appears to be heavily influenced by the critique of carceral feminism that emerged from within feminism. Indeed, the collection includes a contribution from Elizabeth Bernstein, the Columbia University sociologist who first coined the term. Not intent on strictly enforcing boundaries between queer and feminist critique, *The War on Sex* seeks to develop a critical, queer, anti-carceral critique, which recognizes its intellectual roots in feminism. Halperin and Hoppe's book captures the anti-regulatory spirit of queer-inspired work, telling us much more about what law should *not* do than what it *should*. The question of when and how law should intervene to regulate sexual harm is not part of the conversation.

So what does this queer critique add to the Sex Wars 2.0 frame and to our understanding of contemporary debates around sexuality, #MeToo, and the Ronell controversy? First, a caveat about what I do not need it to do. A Google search of "queer" and "#MeToo" returns innumerable stories of LGBT engagement with #MeToo. "Queer" here is largely a stand-in for "LGBT," and the stories explore questions of sexual violence within and against LGBT communities. Kevin Spacey, accused of sexually abusing a young male actor, features prominently, as do stories about the need for a #MeToo reckoning with the LGBT community. Along these lines, the Ronell case could be seen as queer, insofar as it involves a gay man and a lesbian. *My* use of "queer" to supplement the sex-wars frame is rather to unearth its position as a critique, as in its first-generation queer-theory legacy—anti-identitarian, nonfeminist, nonnormative.

So, what *is* the value add? First, it is the nonfeminist (as distinct from anti-feminist). "Queer" brings a focus on sex and sexuality, independent of a feminist lens on the opposition male/female. The feminist sex wars disagree over sexuality, agency, and law from a gender perspective: Is X good or bad for women? Does X contribute to the oppression of women, or challenge this oppression? Queer theory focuses instead on the production and surveillance of sexual norms, behaviors, and practices that are not reducible to gender oppression. The question becomes, How does X contribute to the ways in which sexualities are constituted and policed? Second, and relatedly, the value add is the nonnormative. A queer lens focuses on how some sexual identities, desires, and practices are normalized, while others are often pathologized. It is a lens hypervigilant to the ways nonnormative sexualities are produced, disciplined, and punished. While there is a parallel in the emphasis on danger versus pleasure, and like pro-sex feminism, the queer lens sides with pleasure, this is not because pleasure is good for women but rather because it is good for nonnormative sexualities, desires, and practices.

A queer lens can highlight sexual harms that are not reducible to gender oppression and allow for an exploration of the intersections of sexuality, sex, and gender in ways that are not reduced to the male/female divide. Sex Wars 2.0 becomes not only a debate about what is best for women. With a queer twist, it brings into focus how differing understandings of and approaches to sexuality can negatively impact nonnormative sexualities. A different set of "warring" factions and positions on the meaning and regulation of sexuality comes into view. A tension exists between queer and feminist critiques when it comes to sexual harm generally and the #MeToo movement in particular.[92] While not condoning nonconsensual sex, a queer critique remains hypervigilant to how easily sexuality gives rise to reactions of disgust, righteousness, and virtue signaling, all of which increase the risk of overregulation, particularly of nonnormative sexualities.

The Ronell controversy has brought some of the queer/feminist tensions to the forefront, revealing productive intellectual tracking that can illuminate the underlying disagreements on questions of sexuality. Aya Gruber has explored this tension specifically in relation to #MeToo and Avital Ronell.[93] Gruber rehearses the feminism versus queer sex wars through the well-known characters of Sex Wars 2.0: Catharine MacKinnon and Janet Halley (the stars of "The Return of the Sex Wars" article in the *New York Times Magazine*). Feminism is represented by MacKinnon and queer theory by Halley. Gruber sets up the sex-wars framework through a familiar opposition, sex as danger and sex as play, and uses it to understand what happened. She argues that the feminist critique of Ronell can be seen as a dominance-feminism/sex-as-danger position, whereas those like Duggan, who offered a defense of Ronell, present an example of the queer-sex-as-play position.

Gruber's effort to bring the sex wars lens to bear on the controversy and her deployment of the feminist/queer opposition are helpful. She takes her argument in an interesting but different direction in concluding that these sex wars are in fact proxy wars—that feminists and queers are actually arguing about things not particularly related to sex. We would do better, she suggests, to approach the sex wars through a queer critique, coupled with what she calls a "sex indifferent stance" that gives sex neither the salience in danger nor the salience in play that the feminist/queer sex wars do.[94] I agree that the obsessive focus on sex can obscure the pursuit of other values and goals. Indeed, in the Ronell case some commentators argued that it was less about sex and more about power.[95] The role of sex in the case is contested; as Gruber notes, Reitman appears not to have been indifferent to sex. But, it is also important to recognize the extent to which the problem of power could only be made legible in law by attaching it to a claim about sexual harassment

It was only in its sexual form that the behavior was made actionable under Title IX. The actual role of sex in the Ronell controversy is largely unknowable. Was its emphasis strategic or affective?

However, I want to bracket for the moment this question of whether the Ronell case is really about sex and explore contexts where sex is relevant. Sometimes, the controversy is about the regulation of sex: if and how sexual harm should be regulated, what constitutes sexual harm, and what the harms are of regulation itself. How do feminist and queer critiques diverge on these questions? I would also broaden Gruber's description of the queer side of the sex wars beyond the "sex as play" position. This theme evolves from the earlier sex-positive feminism and develops in distinctively queer directions by those who see sex as affirmation of "the jouissance of exploded limits."[96] As Gruber points out, the focus on Ronell's language as gay coded fits within this "queer as playful" practice. However, this normative affirmation of sex as play is only one of the tenets/strains of queer theory, one that became increasingly associated with queer theory's antisocial turn. Understanding Ronell's defense as a queer intervention also requires resort to other tenets of queer theory—in particular, its critique of regimes of sexual normalization. Duggan and others' so-called defense of Ronell can be tracked to a queer-theory critique of sexuality,[97] which emphasizes the ways in which sex and sexuality are subjects of intense surveillance and normalizing discourses. Duggan and others point to ways in which sexual minorities are more likely to be subjected to sexual harassment claims and less likely to be protected from sexual harassment.

Returning again to Duggan's intervention, I see a quintessential first-generation queer concern: the way the Ronell controversy played out is predictably bad for nonnormative sexualities. According to Duggan, "Because queers are hypersexualized in the public imagination, they are targets for sexual accusations."[98] Admittedly here, Duggan uses "queer" in another one of its meanings, namely, that of nonnormative, minoritized sexualities. Duggan references other cases against queer faculty and argues that there is clear evidence of a selective demonization. The argument is a classically queer one, pointing to the regimes of sexual normalization, wherein nonnormative sexualities are more likely to be targeted and punished. Second, she refers to "the practices of queer intimacy." While baffling to those not versed in these practices and rhetorics, she writes, "Forms of intimacy well outside the parameters of heterosexual (and, homosexual) courtship and marriage are commonplace among queers who do not clearly separate friendship and romance, partnership and romantic friendship." Here, Duggan implicitly references the range of queer scholarship that has explored alternative modes of intimacy beyond the heteronormative. While undeveloped and uncited, it is a distinctively queer critique of regimes of sexual normalization that value certain intimate configurations while disavowing others. Duggan is queerly suspicious of the ways in which sex (here—queer flirtatious banter) in public (here—work e-mails) is subject to surveillance. She suggests that the very idea that romantic language might not signify a sexual relationship is puzzling to outsiders. However, she notes that simply pointing out the possibility of these alternative expressions of queer intimacy "does not establish that a sexual relationship did not occur."[99] What Duggan tries to do is point out the distinct worldviews (or culture clashes, as she calls it) that can be brought to bear on the same texts and behaviors.

Attempting to paint a more complex picture of the Ronell controversy, Duggan did state that she was not defending Ronell and that "queer faculty can be guilty, and should be held accountable."[100] She wrote about endemic power within the academy, particularly between supervisors and graduate students. Indeed, Duggan made common cause with the "not sex but power" critics, noting that the central concern should be whether there were "boundary violations that could be considered harmful. Advisor intrusions do not need to be sexual to be a problem."[10] But, her language also betrayed her. While she did not directly defend Ronell, she defended the letter writers, despite noting the objectionable elitism. She refers to Reitman's husband as "a member of a wealthy New York real estate family" able to fund lawsuits. She pointed to Ronell as "utterly handicapped by the confidentiality requirement." The text positions against the former and for the latter, leaving Duggan's attempt to paint a more complex and contested picture largely unsuccessful. Given the incendiary terrain of the Ronell controversy, Title IX, and #MeToo, it was not language likely to diffuse an explosive controversy. The polarization of the debate, coupled with Duggan's style, became fodder for a "power within the academy" critique. Duggan came to be seen as a defender of Ronell and of the status quo of that academic establishment.

The Ronell case was another round of the sex wars, with its ongoing and familiar contestations over the meaning of sexual harm and the harms of regulating sex. One side defended law's role, through Title IX, in adjudicating the sexual encounter, protecting the victims of sexual harassment, and punishing the offenders. The other side was concerned with an overly negative vision of sex and sexuality and the hazards of using law to regulate it. In many ways, the Ronell case tracked the feminist sex wars around Title IX that I review in chapter 2—contesting both the harms and the regulation of the harms, and the sex wars underlying #MeToo as set out in chapter 3. But, in the Ronell context, the queer difference was one that shifted the focus from the harm to women to the harm to nonnormative sexualities. The debate, as it played out in the public sphere, was one in which #MeToo feminists focused on the harm of sexual harassment in the academy, while the queer critique sought to create discomfort around our definitions of what sexual harassment *is*, and draw attention to the harms of regulating it within the academy.

We start to see a focus on different harms underlying these sex wars. On one side, there is sex as danger; there is the harm of sexual harassment and the harm of underregulation. Nonconsensual sexual behavior has largely gone unchecked, and needs to be recognized and disciplined. On the other side, there is the harm of overregulation. Where the #MeToo feminists see nonconsensual sex and sex as danger, the queer critique raises the possibility that it might not have been about sex, that it might have been consensual, that sex might not be dangerous, and, crucially, that regulating sex might be dangerous. There is the harm of policing nonnormative sexualities under the sign of addressing sexual injury, where consensual sexual behavior is reframed as nonconsensual sexual harm, in the service of normalization regimes. Like the sex wars more generally, the feminist/queer debates are characterized by competing visions of sexuality and law. Sex as danger versus the possibility that sex is not danger. Law as a solution versus the possibility that law is not the solution. The harms of underregulation versus the harms of over-regulation. The sex wars, again, with a queer twist.

Of course, there is much overlap between the sex-positive feminists of chapter 2, the feminist #MeToo detractors of chapter 3, and the queer critique of the Ronell controversy. Not to exaggerate the distinctions in the name of building a taxonomy, but the queer critique aligns with much of sex-positive feminism. Bringing a queer sensibility to bear on the Ronell controversy as a supplement to the exclusively feminist framing of the sex wars adds value and nuance. Sex Wars 2.0 is broadened to include concerns and anxieties about regulating forms of sex that are not reducible to gender subordination. Pro-sex feminism's concern with sexuality as a site of both danger and pleasure for women can be linked with queer theory's exploration of the discursive production of sexualities, normative and nonnormative alike. The feminist anti-carceral concern can be linked to the queer concern with the war on sex. The queer critique that clearly emerged in the Ronell controversy operates as a kind of codicil to the Sex Wars 2.0—a recurrent reminder that a feminist lens—with its focus on gender as an axis of power—might miss other ways in which sex, sexualities, and desires are constituted, disciplined, and disrupted. It is not a perfect fit. Indeed, quite the contrary. But the very dissonance may produce the value add of the queer.

Proscriptively Queer

I have argued that a queer lens can contribute to a diagnosis of the underlying disagreements about sex and sexuality in the Sex Wars 2.0, #MeToo, and debates around Title IX in particular. Now I now turn more proscriptively to queer theory as a means of moving past the sex wars. Queer theory is often deconstructive, anti-normative, and anti-regulatory in tendency, and as such, it might seem counterintuitive to use it for proscriptive ends. But inspired by the later work of Eve Sedgwick and the queer utopian work of José Esteban Muñoz, I try to deploy queer sentiments to think differently about the sex wars and the regulation of sexual harm. In the remainder of the chapter I return to Sedgwick's call for reparative reading and examine the sides of the sex wars beside each other. This sets the terrain for the following chapter, where I explore how we might think differently about regulating sexual harm.

REPARATIVE READING

Eve Sedgwick's essay "Paranoid Reading and Reparative Reading; or, You Are So Paranoid You Probably Think This Introduction Is about You" initiated a seismic critique of what she termed "paranoid reading," a critical reading practice based on Paul Ricoeur's notion of a "herme-neutics of suspicion," which had become a dominant mode in literary and cultural criticism.[102] Paranoid reading reveals and exposes what lies beneath a text, the truth that is hidden within it. At its inception, paranoid queer theory provided a set of analytic tools that revealed the deep structures and discourses of homophobia. But it also led to read-ing that was negative and rigid; that did not like surprises; that relied on exposure assumed to reveal deep truths that lay beneath texts. While paranoid reading was often negative ("X is bad for gays"), it could equally be affirmative ("X is good for gays"). The paranoid element lay in the revealing of deep and unsurprising truths.

Sedgwick did not reject paranoid reading as critique, but rather re-jected the extent to which it had become "nearly synonymous with criti-cism itself":[103] "Paranoia knows some things well and others poorly."[104] Sedgwick argued that it is possible to read otherwise—to engage in what she calls "reparative reading." "The desire of a reparative impulse . . . is additive and accretive." Readers should not only be surprised by but surrender to such a reading:

> To read from a reparative position is to surrender the knowing, anxious, paranoid determination that no horror, however apparently unthinkable, shall ever come to the reader *as new*; to a reparatively positioned reader, it can seem realistic and necessary to experience surprise. Because there can be terrible surprises, however, there can also be good ones. Hope, often a fracturing, even traumatic thing to experience, is among the energies by which the reparatively positioned reader tries to organize the fragments and part-objects she encounters.[105]

Reparative reading is about nurture, about "confer[ring] plenitude on an object." Instead of reading beneath, behind, or beyond, Sedgwick suggests that we learn to read beside: "Beside is an interesting preposition also because there's nothing very dualistic about it; a number of elements may lie alongside one another, though not an infinity of them."[106] Beside, Sedgwick argues, offers "a wide range of desiring, identifying, representing, repelling, paralleling, differentiating, rivaling, leaning, twisting, mimicking, withdrawing, attracting, aggressing, warping, and other other relations."[107]

Sedgwick left no blueprint for "how to read reparatively," but her work produced a tectonic shift in critical reading practices. Elizabeth Weed has described Sedgwick's legacy as "a groundswell of support for new ways of reading."[108] Heather Love writes, "Reparative is on the side of *multiplicity, surprise, rich divergence, consolation, creativity* and *love*."[109] Weak theory—in contrast to the strong theory of paranoid reading— "prefers acts of noticing, being affected, taking joy and making whole."[110] Robin Wiegman has argued that the reparative reader would replace attachments produced by "correction, rejection and anger with those crafted by affection, gratitude, solidarity and love. Under these affective terms, the critical act is reconfigured to value, sustain and privilege the object's worldly inhabitations and needs."[111] Sedgwick's work has generated a multitude of reading strategies, from thinking sideways[112] to reading sideways to lateral reading.[113] Inspired by Sedgwick, each is a queer reading strategy that embraces other ways of reading across texts that better allow us, Dana Seitler argues, "to see in a new light, their connections, challenges, and productive frictions."[114]

* * *

Sedgwick did not eschew the paranoid for the reparative; her call for a reparative reading was not "*only* a call for reparative reading." Sedgwick herself acknowledged the paranoid readings that haunted the first half of her article. She observed that it is "not people . . . but practices—that can be divided between the paranoid and the reparative."[115] Tavia Nyong'o has argued that, for Sedgwick, the "best criticism . . . knew how to interdigitate paranoid and reparative approaches."[116] Accordingly, turning to reparative readings need not mean disavowing the ongoing critical potential of paranoid theory. Reparative reading rather suggests paranoid theory's incompleteness—that there may be more to know than what lies hidden beneath the text, that we can bring a more positive set of affects to our readings and thus see greater possibilities.

The question to which I now turn is how a reparative reading, a "reading beside" strategy, can help us understand the #MeToo controversies. A reparative reading does not disavow the paranoid nature of most of my critical analysis; rather, it can help unearth the common themes and contestations of the sex wars, then and now, and track them to #MeToo in general, or the Ronell case in particular. Not only has my analysis sought to reveal hidden truths of the texts, but my narrative of the sex wars playing out over and over again tracks closely to what Sedgwick calls "paranoid temporality," a kind of structural inevitability, where "yesterday can't be allowed to have differed from today and tomorrow must be even more so."[117] My goal is to break out of the frame of inevitable continuity in order to find other ways of imagining tomorrow. As Sedgwick herself did, and as Nyong'o suggests, I seek to toggle between the paranoid and the reparative. If the intellectual history tracking Ronell and other contemporary controversies from #MeToo to the sex wars leans strongly toward the paranoid, the way forward is a turn to the reparative. How might we read the conflicts with a different critical sensibility? The sex wars and the regulation of sexual harm may seem an unlikely place to look for the possibilities of readings infused with surprise and hope. However, reading *beside* also looks for ways of finding the new, of noticing, of unearthing multitudes. How might this approach shine a fresh, surprising light?

Reading beside the Sex Wars

What might be revealed if we read the feminist and queer claims about Ronell beside each other—if we do not treat them as dichotomous— one right, the other wrong, where only one truth lies beneath the texts? What might we see, understand, feel, if we accepted the truth claims of both sides and held them in tension, beside each other?

In the first round of the sex wars, Carol Vance argued that sexuality is a site of both danger and pleasure in women's lives. Her position represented a refusal of the very terms in which the sex wars came to be framed. Associated with the sex-radical side—due likely to her being a lead organizer of the Barnard conference—she was accused by the other side of downplaying the danger. Her message was either lost or suspect within the ensuing battles. According to Vance, it should not be a matter of choosing one or the other, but of seeking to minimize one and expand the other. Yet, even those terms are dualistic—or became dualistic—suggesting that at any given time, we might be able to locate sex and sexuality, with any degree of precision, on the danger/ pleasure axis—an axis that has stayed with us, through the Sex Wars 2.0 and #MeToo, and remains at play in the feminist/queer version. My argument from the start has been that the positions set out in the sex wars are not as oppositional as they purport to be. Sex may be both dangerous and pleasurable, at the same time, in ways that are difficult to reconcile. Some sexual encounters are ambiguous, located within eroti-cally charged, power-imbalanced, and/or contradictory desires. Reading beside the competing claims might allow us to see the deeply contested and hazy nature of many sexual interactions, how sexual practices elude simple categorization on the danger/pleasure axis, and how seeing them as both may serve us well.

A reparative reading can also be brought to the contested terrain of regulation. #MeToo feminism has staked its regulatory claims around the harms of nonconsensual sex and the failure of law.[118] Queer critics stake theirs around the harms of regulating consensual sex. It is entirely possible to read these two claims beside each other, interrogating how, for example, the under-and overcriminalization of sex can both be valid. Reading reparatively, on the surface, seeing what is in plain sight, tak-ing the intensity of the affective claims seriously, we can acknowledge the harms of the overcriminalization of nonnormative, consensual sexu-ality. We can similarly acknowledge the failure of law to regulate and prevent nonconsensual sexual harms, and the extent to which harms go unacknowledged or unaddressed. This is not to say that there is com-plete commensurability in these claims; there are points of conflict and convergence, to be sure. However, we might begin with what can be si-multaneously held in view. We can notice, value, and sustain the claims of those who aver harm, while recognizing the multiple modalities of harm. Yes, there is a harm, real or perceived. Its affirmation, through a reparative reading, need not imply a particular regulatory response. What if we then explored the implications of the regulatory responses, while holding the multiplicity of harms in view? How can we affirm, make whole, one harm without exacerbating the other?

Returning to the Ronell controversy, a reparative reading might begin with an acknowledgment that #MeToo feminist and queer claims can both be valid. The power operating in the academy makes the harm real. We can recognize that the attention and behaviors directed by Ronell at Reitman were unwanted and that the power differential was such that Reitman did not feel he was in a position to refuse. As I have argued above, the sexual nature of the harassment is unknowable yet clearly relevant in how the conflict played out. It made the allegations both more salacious and more justiciable. This is to suggest not that the claim was false but that its sexual nature is what made it so ripe for public scandal, and legally legible. Reading beside allows us to also hold in view concerns around sexual regulation. The reaction of the university is partially produced by the overregulation of sex and sexuality and the policing of nonnormative sexuality. Reitman experienced a harm that may or may not have been sexual but was expressed as such. Universities have historically not taken these harms seriously, but like other regulatory bodies, may disproportionally discipline nonnormative sexualities. The #MeToo claims and the queer claims are not mutually exclusive. They may feel incommensurable, but a reading beside strategy encourages us to hold these tensions together.

We might also read the power structures beside rather than against each other. The flipping of the gender hierarchy in a case that had no archetypal sexual harassment produced much of the public controversy over Ronell. How to deal with a feminist accused? Can a man be the victim? Some tried to put sexual harassment within its feminist context, as inherently implicating gender hierarchies. Others insisted it be seen neutrally, with sexual injury not specific to gender hierarchies. The reversal was juxtaposed with other hierarchies at play—professional status, supervisor-student. It was an unequivocal power relationship, where supervisors held invisible keys to their students' academic life chances. Some suggested age was a hierarchical factor, although it is unclear where the power lay in that equation. With a fifty-year-old woman versus a thirty-year-old man, it is hard to envision the power lying unequivocally with age; rather, gender comes back into the equation with the societal disregard for older women.[119] In a reading beside strategy rather than choose between these hierarchies, we recognize that they are each at play, pulling the conflict in different directions and allowing the contested claims, operations of power, and harassment, sexual or otherwise, to be approached with more complexity.

A reparative reading also allows us to examine the affect on all sides. Graduate students—current and former—experience a sense of powerlessness, of being subject not only to the whims of their supervisors but to the changing landscapes of higher education, where tenure-track employment is increasingly elusive and the American Dream: Academic Style is disappearing. Fear, resentment, and anxiety simmer, barely beneath the surface, erupting in moments of contestations that highlight their precarity. Senior academics fight entire careers as outsiders, experiencing a range of individual and structural discrimination and harassment. They, too, are anxious, always waiting to be scapegoated, attacked, sidelined, or ignored by the department, faculty, university. Even the misconceived letter can be read in this light—paranoia, fear in the face of the persecution of a scholar. This in no way excuses the letter, which was, in language if not intent, inexcusable. But, it is an attempt to grasp the affect that motivated such a smart group of people to do such an unwise thing. Ongoing low-grade anxiety bursts into full-blown paranoia and panic in moments of challenge. Fear and paranoia transform into anger and outrage, on both sides. Reading beside allows all these affective feelings and the behavior they animate to be held simultaneoulsy in view. Neither is more real or more right. They just are.

Affirming the affective nature of contestation creates space for reflection and reflexivity of the self and the other. Consider for a moment Judith Butler's expression of regret regarding the letter.[120] She admits the obvious: that they "surely ought to have been more fully informed of the situation if we were going to make an intervention." The regret is in relation to two elements of the letter: the motives attributed to the complainant, and the suggestion that status and reputation should have any bearing on the adjudication of sexual harassment. She directs an apology exclusively to the MLA, of which Butler was the incoming president. She had signed the letter under that affiliation and apologized to the officers, staff, and members for having done so. Butler ends on a note of reflexivity: "We all make errors in life and in work. The task is to acknowledge them, as I hope I have, and to see what they can teach us as we move forward." Some may say that this was too little, too late; that it did nothing to change the underlying power inequalities; that it was easy for a senior academic superstar to express regret where there are no material repercussions. But we miss the potential of the moment if that is all we see. It is a remarkable statement of apology, of wrongness, in a world characterized by very little of such humility. The sex wars remain wars in part because the contestants rarely admit wrongdoing or even the possibility of wrongness. The paranoid readings of others continue: never to be surprised. Indeed, the quick dismissal of the apology is classic paranoid reading—an absolute refusal to read the controversy as containing any truth other than sexual harassment. A reparative reading might create space to read Butler's words on the surface as: we make mistakes, we can admit to them, and we can try to change. In the world of academia and in the sex wars, that is a surprising admission.

* * *

Taking responsibility for wrongdoing is more than just a gesture of regret for the letter and the role it played in the Ronell controversy. It might also help as we turn to the more difficult question of the appropriate regulatory response. How can/should we respond to allegations of sexual injury, when the terms of consent and sexuality are themselves contested, and where the regulatory response sits precariously on the over-/undersurveillance axis? Underregulating risks reinforcing the failure to notice harm and power. Overregulating supports more surveillance of consensual, nonnormative sex and its harms. Both risk fetishizing the consent/nonconsent distinction; as Joe Fischel has argued, consent cannot always do all of the work in describing problematic sexual encounters.[121] How might reparative readings allow us to reimagine the regulation of sexual harm? These are the questions to which I turn in the next chapter: How can keeping the seemingly conflicting claims in view help us in crafting regulatory responses? How might these reparative readings help us resolve individual disputes? The Ronell/Reitman conflict, for all its publicity, requires a resolution. Can we reimagine what is possible or desirable? As a start, reading beside expands our understanding of the disputes, and their broader discursive meaning. It can help us hold onto the contradictory claims of the sex wars and #MeToo and the affects that they produce.

Reading beside Harder Cases

While I use the Ronell case to bring the queer dimensions of Sex Wars 2.0 into focus, and demonstrate the promise of a reparative "reading beside," there are important ways in which it might be an easy case study. There were a host of exonerating discourses involved (like the "campy" sexuality discourse Ronell references), the role of sex was ambiguous (the female harasser and male target were both gay/lesbian), and the structural inequality issues were more complicated (the female harasser breaks from the usual male/female hierarchy but a professional hierarchy remains).

How might other contested cases of #MeToo lend themselves to reading beside? The Al Franken case is interesting to reexamine, particularly in light of a second flashpoint—feminist and otherwise. In the spring of 2019, a few articles appeared revisiting the controversy. Emily Yoffe—feminist #MeToo detractor—argued that the Democrats needed to learn from their rush to judgment of Franken. While condemning sexual misconduct, she argued for a fairer sense of proportionality in response to different degrees of misconduct. But the flashpoint erupted with the publication of an article by Jane Mayer in the *New Yorker* in July 2019,[122] which, after a thorough fact checking that had not been done when the story broke in 2017, found many holes in Tweeden's story. Contrary to Tweeden's claims, the offending skit had not been written specifically for her but had been performed many years earlier. The offending photograph was not taken on Christmas as "a final taunt" but several days before, and had not just been sent to Tweeden; rather, a CD containing multiple photographs had been given to many people on the trip.

The article placed Tweeden's allegations within the context of her role as a right-wing operative, flagging the timing of the release of the eleven-year-old photograph a week after Republican senatorial candidate Roy Moore was accused of sexually abusing teenage girls. Mayer interviewed many of Franken's colleagues over the years who declared him too nice a guy to have engaged in this kind of misconduct. Some described him as awkward, or physically obtuse, but definitely not a sexual predator. Mayer also included statements of regret from many of the senators who demanded Franken's resignation in November 2017. Patrick Leahy, D–Vermont, described his decision to join the ranks against Franken as "one of the biggest mistakes I've made" in forty-five years.[123] Heidi Heitkamp, the former senator from North Dakota, said it was the one decision she would take back. Tammy Duckworth, D–Illinois, said she wished the Senate Ethics Committee had moved forward. "We needed more facts. That due process didn't happen is not good for our democracy." Senator Jeff Merkley, D–Oregon, expressed his regret over the hurried condemnation. The list goes on.[124] The theme of the piece was one of a rush to judgment in the absence of facts that eventually painted a more complex picture.

Mayer's article produced a flurry of criticism. A number of #MeToo feminists jumped into the fray. While they recognized that Tweeden's allegations were problematic, they argued that the Mayer article was, too. #MeToo feminists critiqued Mayer for focusing only on the allegations by Tweeden and not on those of seven other women, most involved in Democratic politics, for minimizing the nature of the alleged misconduct, and for relying on character evidence. The attempted rehabilitation of Al Franken, they argued, played into familiar tropes of excusing male behavior, of distrusting overly sensitive women, of feminists unable to take a joke.[125]

Jill Filipovic, for example, reflected that Mayer's article raised questions of Tweeden's "less than legitimate motivations" and that "we are still figuring out a fair process to handle these #MeToo claims."[126] However, Filipovic also questioned the minimizing of Franken's conduct. She responded to claims that Franken was socially awkward or inept by insisting that women should not be expected to "tolerate behavior that is neither standard nor socially acceptable—that is frankly gross."[127] As to whether it would have been better to slow down and investigate, Filipovic says perhaps, but she deemed the Democratic decision politically motivated—just as Mayer argued Tweeden was—noting that it would have been damaging to have Franken on the Senate Judiciary Committee for the Kavanaugh confirmation hearings. Other feminists made this point more strongly: Amanda Marcotte wrote, "What happened was good for Democrats."[128] She argued that by going after Franken, "those same Democrats had the moral authority to go into the Kavanaugh hearings" (which did not turn out well, but that is another story).[129]

Filipovic's argument was more nuanced than many others, including Mayer's that Franken had been "railroaded." She observed how "intent" had worked in favor of Franken's rehabilitation—"he didn't mean it"—but against women like Senator Kirsten Gillibrand, who was held responsible for forcing him out.[130] In refusing a categorical conclusion, Filipovic gestured towards what a reading beside strategy might bring to bear. She reflected, "It is possible to think Democrats got it wrong on Franken without concluding that Franken was in the right. It is possible to recognize that some #MeToo cases end up with an imperfect result without concluding that the movement has gone too far." She calls for more ambivalence, neither outright condemning Franken nor letting him off the hook, neither condoning the speed and rigor of the reaction to him nor going full throttle on the deprivation of due process. With the benefit of critical reflection, Filipovic saw both sides, and did not fully agree with either.

A strategy of reading beside in the Franken controversy parses out the competing claims and refuses to read them dichotomously. #MeToo feminists saw in Franken, then and now, the kind of nonconsensual sexual behavior—sexual harassment and sexual misconduct—that men have long gotten away with. They saw women forced to tolerate the behavior because the men are more powerful, because they would not be believed, or because they would be considered overly sensitive to a joke or a friendly gesture. The critics, feminist and otherwise, saw mob justice that sacrificed fairness and due process in a heated moment of judgment. It is a familiar opposition—unaddressed sexual harm versus overregulation of the sexual.

Reading reparatively, on the surface, seeing what is in plain sight, taking the intensity of the affective claims seriously, can help us understand these competing claims. Much of the debate surrounds the photograph that showed Tweeden asleep in a chair aboard a military aircraft, dressed in a helmet, fatigues, and a body armor vest. Franken is leaning towards her, hands spread over her breasts, his face turned to the camera with a wry smile that many described as leering. The visual produced deeply divergent reactions. For some, it was an obvious example of egregious conduct—a kind of #MeToo caught-in-the-act, where Franken visually becomes the poster boy of sexual misconduct. He was touching (or almost touching) the breasts of a sleeping, and hence nonconsenting, woman. For others, it was obviously a joke by a renowned jokester. The photograph was taken during a U.S.O. tour, described as a "notoriously burlesque" event, and Franken's joke lay in his inability to touch Tweeden's breasts because of the body armor vest. Reactions to the photo were polarized. The intensity of the affect of each side flowed from their respective obviousness: How can you not see what I see?

Photographs have long been ascribed a unique claim to truth, based on realism and mechanical objectivity. As Susan Sontag famously observed, "Photography furnishes evidence. Something we hear about, but doubt, seems proven when we're shown a photograph of it."[131] Critical scholars of photography, however, have revealed the many ways in which photographs are "never as easy to decode as they may appear and they are usually open to a number of readings."[132] Photography studies has explored, through widely divergent theoretical perspectives, the ways in which meaning is produced and interpreted. Some explored the political, ideological, and functional role of photography in reproducing power relationships. Others examined the particular ways in which meaning is produced and contested through photographic frames. Roland Barthes, whose writing has had a formidable influence on photography studies, explored photography's role in constituting and reproducing power relationships while simultaneously naturalizing them. Photographs were also deeply malleable: "[A] photograph can change its meaning as it passes from the very conservative *L'Aurore* to the communist *L'Humanité*."[133] While Barthes moved away from this structuralism in his later work, focusing instead on the subjectivity of spectators' responses and developing a semiotic theory of photographic meaning, others picked up on the more political critique. For example John Tagg, a photography theorist and art history professor at Binghamton University, examined how photographs only have meaning within specific historical contexts: "*Every* photograph is a result of specific and, in every sense, significant distortions which render its relation to any prior reality deeply problematic."[134] Tagg explored the truth claims of photography not as lying in the workings of an internal semiotic code but instead as the product of "their discursive mobilization, their channels of circulation, or their 'currency.'"[135]

These, and the many other theories of photography, offered up what Sedgwick would describe as strong theories with their paranoid readings: looking for meaning that lay buried beneath the surface, unearthing deeper meaning through multiple forms of critique. Susan Sontag said as much: "Photography implies that we know about the world if we accept it as the camera records it. But this is the opposite of understanding, which starts from *not* accepting the world as it looks."[136] For Sontag—and in sensibility, much photography scholarship—we need to reject the surface reading to find what is hidden underneath. This is not to dismiss the scholarship but to locate it within a history of critical thinking that may lean toward the paranoid in interpreting photography as that which is not simply an objective reflection of the real.

More recently, scholars, particularly those influenced by queer theory and its affective turn, have explored the affect of photography—the way in which photographs produce affect, feelings, and emotions. Elspeth Brown and Thy Phu argue, "That we feel photography can hardly be doubted. Photography excites a spectrum of feelings: faced with a violent image, you may respond with both horror and pity. The portrait you carry in your wallet may be of your beloved, whom you cherish. The photograph on your desk reminds you of one you've lost and may always mourn."[137] Yet, Brown and Phu argue that photography theory has failed to explore affect and feeling. In contrast to the "thinking photography" approach that had previously dominated photography studies, Brown and Phu's collection explores the implications of feeling photography and is simultaneously a queering of photography, focusing on "queerness and feeling in terms of both sexualities and marginal subjectivities."[138] They focus on how photography represents through emotions. Their approach, though not expressed as such, comes closer to the reparative, suggesting that we feel what is in the photograph, and also seeks to uncover hidden meanings, interdigitating between the paranoid and the reparative.

This brief foray into photography studies helps us understand the recurrent role of the photograph in the Franken controversy. On one hand, photographs continue to hold a special persuasive effect, a "lingering evidentiary trace" of an objective reality. Admittedly, photoshop and other digitally altering technology has cast doubt on the literalness of images in the public imagination. Yet, in the absence of claims of digital alteration—and there were none here—viewers often still process a photograph as proof. On the other hand, their meaning is produced through networks of circulation and diverse worldviews that shape what the photograph proves. The Franken photograph provided evidence, although opinions were deeply divided on what the proof revealed. Contexts, belief structures, and values all shaped interpretations. On one side, feminists and those sympathetic to #MeToo saw sexual misconduct. It was obvious: she is sleeping and he is touching her breasts. The other side, feminist #MeToo detractors, nonfeminists, and anti-feminists alike, saw a joke. Christine Zander, a writer for *Saturday Night Live* quoted in the Mayer article, said, "When I saw the photo, *I knew exactly what he was doing.* The joke was about him. He was doing 'an asshole.' . . . It was a mockery of someone acting in bad taste" (emphasis added).[139] Fo

Zander, and for many others, it was obviously a joke. Competing claims intensified the feelings. Disgust and ire at the image of sexual misconduct in progress becomes anger when others cannot see what is in plain sight. Amusement at an "off-color joke" becomes outrage and frustration that people cannot take it. For one side, reactions to the photograph provided evidence of the #MeToo claims. For the other, they proved that #MeToo had gone too far. Rather than appreciate the possibility of multiple meanings, everyone dug in their heels.

Lauren Berlant, in the first round of the Franken controversy, reflected on it through the lens of "the predator" versus "the jokester"—opposites with interesting equivalencies:[140] "Where the predator creates a situation they can exploit, it is often cushioned by a menacing sense that they control the interactive space and that they're unavoidable. When a goof performs a joke, which is mostly spontaneous and casual, it is shaped by the play of surprise and hard to process in the moment. Time and fresh awkwardness provide the jokester's cushion, however slight. In both cases the target suddenly feels baffled or overwhelmed."[141] Berlant argues that they are additionally linked by power;[142] those with less structural power are the most vulnerable to "the harassment and teasing, the world of humiliation and dings, sexualized, racialized."[143] Berlant describes these encounters "as a predictable kind of unwanted overcloseness, whether or not it's darkly predatory, jokey, or both. It's often both" (emphasis added).[144] As many things are. A reading beside strategy can allow us to view the photograph as both an unwanted sexual joke—it is a joke—and predatory. Both interpretations are partially right, but without the other, each is only partial.

Berlant explores the link between pleasure and aggression in comedy, and their relationship to power, in ways that bring insight to both sides of the Franken photo response. She asks us to consider the following: The next time you hear your voice bleat, 'It was just a joke,' ask yourself: who made you the boss of genre? And when something affronts you, slow things down: who made you the boss of genre?"[145] These are precisely the dueling responses that viewers had to the photograph. It was just a joke. It was offensive sexual misconduct. How can you not see this? It is right there in the photograph. As Berlant suggests, despite the differences, a given encounter can be both. Reading beside might help us appreciate that the photograph represents both. It makes Franken the jokester that he is, and accordingly, those who cannot see the joke, humorless. On the flip side, it makes Franken the sexual harasser, caught in the act of pretending to touch a woman's breast while she sleeps. For the latter, the fact that it was supposed to be a joke—he is laughing—only makes it worse, and more obvious.

When it comes to the photograph, the facts revealed by Mayer that it was taken on a different date and circulated to more people than Tweeden had originally claimed does nothing to alter its content or the affect of the viewer. Small inconsistencies are not uncommon in older accusations. Memory fades, affect remains. Would we hold this against Tweeden because she was a conservative? It is not about the small inconsistencies in the photograph; it is about what the photographic evidence seemingly presents. That Mayer's article focused so exclusively on the photograph was itself telling. The allegations by the other seven women simply fade away, made invisible by the photo that establishes the story of Tweeden as its central and discredited character. "Don't believe what you see" is the message of Mayer's read on the photograph—it is simply not all true. But Mayer's narrative also supports the jokester lens—look, it was all in fun—and the political operative lens—Tweeden lied about the photo to discredit Franken. She simultaneously relies on the conventional wisdom of the photo's objective realism, while challenging it.

Reading the competing claims beside each other allows us to contemplate the validity of both. Franken intended to make a joke. He made a bad one. The photograph captured inappropriate sexual conduct, with an apparently sleeping subject unable to consent. These are not—nor do they need to be—mutually exclusive interpretations. We also need to factor in the feelings of the spectators, to understand the intensity of the contestations. Acknowledging the affective responses as real may go some distance to reconcile the partiality of the claims they accompany.

* * *

The politics operating in the Franken controversy might also benefit from a reading beside. That Tweeden was a right-wing operative with questionable timing does not negate what happened, or make it less inappropriate. Nor does it mean that the release of the photograph was not political. Similarly, the politically expedient Democratic response in a moment of hypervigilance to sexual misconduct was riddled with its own contradictions. Eager to prove that they took the issue of sexual misconduct seriously, the Democrats turned on one of their own, rushed to judgment, supported Franken's ouster, and subsequently expressed regret. And even if the demand for Franken's resignation gained them higher moral ground in the subsequent fight against Brett Kavanaugh's Supreme Court confirmation hearings, it also placed them on the slippery slope of failing due process. The Republicans cried for some imbalanced form of due process during the hearings, supporting Kavanaugh, who had wrapped himself in the due process flag. Political calculations were made, some of which proved to be right for some contexts and wrong for others. Politics were played on all sides; it makes neither more true.

Reparative reading clarifies why the Franken case was so much more controversial than other political sex scandals at this time, and why it remains so contested. Five other members of the 115th Congress were forced to resign over sexual-misconduct scandals, while three members were pressured not to seek reelection. Of the five who resigned, four were Republicans. Of the three not seeking reelection, two were Democrats. All but Franken were members of the House of Representatives. Of the accused (resigned and no reelection), all but one were men. There was a range of misconduct. Representative Tim Murphy–R was forced to resign for asking a woman with whom he had an extramarital affair to have an abortion. Initially, he planned not to seek reelection, but was pressured by Republican leaders to resign, thereby removing himself as a distraction to the GOP agenda.[146] Three members of the

House of Representatives resigned after revelations that they used tax-payer money to settle sexual harassment suits (Pat Meehan–R, Blake Farentheld–R, and John Conyers Jr.–D). Two were accused of sexual harassment and misconduct by staffers (Trent Frankes–R and Rubin Kihuen–D); the former resigned and the latter was pressured to not seek reelection. Of those who refused to resign but were pressured not to seek reelection, one was a woman: Elizabeth Etsy–D, who was herself accused not of sexual misconduct but rather of failing to fire her former chief of staff accused of sexual harassment. An eighth member of Congress, Joe Barton–R, did not resign but decided not to seek reelection in the wake of a nude photo and explicit message. None of the #MeToo-related resignations created the same due process furor.

What, then, was so unique about the Franken allegations? We may not need to look behind or underneath or beyond to see what is argu-able in plain sight. It is not that the conduct of which he was accused was worse than—or not as bad as—that of others. It was not that he was a Democrat—there were others. Admittedly, Franken was the only senator, and his star was rising. And he was caught in the "act," whatever that act was. It comes back to the photograph and its deeply, affectively contested nature. The photograph operated as visual evidence that was both exculpatory and inculpatory, depending on the viewer.

The seeming incommensurability of responses to the photograph became even more unsettled in the second round of the Franken controversy, where regret abounded. A queer exploration of affect would have us examine the way the emotion played out in the controversy and the extent to which it animated and shaped it. Mayer's article high-lighted the many expressions of regret among Democrats for their role in demanding Franken's resignation, related almost entirely to a rush to judgment, failure of due process, and, specifically, not allowing the allegations to proceed to a Senate ethics committee. Franken himself expressed regret at resigning.[147] Regret manifests as blaming ourselves for bad outcomes, wishing we had made different choices. It is a look-ing back, a "staying with" the past.[148] Brian Price suggests that looking back has political potential, making us reflect on choices we might have taken, or could take in the future. He suggests that regret conjures two sets of images—what did happen and what should have happened—that become superimposed. Some suggest that Price has an overly positive vision of regret that encourages clear thinking, while "cleansed of all its negativity" and messiness.[149] Reinvesting regret with some of this messiness, this *feeling backwards*, as Heather Love would describe it,[150] may help explain some of what was occurring in this second round of the Franken controversy.

A number of senators wished they could undo their demand for resignation before an ethics committee had an opportunity to investigate. But regret does not produce crystal-clear hindsight; the vision remains messy. It is unclear whether they think that his resignation should not have happened or that the allegations were not in and of themselves substantial enough to justify it. Their views, whatever they might be, are hidden behind their eulogy for due process. They are, after all, politicians who tend to resist expressions of regret. There was no due process regret around the members of Congress who resigned. Something in the expression of regret around Franken speaks to the ambivalence of the allegations and is accelerated not only by partisan politics but also by the seemingly unimpeachable facticity of a photograph. To the extent that the photograph initially "spoke for itself," the expressions of regret suggest that alternative readings were possible. Maybe the photograph was not all the evidence needed to confirm what happened. It may have depicted inappropriate sexual conduct *and* a joke gone wrong. If so, a process was required to assess the claims and determine a proportional response. Regret sticks to the senators,[151] an awkward discomfort with choices that cannot be undone, even if the allegations and the photograph are now seen differently.

Reading the multiple opposing claims beside each other allows us to move beyond the either/or of the sex wars and the culture wars that played out in the Franken #MeToo controversy. If we can surrender to ambivalence, it lets us see the validity of both sides without condoning sexual misconduct. Interactions can be mistakes, jokes, and sexual misconduct, all at once. Regret, read reparatively, may allow us to recognize what we might have done differently, what we could still do differently, and acknowledge the ambiguity in our judgment. My goal is not to produce a relativistic or nihilistic reading, absent of normative judgment, but to hold onto the idea of sexual harm and sexual misconduct as real harms, as pervasive and unacknowledged, while also suspending our certainty. We might reasonably conclude that what Franken did was wrong, that the photograph does not speak for itself, that he was a prankster, that his jokes were predatory and from a bygone era, that his behavior touching women was inappropriate, that he didn't "mean it," and that he might not have been treated fairly—whatever that may mean.

CONCLUSION: FROM REPARATIVE READINGS TO REPARATIVE JUSTICE

Reparative reading may help us with many other more complicated #MeToo cases, allowing for seemingly contradictory claims to be kept in view and for an appreciation of their deeply affective nature. To return momentarily to the Ansari case, consent was complicated and there was a male/female hierarchy, but it was not in a professional context. Criminal lines were not crossed, and sexual harassment would not apply. Yet, a sexual harm was experienced. Can a reparative reading help hold the competing claims—there was an injury and the injury was not justiciable—to be simultaneously valid? Can a reparative approach help us think about alternative modes of accountability for such harms? What about Neil Degrasse Tyson, whose allegations of sexual misconduct were intricately connected to questions of race? Or Kevin Spacey, where the focus shifts to nonnormative sexualities and an absence of a male/female hierarchy, but clear hierarchies of age and profession existed? Spacey came out as gay in the immediate aftermath of the allegations. He was broadly condemned, including by many in the gay community—though there was a sotto voce queer critique, one that emerged if no exactly to defend Spacey, then to suggest the troubled discourse around his condemnation.[152]

Of course, then there is Harvey Weinstein, the consensus villain of the #MeToo movement. We could add Jeffrey Epstein. Or Larry Nassar. Is there a role for reparative reading, or reading beside, when it comes to these archetypical cases of serial sexual assault? Are there limits to a reparative paradigm? Can it take us to a slightly different set of questions than in the contested cases? These are not "hard cases" with competing claims to the legitimacy of sexual behavior. However, a reparative reading can call into question the faith we place in the criminal law to prosecute away sexual injury. It is useful not to reduce all of #MeToo to the Harvey Weinsteins, to recognize that the spectrum of sexual harms requires different thinking about accountability. Such a recognition might lead us to broaden our lens on the role of law beyond the criminal. These are some of the questions to which I now turn.

But before I do, I go back to where this chapter started: the Ronell controversy. Lisa Duggan ended her essay with a gesture towards a rethinking of harassment and power within the academy: "Perhaps we should begin to think about a restorative justice process that would center in departments, be transparent, hold faculty responsible, and assess the question of boundaries in local context? Perhaps impose confidentiality as the exception, not the rule—to be invoked when a need is demonstrated."[153] In this gesture toward the restorative, Duggan's critique is not anti-regulatory; rather, it points, however tentatively, towards an alternative model of regulation. In this moment, Duggan is in common cause with her critics, and those protesting NYU's handling of the Ronell case. The NYU Graduate Student Union's demands for institutional reform similarly called for a restorative justice option in addressing sexual misconduct. Of course, the devil is always in the details, and it is unclear whether the restorative justice model envisioned by the NYU Graduate Student Union is similar in form to the restorative justice process that Duggan has in mind. The same document called for Ronell's firing; the call for the restorative sits uncomfortably with the call for the punitive.

For now, I simply highlight a point of overlap in the otherwise highly polarized debate, specifically in relation to alternative modes of regulation. Both see a restorative future.

Restorative justice is a popular, broad, and vague concept that captures a range of alternative approaches to harm. At its most general, it seeks to bring the wrongdoer and the victim together to repair the harm done. I return to the contested notions of restorative justice in the next chapter. What are we to make of the echoing calls from the warring factions within the Ronell controversy? It may be worth paying attention to how carceral critique has taken hold, and the call for restorative justice is cutting across political differences in the analysis of sexual harm. While the carceral critique focuses in particular on the use of the criminal law to punish and incarcerate, it has translated into a broader critique of the punitive imaginary. We have seen the carceral logics at play within the dominance-feminist side of the sex wars, as well as its instantiations in #MeToo feminism. The call is for greater punishment—criminal *or otherwise*. In the context of campus sexual violence, the call is not for incarceration but for other forms of punishment. However, in the Ronell controversy, there was a tacit agreement among opposing voices (though certainly not all who weighed in on Ronell) on the carceral critique, which recognizes the devastating impact of incarceration and rejects its expansion as a mode of governance, and on the need for a restorative future. In the next chapter, I explore this future with a reparative sensibility, intriguing precisely as a call for an alternative form of regulation that gestures towards the possibility of approaching sexual harm differently.

5

REGULATING REPARATIVELY

On February 24, 2020—two and a half years after the *New York Times* broke the story of his predatory sexual assault and sexual harassment— Harvey Weinstein was found guilty. The allegations had been a galvanizing force behind the #MeToo movement; by the end of October 2017, over eighty women had come forward with accusations. The trial itself addressed five sexual-offense charges brought by two women. Weinstein was charged with two counts of predatory sexual assault, an alternative count of rape in the first degree, a criminal act in the first degree, and rape in the third degree. He was found guilty of a criminal sexual act in the first degree against Miriam Haley in 2006 and rape in the third degree against Jessica Mann in 2013. Despite being acquitted of the three most serious charges, which could have resulted in a life sentence, he was sentenced to twenty-three years in prison. While Judge James Burke cautioned the jury not to see the case as a referendum on #MeToo, in the public sphere, it was almost impossible not to do so. The trial was described as a landmark, a watershed, a turning point for the movement. The feminist reaction to the conviction was one of overwhelming relief[1] and celebration: "The conviction of Harvey Weinstein is a stunning victory for every single woman who refused to remain silent any longer."[2] Many were gratified, if surprised, that the rich and powerful producer had not been able to buy his way out and would go to jail. Jessica Valenti, an American feminist writer and blogger, captured a common sentiment when she tweeted, "It says a lot about rape culture and how accustomed women are to losing that nearly every

female friend I have was expecting a 'not guilty' verdict in the Weinstein trial."[3] Broad gratitude and support were expressed for the women
who had come forward and broken the silence at significant personal
cost. Others were pleased that Weinstein was going to jail. Roxanne Gay
tweeted, "May Harvey Weinstein spend what remains of his life behind
bars, thinking about all the terrible crimes he committed against women
and may [he] find some measure of peace in his punishment."[4] When
criticized for her carceral sentiment, Gay responded, with candid emotional honesty, "I am fine with rapists sitting in prison. Prison reform is
desperately needed but I am not so evolved as to not want rapists to rot
there. I am glad people like you are."[5]

A few were more ambivalent. Ashley Judd, one of Weinstein's accusers, wrote that she would have preferred a different process: "I would
love for Harvey to have a restorative justice process in which he could
come emotionally to terms with his wrongs. The criminal justice system
is a distant second to a more humane kind of process. This is what he
has created for himself: prison, lack of remorse, lack of accountability.
The man is going to prison for sex crimes."[6] Aya Gruber, Lara Bazelon,
Megan Nolan, and Melissa Grant, among others, used the verdict to
reflect on the limitations of a criminal justice system that reinforces a
punitive, carceral state as an appropriate response,[7] and to suggest alternative restorative approaches.[8] Grant noted the work of prominent
abolition feminists[9] and specifically flagged the system's failure to repair
the harm to the victims.

The feminist reaction to the Weinstein conviction reflects the complicated, multilayered, and contested legacy of #MeToo. Weinstein was
the consensus villain, the "monstrous" predator, whose behavior was
not ambivalent "sexual misconduct" but fell smack in the middle of rape,
sexual assault, and quid pro quo sexual harassment. Given the current
system for dealing with sexual violence, how could he not be prose-
cuted? Criminal charges seemed the only game in town to address his
egregious behavior, and pressure was on the district attorneys to take
action. Given the criminal justice system's many failures in relation to

sexual violence, there was great anxiety that Weinstein too would be exonerated. An acquittal would have been a blow to #MeToo, suggesting yet again that complainants were not believed and that even the most serial of sexual offenders could act with impunity. Yet, Weinstein's prosecution, conviction, and imprisonment raised the specter of the carceral state, of the power of the criminal justice system and mass incarceration. The feminist consensus on Weinstein's conduct faded a little when it came to the appropriate remedial response.

The understandably diverse feminist reactions to the Weinstein verdict gesture towards some of the fault lines of the sex wars.[10] Some focused on the harms his sexual injuries had caused, while others worried about the harms of regulating sexual injury. In some ways, Weinstein's was an easy case with little dispute over whether the alleged conduct was problematic and no concerns around due process—something he had been afforded in great measure as a criminal defendant. Yet, for some feminists, there was lingering equivocation about the turn to the criminal justice system. Others might well respond that he was a serial rapist and deserved the full weight of the criminal law, that there was no alternative. But is there? This chapter explores precisely that question: What else could be done?

Broadening the lens beyond Weinstein, this chapter explores how to think differently about regulating sexual harm using the fault lines of the sex wars, and the debates they raised about when and how to use law to redress sexual harm. On one side, feminist claims staked in the harms of nonconsensual sex and the failure to regulate it call for more law—broader definitions of sexual harms, more robust notions of sexual consent, more effective enforcement and punishment. On the other side, sex-positive feminists and queer critics remain more concerned with the overregulation of consensual sexuality and the "carceral creep" of anti-violence feminism[11]—and call for less law, with an anti-regulatory impulse. The division has long played out on the terrain of criminal law although more recently, as controversies around Title IX have demonstrated, the civil context is also at play. The two sides of the sex wars are not easily reconciled—increased versus less criminalization, broader definitions of sexual harm and affirmative consent versus narrower ones, tougher versus more lenient penalties.

Using the reparative reading tools discussed in the previous chapter, I argue that it is possible to read these two claims beside each other, interrogating how the under- and overregulation of sex can both be valid. The harms of sex can be read beside the harms of regulating sex. Reading reparatively, seeing what is in plain sight, and taking the intensity of the affective claims seriously illuminate the potential harms of criminalizing nonnormative, consensual sexuality at the same time as they make clear the failure of law to regulate and prevent nonconsensual sexual harms, and the extent to which those harms go unacknowledged or unaddressed. I do not mean to suggest that we will find complete agreement; there will be continuing points of conflict and divergence. But, we might be able to see different possibilities if we hold the multiple positions simultaneously in view.

The reparative sensibility that I advocate seeks new ways to repair sexual harms that heed the decades of advocacy and warning from both sides of the sex wars. The reparative approach takes sexual harms seriously while simultaneously interrogating what it *means* to take it seriously. The approach is not simply a "middle" position within the various debates but rather, an argument to displace the centrality of the criminal law and its binary corollary—criminal law or no law, criminal harm or no harm—that has long plagued both sides of the sex wars. Loosening the criminal law's hold on the definition and regulation of sexual harms could go some way in allowing for deeper feminist and queer conversations that affirm sexual harm, without endorsing a carceral state. However, the site of contestation goes beyond criminal law. From Title IX to workplace sexual harassment, we hear calls for broader definitions and tougher punishment. Indeed, as anti-violence advocates increasingly embrace a critique of the carceral state and its remedies, more attention gets shifted to civil and administrative law. Yet a carceral logic informed by a retributive justice model remains embedded—one that emphasizes punishment, albeit not incarceration.

Critiquing and rejecting the role of the criminal law, and the carceral logic of the civil, do not necessarily imply rejecting the role of law in the regulation of sexual harm. Building on the growing body of literature considering alternatives to the criminal justice system, the chapter explores ways to address and regulate questions of sexual harm differently. How might we use the creative sensibilities of reparative readings, of reading otherwise, of reading beside, to think otherwise about remedial approaches? Reading beside can help us hold contradictory claims, and the affects that they produce. The chapter seeks to bring Sedgwick's reparative reading to the regulation of sexual harm and explore the possibilities of a reparative sensibility for sexual justice. My objective is not to set out precise definitions or alternative models of dispute resolution, but to gesture toward the intellectual sensibility required in their design.

THE CRITIQUE OF THE CRIMINAL JUSTICE SYSTEM AND THE SEARCH FOR ALTERNATIVES

The last two decades have seen a growing critique of the criminal justice system, the exponential growth of prisons since the 1980s, and prison populations made up disproportionately of people of color. Called "the prison industrial complex" by Angela Davis and "prison nation" by Beth Richie,[12] this phenomenon has been addressed by scholars, activists, journalists, and filmmakers who have tracked the rise of mass incarceration and its devastating impact on Black communities.[13] From Michelle Alexander's best-selling *New Jim Crow: Mass Incarceration in the Age of Colorblindness* (2010) to Ava DuVernay's award-winning documentary, *The 13th* (2016), alongside the emergence of the Black Lives Matter movement, the critique of the prison industrial complex has entered the mainstream consciousness, driving a growing progressive consensus that the United States incarcerates too many people, and that too many of them are Black. There is growing awareness of the deeply racialized impact of a state that punishes and incarcerates at rates higher than in any other country in the world.

This critique of the criminal justice system was forged by women of color[14] with a specifically feminist tone. Angela Davis, Beth Richie, and Ruth Wilson Gilmore are among the Black feminist activists and scholars who have highlighted the devastating differential impact of mass incarceration on Black people. While they have joined issue with the prison abolition movement, they insist that attention be addressed to sexual violence, something often missing within the broader movement. In 2001, INCITE! and Critical Resistance came together to articulate the failings of the prison abolition movement and the feminist anti-violence movement in their "Statement on Gender Violence and the Prison Industrial Complex": "We share the feelings of outrage experienced by rape victims; we believe that repetitive rapists must be restrained from committing further acts of violence. On the other hand, we do not support the response of imprisonment. We challenge the basic assumptions that punishment, harsh sentences and retributive attitudes will serve to lessen victims' pain, re-educate rapists or genuinely protect society."[15] Beth Richie focused on the negative effect of criminalizing and incarcerating racialized survivors of gender-based violence. Her book *Arrested Justice: Black Women, Violence, and America's Prison Nation* (2012) focuses on the plight of Black women, socially marginalized through structural racism and economic inequality, left susceptible to both male violence and state incarceration.[16] In 2013, Angela Davis gave this movement a name—abolition feminism.[17]

* * *

Elizabeth Bernstein coined the term "carceral feminism" in 2007 to describe the commitment of many anti-violence feminists to "a law and order agenda . . . and a drift from the welfare state to the carceral state as the enforcement apparatus for feminist goals."[18] While the term was used to describe the turn to the criminal justice system by anti-trafficking activists, it has gained traction to critique anti-violence feminist strategies more generally. As Mimi Kim describes, carceral feminism now "points to decades of feminist anti-violence collaboration with the *carceral state* or that part of the government most associated with the institutions of police, prosecution, courts, and the system of jails, prisons, probation, and parole. . . . [T]he carceral state focuses on activities of surveillance, arrest, and incarceration."[19] Critics of the criminal justice system, including abolition feminists, who have led so much of the resistance, adopted "carceral feminism" to signal anti-violence feminism's implication in mass incarceration.

Similar influential critiques followed. Kristen Bumiller's *In an Abusive State* (2008) tracked the mainstream success of anti-violence feminism with the rise of the neoliberal law-and-order agenda, which created a problematic alliance between increasing criminalization and penal welfare state surveillance of victims of violence, particularly of low-income women.[20] The racialization of sexual violence was front and center in Bumiller's analysis of high-profile trials such as the Central Park 5, the impact on Black communities of the turn to mass incarceration, and the unintended consequences for Black and low-income women caught up in a web of social-service surveillance. Bumiller argued for a move away from criminalization. While she did not develop specific proposals, she advocated a reconsideration of the regulation of sexual violence that would include "a recognition of the dangers of counteracting it primarily through the punitive and regulatory mechanisms of the modern state." Aya Gruber similarly writes about how the feminist war on crime has contributed to the problem of mass incarceration.[21] From early feminist efforts to oppose domestic violence and rape to second-wave feminist campaigns to toughen laws against sexual violence to more recent campus anti-violence activism and #MeToo, Gruber argues, the feminist tendency has been punitive, dependent upon and reinforcing of an increasingly carceral state. Gruber posits that feminists must take a step away from criminal law and toward non-carceral gender justice."[22] Supporting abolitionism as a position, she supports feminists taking "a firm stance against policing, prosecution and punishment as the preferred solution" and turning towards the work of abolition feminists like the members of INCITE!

This critique of the system is not an abdication of responsibility and accountability for harms, including sexual harms. It is, rather, a plea to reimagine what that might look like outside the punitive regime of mass incarceration. Abolition feminists have long been on the front line developing transformative models of justice to address sexual harm from outside of the criminal justice system. Others have looked to alternative justice modalities that supplement the criminal justice system, advancing restorative, transitional, and/or reparative models. The visions have their advantages and disadvantages and often overlap. With broad definitions, multiple visions, and multiple processes, each has gained traction, though none more than restorative justice. All the approaches share an underlying dissatisfaction with models currently grounded in the criminal justice system. Some scholars have explored the possibilities of these alternative justice models in responding to gender and sexual harms, and a few have considered how they might apply to #MeToo. In the remainder of this section, I set out each of the models in broad strokes, and explore their relevance to feminist responses.

Transitional justice developed as a mechanism for states to address violent legacies post- conflict and/or post–authoritarian regimes. Colleen Murphy describes it as an approach used in the aftermath of massive human rights violations, committed for political purposes, by agents of government or those with the government's tacit permission and where the legitimacy of the state itself is in question, "where the authority of the state to deal with past wrongs needs to be established, because the state is often implicated in the wrongs that are now the focus of transitional justice processes."[23] Societies in transition face "serious existential uncertainty," yet despite the fragility, "there is a credible aspiration to end conflict and/or repression and democratize." Transitional-justice models include criminal prosecutions of those individuals responsible for the most serious violations, truth and reconciliation commissions reparations, and law reform. Transitional justice looks both backward and forward—telling the story of the past and providing accountability for transgressions, while also looking to build a better future.[24] In this way, it seeks to address broad-based violations while bringing about the kind of structural change necessary to prevent future ones.

Restorative justice has emerged as an increasingly popular alternative to the current criminal justice model. While there is no universal definition, at its most general, it is a "process where all stakeholders affected by an injustice have an opportunity to discuss how they have been affected by the injustice and to decide what should be done to repair the harm."[25] Restorative justice typically focuses on addressing harm by holding offenders responsible and providing an opportunity for victims and communities to name the harm and their needs in the aftermath. Restorative justice is often presented in opposition to retributive justice: "Retributive justice essentially refers to the repair of justice through unilateral imposition of punishment, whereas restorative justice means the repair of justice through reaffirming a shared value-consensus in a bilateral process."[26] Sometimes restorative processes are used to supplement the criminal justice system, and are deployed at its various stages. Restorative justice has also been advocated as an alternative to the criminal justice system as a whole. Either way, restorative justice is seen as redressing limitations: "The criminal justice system can fall short in supporting victims and enhancing offender accountability on a number of levels. In a criminal prosecution, the defendant is not incentivized to take true responsibility for his actions. He is discouraged from testifying on his own behalf—even during sentencing after a conviction or guilty plea."[27] In contrast, restorative justice promotes offender accountability, victim reparation, and reintegration.

Transformative justice builds on the principles of restorative justice but moves beyond the impact of harm on individuals and communities involved to focus on the structures and underlying social circumstances that produce harmful behavior. Transformative justice embraces the restorative justice goals of victim healing, offender accountability, and community engagement but also seeks to understand and change unequal social conditions that perpetuate violence. It is a model that decenters the criminal justice system, by developing modes of accountability outside the carceral state. Grown out of grassroots movements, led by communities of color often associated with abolitionist politics and abolition feminism, it has received attention from critical criminologists who see transformative justice as an opportunity for broader structural change.

Feminists—including legal scholars—have taken up each of these models as possible alternatives to the contemporary regulation of gender and sexual harm.[28] While transitional justice might seem the least relevant to rethinking the regulation of sexual violence in nontransitional contexts like #MeToo, some feminists like Lesley Wexler suggest that comparing contexts is useful in guiding reform efforts.[29] Similar to post-conflict settings where transitional justice is often applied, #MeToo emerged against a backdrop of "widespread patterns of misconduct, structural inequalities, a history of denial, and the normalization of wrongful behaviour." Wexler and her coauthors argue that transitional justice has the advantage of linking individual "wrongs with broader institutional change," exemplifying the ways in which transitional, transformative, and restorative justice overlap—indeed the terms often get used interchangeably—and building on the advantages and/or limitations of each.[30]

Restorative justice has attracted considerable feminist attention, with robust legal scholarship exploring its potential in the context of gender and sexual harms.[31] The literature points out the limitations of the current criminal justice system and highlights the potential for a restorative approach to reduce the focus on punishment and the sidelining of victims, while better meeting their needs and promoting offender accountability. Barbara Hudson was an early advocate for restorative justice in the context of gendered violence.[32] In the late 1990s and early 2000s, Hudson explored a restorative approach not simply to divert certain offenses away from criminal justice processes but to provide a more effective model of justice for victims of gendered violence. Her work ze-roes in on the extent to which criminal censure is seen as "the expressive yardstick for the condemnation of behavior," and argues that restorative justice can and should take on this expressive function.

Leigh Goodmark's work explores the possibilities of restorative jus-tice in the context of domestic violence.[33] A law professor and director of the Gender Violence Clinic at the University of Maryland, Goodmark argues that the criminal justice system, with its adversarial nature and focus on retributive punishment, is hostile to victims of violence, who are "frequently silenced or blamed for the victimization,"[34] and rarely gives victims "the reparation they seek." Goodmark cites multiple studies where victims "stressed their preference for prevention and rehabilita-tion over punishment and for holding offenders meaningfully account-able outside of penal institutions. Other studies suggest that victims of violence want offenders to experience and express remorse, develop empathy, and, most importantly, stop hurting others."[35] The existing criminal justice system, she suggests, fails on all fronts; it "discourages offenders from accepting responsibility for their actions in the hope of escaping criminal culpability. Prosecution hardens offenders' attitudes toward their victims, making the development of empathy and behavior change unlikely at best. Incarceration does nothing to change offend-ers' attitudes toward their partner or their use of violence."[36] Restorative justice is better positioned to deliver on these needs with processes that center the victim, promote offender accountability, and encourage com-munity involvement, thus delivering on the justice objectives of voice, validation, and vindication.[37] The process itself can serve "the feminist goals of amplifying women's voices, fostering women's autonomy and empowerment, engaging community, avoiding gender essentialism and employing an intersectional analysis, transforming patriarchal struc-tures and ending violence against women."[38]

Many others have taken up the restorative cause for sexual violence, some specifically in the post–#MeToo context. Lesley Wexler and Jen-nifer Robbenolt have explored how key components of restorative justice—including acknowledgment, responsibility taking, harm repair, nonrepetition, and reintegration—might be helpful in the context of #MeToo.[39] Laurie Kohn has similarly argued for this approach to pervasive sexual misconduct in the wake of #MeToo.[40] Quoting Howard Zehr, she describes restorative justice as a process that involves all those "who have a stake in a specific offense," enabling them "to collectively identify and address harms, needs, and obligations, in order to heal and put things as right as possible."[41] Kohn argues that restorative justice is a process uniquely suited to the needs of victims of sexual violence: "[T]he offender has to face the victim and take responsibility for his or her actions that caused harm. The process gives victims back some of the power they lost during the sexual misconduct by allowing them to confront those who wronged them and participate in the process. Restorative justice is uniquely poised to invite and host a conversation about the critical question, 'why?'"[42]

While there is still less uptake within feminist legal scholarship, some feminists are looking towards transformative justice to go beyond what restorative justice offers victims of gender and sexual harms. Abolition feminists have led the way. Organizations like IN-CITE! promote grassroots organizing and community accountability,[43] seeking not only individual remedies but structural change to the very conditions that create sexual violence. While building on restorative justice's emphasis on participation, collaboration, and repair, the abolition-feminist approach to transformative justice breaks from restorative justice's ties to the criminal justice system. This break with state-based responses may account for the relatively low traction of transformative-justice models within feminist *legal* scholarship and activism, to the extent that law seems to necessarily implicate state-based models. Yet some have taken up the mantle, claiming that transformative justice can go further than restorative justice. Donna Coker for example argues, "Restorative justice processes do not generally address these sources of battered women's inequality nor do they address the subordinating systems that may operate in the life of the batterer

The concept of *restoration* suggests that a prior state existed in which the victim experienced significant liberty and the offender was integrated into a community; in many cases neither is true. Rather than restorative justice, battered women should have the option to choose processes that operate with a *transformative* justice ideal."[44] Coker argues that it is a means of confronting pervasive structural inequalities that give rise to sexual violence.

Transitional, restorative, and transformative models share a critique of the inadequacy of the current criminal justice system and a belief that new and different ways of taking harm seriously are possible. I build on this sentiment, arguing for a reparative sensibility to regulating sexual harm that decenters criminal law and carceral logics. Angela Davis has warned that prison abolitionists need to "let go of the desire to discover one single alternative system of punishment" and imagine instead "a constellation of alternative strategies and institutions."[45] A reparative approach to sexual harm must similarly remain open to the array of strategies and possibilities emerging from alternative models of justice. The approach I advocate returns to Sedgwick's reparative reading, which holds contesting positions and strategies in view. It is different from what is sometimes referred to as "reparative justice," another alternative model focusing on broad-based reparations, with a restitutive and expressive function primarily in relation to historical wrongs.[46] Reparative justice may have a role to play alongside other alternative models in addressing sexual harms, but the approach I propose as a basis for regulation invokes the spirit of Sedgwick's reading beside—an openness to things being otherwise. Sedgwick, and those who followed in her footsteps, have sought to read with plenitude, affection, generosity, solidarity, and, I would add, grace. A reparative sensibility brings these affective strategies to bear, building on the critique of the criminal justice system while heeding decades of advocacy on both sides of the sex wars. While a reparative approach imagines different ways of thinking about sexual harm, it never dismisses it. An interrogation of what it means to take sexual harm seriously remains at the core.

REGULATING REPARATIVELY

How might we think about regulating reparatively? Some might eschew the very idea of state regulation as being compatible with queer reparative justice, which, as discussed in chapter 4, tends towards an anti-regulatory stance. Some anti-carceral feminists like Chloe Taylor reject engaging with the state *tout court*, seeing feminist law reform as de facto carceral, endorsing instead only those projects independent of the law and the state.[47] Many such critics point to the transformative-justice work of abolition feminists like the members of INCITE!, who view change as deriving from the local, community level. Based on this premise, INCITE! develops "community-based alternative responses to addressing domestic and sexual violence so that survivors are not forced to rely on police and prisons."[48] But abolition politics are not inherently opposed to law reform.[49] While advocates of abolishing the penal system distinguish their position from reformism, they do support law reforms that move towards abolition. Critical Resistance, an activist organization founded in 1997 in Berkeley, and other such organizations, champion reforms that advance abolishing the prison industrial complex, such as eliminating the death penalty, decriminalization, shorter prison sentences, improved parole directed at decreasing recidivism, supporting prisoners' rights to organize politically, and doing away with mandatory minimum sentences. With eliminating prison altogether as the ultimate goal, the question defining strategies is whether reforms are directed at "fixing" the system or decreasing its footprint.

Anna Terwiel interrogates the meaning of carceral feminism and argues for an expansive feminist abolition politics that eschews the carceral/anti-carceral binary and, by extension, engaging/not engaging the state.[50] Terwiel argues that both carceral and anti-carceral feminism are contested terrain and that "a binary understanding of carceral feminism that pits feminists who are willing to engage with the state or the law against feminists who see transformative justice as the only route to justice, obscures that feminists *within* each camp (and not just the people they wish to hold accountable) may disagree about what sexual (in)justice looks like."[51] Indeed, Terwiel draws parallels with the disagreements about sexual harm that characterized the sex wars. She argues that the either/or of those debates may be counterproductive to an expansionist feminist politics. She advocates instead a spectrum of decarceration that does not perpetuate an opposition between the restorative and the transformative, the state and the community, the carceral and the anticarceral.[52] For Terwiel, the question should not be whether to engage with the state but rather how to do so in ways that advance decarceration.

My imagined reparative regulation returns to the terrain of law and builds on the idea of rejecting the either/or. I do not pit the reparative approach against the more transformative visions, although I appreciate that engaging with the legal apparatus of the state risks reinforcing its power. I return to law, however, to envision a better way to regulate sexual harm and acknowledge the risks inherent in regulation itself. Beyond a move away from criminal law, my reparative approach is a move away from the carceral logics that inform regulation and cast a disciplinary and punitive surveillance over vulnerable populations.[53] Developing approaches to regulate sexual harm must keep those harms in sharp relief.

The promise of restorative-justice approaches, including those incorporated into transformative strategies, lies in centering the victim/survivor. A reparative approach can do this while simultaneously holding in view queer and sex-positive feminisms' critiques of victimization. In the current system, allegations of sexual assault by victims lead to the criminal law, where they lose all control. More often than not, allegations do not lead to charges, charges do not lead to prosecutions, prosecutions do not lead to convictions, convictions do not lead to significant imprisonment. Critiques of the way criminal trials sideline and traumatize victims abound. Even in cases where the offender is convicted, there is reason to ask what the victim received in return. Retributive justice, where incarceration of the offender is equated with vindicating the allegations, is understood to recognize the harm done to the victim. Longer sentencing is equated with taking the harm more seriously.

It is easy to see how we got here, and even why we continue to imagine that the criminal justice system provides validation for harm done. Feminist resort to the criminal law was part of a broader discursive struggle to make sexual harms both legible and serious in order to signal in the strongest way possible that the conduct was socially impermissible. As Tanya Serisier argues, the promise of the criminal law has been one of recognition and condemnation: "The criminal justice system offers the chance of official validation, social condemnation of the harm suffered by survivors and accountability or at least punishment for the perpetrator of that harm, even if that offer is largely illusory."[54] The expressive promise is, Serisier points out, a far cry from what it actually delivers. While arguing against the framing of sexual harm as a crime suggests that it be taken less seriously, the starting point should rather be the failure of criminal law itself. Criminal justice rarely provides either validation for complainants or accountability for offenders. Bracketing the equation of recognition with incarceration, we might reasonably ask if there are better approaches for recognizing harm.

Many studies have shown that victims/survivors seek above all to have their injury acknowledged and recognized. The criminal justice system operates at cross-purposes with recognition; indeed, as critics have pointed out, everything about it incentivizes the offender to deny responsibility for the wrong. The very structure of a punitive system is to encourage denial, not accountability. Allegations of sexual assault, precisely because they are criminal with potentially carceral consequences, are necessarily met with denials, rigorous defenses, and the marshaling of all the due process safeguards that the criminal justice system provides. Remorse is taken into account at the sentencing stage, but it only comes—if it comes at all—at the end of the criminal justice process.[55] Long before there is any role for remorse, victims are met with a form of structural gaslighting: the denial of their memory, perception and judgment. The common refrain that the criminal trial revictimizes the victim is based on the systemic structure of denial. To advocate regulating reparatively is not simply a call to #BelieveAllWomen, presume innocence, or reverse the burden of proof. It is rather an invitation to think about what repair might look like and affirm the importance of recognition as a justice goal. Instead of punishment, what if recognition and responsibility were prioritized? What if remorse, as a part of accountability, was not only relevant when the accused is about to be criminally sentenced? It may require a fundamental reorientation, a shift in our legal and political imaginary, a redefining of "recognition" and "responsibility" that veers away from punishment.[56]

What if allegations of sexual assault did not necessarily lead to the criminal law? What if the stakes were not carceral? As I mentioned above, many rightly worry that a call to decriminalize sexual violence signals that the harm is not serious—an anxiety based on the underlying assumption that the criminal law is required to indicate the gravity of the offense. But, abolition is not about sexual harm alone, or singling it out for decriminalization. It is a move to seek alternative, and arguably more effective, ways of signaling the undesirability of conduct, calling for accountability, and thinking about repair. There are many modalities of regulation beyond the criminal; civil law, public law, and administrative law offer many alternatives. From labor law to occupational health and safety law, environmental law to human rights law, there is a broad range of options for thinking about appropriate regulatory responses to harms. None offers a panacea in its own right; each presents its own challenges and limitations. But, collectively, they point to legal methods that go well beyond the criminal. Redesigning a regime to address sexual harms could also involve incorporating alternative dispute-resolution processes that build on restorative and transformative strategies and goals. With punishment and retribution giving way to recognition and responsibility, the resulting regulatory model, designed to affirm victims of violence and promote the accountability of offenders, could take harm more seriously rather than less.

In thinking about alternative modes of regulating reparatively that produce less harm, many claims need to be held beside each other—like the harms of sex and the harms of regulating sex. But, the "sides" do not only disagree on appropriate modes of regulation (criminal versus noncriminal, punishment versus restitution, retribution versus restoration); they also conflict on sexuality as danger/pleasure and woman as victim/agent. This dispute often manifests itself in the legal definintions of sexual harms. If the standard is one of consent, then how broadly or narrowly should consent be defined? If the standard is something other than consent—say, unwanted—how do we define that? To answer these questions, we must address the underlying understandings of sexuality and sexual agency. How can we hold the sides in tandem, attentive to sexuality as a site of both danger and pleasure and to women as both victims of sexual violence and agents of sexual negotiation?

The victim/agency dichotomy is one that plagues the sex wars and demands a reparative reading. How might the critique of victimization be held beside the conditions of inequality that limit women's agency and result in sexual injury? Women are subject to sexual violence. The way that the law recognizes (or fails to recognize) sexual violence can contribute to what Wendy Brown calls "wounded attachments" or what Janet Halley calls "a politics of injury and trauma sensibility."[57] Brown argues that victims run the risk of becoming overly attached to the harms they have incurred; indeed, the harms can become the basis of a political identity. Halley has similarly argued that feminist politics contribute to an inflated sense of victimization. The critique of the way in which anti-violence feminism has relied on and reinscribed gendered constructions of women as vulnerable and passive is a powerful one. Rebecca Stringer describes the 1990s popular and academic feminist critique as part of a broader victim politics that left no room for women's agency. Stringer suggests that "to represent women as vulnerable victims is disabling, misleading, regressive, and harmful, whereas to recognize women as agents is enabling, progressive, and liberating."[58] She calls this "the 'victim-bad/agent-good' formulation," a reductive logic that begs more critical scrutiny. Stringer argues for a feminist reconceptu- alization of the meaning of victim, victimhood, and victimization that moves beyond this narrow framing and reconsiders the bad name given to victimization and the good one to agency. Stringer agrees with those who believe that victim feminism has supported the rise of the carceral state, as part of the neoliberal war on crime, but suggests that the affirmation of agency runs the risk of reinforcing a different element of neoliberal governance: an emphasis on personal responsibility in place of structural subordination. Feminist and other critical scholars have revealed a fundamental shift in governance under neoliberalism towards individual responsibility and the privatization of risk.[59] Stringer sees overlap between the neoliberal anti-victim talk and the feminist critique of victim politics. Not eschewing agency, she rather suggests the need for a more critical approach that recognizes how the agency-good trope lends weight to an individualized model of responsibility and risk reduction for sexual violence. Stringer argues that we also need to explore the victim-bad trope. She looks to the work of Carine Mardorossian, who has argued that in 1960s and 1970s feminism, the idea of women as victims of male violence was not coterminous with an absence of agency: "Being a victim did not mean being incapacitated and powerless. It meant being a determined and angry (although not pathologically resentful) agent of change."[60] Mardorossian's work is a reminder of the powerful agency of the anti-violence feminists of the earlier sex wars set out in chapter 2, before it was obscured through the narrative of victim feminism.

In refusing the binary, Stringer's work gestures towards the kind of reparative reading I advocate, standing neither *for* victimization nor *against* agency. Rather, she advances a critical sensibility towards rethinking victimization that "resist[s] the facile opposition between passivity and agency."[61] Her critique recalls a problem that has long plagued the sex wars: overstating the claims of the opposing side and hurling caricature across the divide. The critique of victim feminism, even at its most scholarly (Brown, Halley, and others), runs the risk of overgeneralizing, in a kind of baby-with-the-bathwater maneuver. Returning, then, to their critique of wounded attachments and the politics of injury and trauma, it seems entirely possible to affirm the importance of this critique without giving it the last word. Consider Michelle Anderson's observations on Halley's critique that the law of sexual harassment and sexual violence "might well have a shaping contribution to make to women's suffering when, for instance, it insists that a raped woman has suffered an injury from which she is unlikely ever to recover."[62] Anderson argues that Halley's argument is undergirded by problematic stereotypes: "Today's lying female is confused, misled after the fact into believing that she was victimized by sex when she never previously considered the sex bad, nor herself a victim. In a fit of 'erotic imagination,' she has been duped—by feminists—and is now a fool who fools others."[63] One need not accept the full vitriol of Anderson's polemic—more proof of the overstatement of the claims of the other—to appreciate the need to interrogate the discursive underpinnings of Halley's and others' critique of victimization. The idea that legal discourse constitutes the very subjects that it regulates does not only play in one direction; we need to be attentive to the multiple and contradictory ways even the critical language we deploy is itself embedded in deeply gendered discourses and runs the risk of reinscribing them. We should have to choose neither between victim and agent nor between traumatized sensibility and manipulative fabrication. A reparative reading allows us to sit within these tensions, while bringing the polemic down a notch.

Equipped with a reparative sensibility, we must return to the question of legal regulation that recognizes discursive dilemmas on all sides. The criminal law of sexual assault has demanded not only the performance of victimization but a very particular one. *Successful* complainants have to be very specific types of victims, who carefully follow a script. Interestingly, within this prescribed victim stance we can hold the views of MacKinnon and Halley side by side, admittedly in ways that they might not recognize. For both, the victim script is a problem.[64] For dominance feminists, it fails to see the many ways women are subject to sexual violence. For sex-positive feminism, the script itself produces the subject position of victim and an attachment to it. These two positions push in different directions. Dominance feminism wants more conduct classified as sexual violence and made actionable. Sex-positive feminism wants less. What might be revealed if we inhabit the space of this tension, where the victim script is a problem of both over- and underregulation, further complicating the MacKinnon/Halley, victim/agency opposition? The specific script the law requires is embedded with elements of both victimization and agency. While Sharon Marcus powerfully argued that rape scripts construct women as "always already raped and rapeable," Stringer observes that a particular female agency has always been embedded in rape law, which has long sought the perfect victim who resists. "Rape law is replete with images of women as capable agents; indeed, a defining feature of rape law has been its recourse to this imagery to establish women as always already responsible."[65] The law itself is located at a problematic intersection with victim/agent, where good victims must display just the right amount of agency and no more. The problem is not victimization or agency per se, but the particular script embedded in the law that reinscribes deeply gendered norms.

Can we not imagine a standard where a complainant need be constituted neither a legal subject in and through the script of victimization—a victim "through and through"—nor an agent responsible for avoiding sexual harm?[66] Where a legal subject's harm can be recognized without reducing the subject to only that harm? Where the harm does not define identity and subject position, nor exaggerate the damage? There are many ways the law can potentially make the harm worse. Brown and Halley address the law's production and potential exacerbation of the injury, insisting it be the "worst thing that ever happened." On the contrary, there is law's refusal to recognize at all, which performs an elaborate gaslighting referred to as a "secondary harm." Stringer describes this second-order vulnerability as "the ability to be wounded and to then have that wounding effaced, in language, by others, by the law."[67] Both of these harms must be held in view; law can harm in the way that it recognizes and in the way that it does not. Regulating reparatively refuses the either/or, and the "there is no alternative" thinking. There is always an alternative, if we imagine it. It should be possible to recognize and validate the harm, while ensuring it does not become all-consuming, or all-constituting. Complainants should not have to become their injuries in order to have them validated.

A process for redress designed to recognize, validate, and restore can help break the victim script and the wounded attachments it often creates. For example, Goodmark has argued that restorative justice can "foster agency rather than demanding a disempowered stereotype of victimization."[68] According to Goodmark, "People who have been harmed choose to participate in the proceedings and play an active role in the process, deciding what their goals are for the process and how those goals should be actualised. Victim-survivors who opt into RJ can choose who will be there to support them, share and guard information as they see fit and request the reparations that will best meet their justice goals."[69] Goodmark claims that restorative justice resists the gender essentialism inherent in the current legal system "by 'insist[ing] that survivors and responsible parties be viewed as something other than predetermined caricatures of victim and offender,' categories that 'rel[y] upon polarized gender roles of maleness and femaleness.'"[70] A more reparative process for redressing sexual harm can disrupt the victim script, while paying heed to limitations on both sides of the victim/agency divide.

FEMINIST FLASHPOINTS REDUX

The feminist conflicts of #MeToo and the sex wars will not be resolved in the abstract. Indeed, their abstract nature likely contributes to the binary antagonisms, the caricatures, and the affective outrage. If we return to some of the feminist flashpoints of the Sex Wars 2.0 and #MeToo, we can focus on the precise nature of the disagreements and read them with a reparative sensibility. In chapter 4, I suggested ways of applying this approach to both the Avital Ronell and the Al Franken controversies. Here, I revisit one of the contestations, the Battle of Cambridge[71] and the ensuing Title IX fracases that specifically invoked the question of appropriate regulation of sexual harm at Harvard and did so as a classic sex-wars performance. I revisit the controversy, and its follow-up in the new Title IX regulations, to explore how we might think through these conflicts more reparatively.

Never about criminal law, the Battle of Cambridge, and broader debates around Title IX, are useful in thinking about decentering the criminal justice system. Title IX is an administrative process, albeit one implicated in carceral logics. The law professors who opposed Harvard's sexual harassment policy did not oppose all sexual harassment policies. Their critique was quite specific, in both substance and procedure. Substantively, they opposed the definition of sexual harassment that went beyond what was required by Title IX. The professors also objected to the expansion of prohibited conduct regarding the sexual behavior of students who were impaired or incapacitated, in ways they claimed were one-sided. Procedurally, they objected to the policies' failure to provide an opportunity to discover the facts, to examine witnesses, and to mount a defense, as well as to specific provisions of the policies and procedures they considered overly broad and unfair. Finally, they opposed the combination of investigation, prosecution, fact-finding, and appellate-review functions in one office, as well as the failure to provide adequate representation for the accused. Following the high-profile letter, Martha Minow, the dean of Harvard Law School at the time, established a faculty committee with law professor John Coates "to develop 'local' procedures for Harvard's Title IX policy."[72] After meeting with law students, faculty members, and university administrators, including university Title IX officer Mia Karvonides, the committee drafted a new set of procedures for Title IX complaints at the law school. The new policy, approved by the faculty in December 2014, primarily addressed the procedural critiques raised in the letter, separating the investigative and adjudicative functions, allowing students accused of sexual misconduct to retain a lawyer at the law school's expense, providing the same right of appeal to the accused as to the complainant, and allowing the parties the opportunity to face each other in a hearing.[73] However, the substance of the procedures, in particular the contested preponderance-of-evidence standard and the unwelcomeness standard, remained in place. The original critics, including Janet Halley and Jeannie Suk Gersen, both commented that the revised policies were much improved.[74]

Cory Cole described the revised policy as a hybrid representing "a masterful compromise" between the model proposed by OCR's 2011 Dear Colleague Letter and the procedural protections demanded by the law professors. It is an interesting observation, insofar as the new policy represents a middle ground between the original policy and the critics—more procedural protections within the same substantive provisions. It is a compromise, not a break with the prevailing models of civil justice, remaining predicated on an adversarial and punitive paradigm. Harvard Law School operated within a confined legal environment, obligated to comply with OCR requirements. It could only search for a middle ground, not construct something new. These very real limitations left the new policy plagued by the problems of a carceral model, based in adjudication and punishment. Its relatively broad standards—of preponderance of evidence and unwelcomeness—needed to be balanced with due process protections, precisely because the standard is broad and the remedial consequences potentially severe.

But the original critics did not rest on their laurels. In 2017 Elizabeth Bartholet, Nancy Gertner, Janet Halley, and Jeannie Suk Gersen (the Harvard Four)—submitted a brief to the US Department of Education that advocated for reform to the policies on sexual violence on campus.[75] In May 2020, the Department of Education released new Title IX policies and procedures. Unlike the guidelines issued by the Obama administration, these are regulations with the force of law. The new regulations addressed many of the concerns raised by the Harvard Four. Definitions were refined,[76] due process rights were buttressed, investigation was separated from adjudication. Not unlike the Harvard Law School model, the new regulations operate to rebalance the rights of the complainant and the accused, in what remains a largely adversarial model, grounded in a carceral logic of punishment. However, the new regulations included the possibility of using nonadversarial dispute

REGULATING REPARATIVELY > 187

mechanisms, giving colleges and universities discretion "to offer and facilitate informal resolution options, such as mediation or restorative justice, so long as both parties give voluntary, informed, written consent to attempt informal resolution." The regulations provide that schools may not require parties to participate in such a process and may not offer an informal resolution process unless a formal complaint is filed.[77]

Criticism was swift; not surprisingly, many were skeptical of an anti-sexual violence initiative coming from the Trump administration. Colleges were given a deadline of August 14, 2020, to implement the new guidelines in the midst of a pandemic. The American Council on Education, made up of seventeen hundred college and university leaders, stated that the Department of Education "is not living in the real world. . . . As a result of the pandemic, virtually every college and university in the country is closed. Choosing this moment to impose the most complex and challenging regulations the agency has ever issued reflects appallingly poor judgment."[78] And the campus-sex-war foes responded predictably. Campus anti-rape activists condemned the new regulations. Sage Carson, manager of Know Your IX, stated, "Today, Betsy DeVos and the Trump administration have shown, once again, that they have no interest in supporting student survivors and their rights. . . . The final rule makes it harder for survivors to report sexual violence, reduces schools' liability for ignoring or covering up sexual harassment, and creates a biased reporting process that favors respondents and schools over survivors' access to education."[79] Janet Halley, on the other hand, welcomed the regulations: "The new system is vastly better and fairer. . . . The fact that we're getting good things from the Trump administration is confusing, but isn't it better than an unbroken avalanche of bad things?"[80] There is nothing new in this latest volley. One side wants narrower definitions and more due process for respondents. The other wants broader definitions and more protections for complainants.

It is a kind of sex wars of infinite regress, with no end in sight. A week after the new rules were passed, Know Your IX, the American

Civil Liberties Union, and other advocacy groups filed a suit seeking to overturn them.[81] Shortly thereafter, eighteen attorneys general filed a similar suit.[82] We are a far cry from the final word on Title IX. President Biden's campaign criticized the DeVos regulations and vowed to restore the 2011 guidelines.[83] While the precise action to be taken by the Biden administration remains to be seen,[84] the change on the horizon presents an opportunity. How might a more reparative sensibility allow us to approach the regulation of campus sexual violence and avoid déjà-vu all over again? Victims of sexual violence want recognition of the harms done to them. Critics want to ensure that those accused are not treated unfairly in the absence of due process protections, recognizing that it is the most vulnerable who will bear the burden. These are reasonable positions that need to be read together. But, the revised regulations are not a reading beside; they are a compromise. Much like the Harvard Law School's, they remain predicated on an adversarial and punitive paradigm. Those involved in designing the new regulations speak of achieving a better balance between the rights of the complainants and those of the respondents. Critics argue that the new rules are now off-balance. But, the very rhetoric of balance is one of fine tuning, of compromise within an existing system, not a fundamental rethinking.

The kernel of reparative possibility in the revised regulations is the discretion to offer informal resolution options—a nod to restorative justice. Whether there is uptake of these informal resolution options by the institutions themselves in designing the processes and by the complainants and respondents who must consent to the process remains to be seen. Of course, when restorative justice merely supplements the criminal justice system—or the carceral logics of civil processes—informal resolution options will be subject to the limitations of the regulations themselves and existing definitions of sexual violence. But, it is a small crack, a pressure point, that offers the possibility of broader change. Ideally, regulating reparatively would call for a more complete break with the existing system, but pushing on these informal processes is an incremental step towards promoting recognition and accountability.[85]

The promise of the campus model lies precisely in the fact that it is not criminal. While rooted in the carceral logic of retribution and punishment, these processes offer a window into an alternative register. Contestations over Title IX regulations will continue. In the meantime, the possibilities of these alternative processes should be engaged.

Reparative approaches would break most successfully with existing processes if they included a rethinking of definitions, standards, and remedies for sexual harm. Stepping back from the specificities of the ongoing battle over Title IX, we need to address difficult questions of what constitutes harm and when it should be actionable, and revisit the multiple legal standards in play, from unwelcomeness to consent. A reparative approach would begin by recognizing the legitimacy and partiality of each of the multiple feminist positions. Women negotiate sexual relationships in conditions of inequality, of partial or obstructed agency. Law constitutes the harm it regulates in ways that are deeply gendered, contradictory, and undermining of the recognition of sexual harm. While these questions are unlikely to be queried in any substantive way in the struggle to rebalance Title IX, they need to be engaged in specific regulatory contexts to design more complex responses to sexual harm.

Debates around the legal definition of consent are thorny, technical, multifaceted, and increasingly entrenched. "Affirmative consent," for example, is a loaded concept, deeply grounded in the sex wars. One side sees it as the answer, the other as a road to sexually repressive hell paved with feminist intentions. There is little consensus on what it even means. Sometimes, affirmative consent is conflated with "enthusiastic consent," by both sides. At other times, it is a more specific legal standard. Perhaps the terminology is too rhetorically encumbered to reparatively recuperate. But still we should explore the actual legal standard of affirmative consent, the ways it has been operationalized and used in other jurisdictions for decades.[86] An evaluation of the criminal law of sexual assault would suggest that it is neither the panacea nor the apocalypse that each side imagines. Contra the hopes of anti-rape feminists, charges, prosecutions, and convictions are elusive in many jurisdictions with affirmative consent standards. And contra the claims of the critics, the standard has not produced a sexual landscape where individuals enter into contracts before a sexual encounter. It does not include sex that is "merely" unwanted and unwelcome; it does not require enthusiasm or desire. Yet, the affirmative consent standard is embedded in a criminal justice system where rape scripts have changed little, where complainants' credibility is challenged, and where the carceral consequences of conviction make the rights of the accused crucially important. Examining the ways affirmative consent has been interpreted might help turn down the volume of the debate, allowing the possibilities and limitations of alternative conceptualizations of consent to be considered with more nuance. I do not endorse a particular conception of affirmative consent, for criminal or civil purposes, but suggest we delve deeper into a reconceptualization of legal standards with a little less binary thinking and antagonistic affect. Reading beside might allow us to see not only when both sides are partially right but when they are partially wrong.

Precisely because it is not a criminal process, Title IX and ongoing legal battles over policies and procedures provide a productive space for the kind of rethinking that, if done correctly, could serve as a kind of prototype for noncriminal approaches to sexual violence. However, there is a risk in placing too many reparative eggs in the Title IX basket. The burden is on universities and colleges, alongside the Department of Education, which may neither be well positioned nor have the institutional capacity to design alternative dispute-resolution mechanisms. Title IX may also already be constrained by path dependencies, meaning present and future decisions are limited by those made in the past, even though the circumstances may no longer apply. In the context of developing public policy, once a direction has been chosen, it is hard to change it. As Margaret Levi described, "Once a country or region has started down a track, the costs of reversal are very high. There will be other choice points, but the entrenchment of certain institutional arrangements obstruct[s] an easy reversal of the initial choice."[87] Tinkering with the balance between victim support and offender due process within Title IX legal battles reflects precisely such path dependency, where larger rethinking becomes increasingly impossible to imagine. Indeed, the sex wars, then and now, have come to embody path-dependent feminisms, where choices made and positions staked out make it difficult to change course.

Reparative regulation and the kind of rethinking it demands is a direct challenge to path dependencies and entrenched visions of no alternatives. The route to achieving it should look for inspiration to disrupting concepts like queer futurity. José Esteban Muñoz sees "queerness [as] an aspiration toward the future. To be queer is to imagine better possibilities."[88] Regulating reparatively is about seeing things differently and maintaining the capacity to be surprised. In this regard, the Sedgwick quotation from chapter 4 bears repeating. "To read from a reparative position is to surrender the knowing, anxious, paranoid determination that no horror, however apparently unthinkable, shall ever come to the reader *as new*; to a reparatively positioned reader, it can seem realistic and necessary to experience surprise. Because there can be terrible surprises, however, there can also be good ones."[89] Feminist approaches to Title IX, like the feminist debates around the sex wars more generally, have recoiled from surprise. Both sides more closely approximate the "knowing, anxious, paranoid" reader, for whom new paths forward are hidden by the rigid belief that we already know all there is to know. Regulating reparatively, reading the sides beside each other, requires abandoning that certitude and opening ourselves to the possibility of surprise—which may be one of the clearest routes to imagining new possibilities.

CONCLUSION

My discussion of reading and regulating reparatively has touched on a range of controversies and could be brought to bear on many more. From Brock Turner to Aziz Ansari, revisiting the flashpoints through its lens could produce increasingly nuanced understandings of disputes that can contain conflicting positions simultaneously. Beyond sexual violence, the sensibility of regulating reparatively has the potential to address a broad range of issues that have long plagued the oppositional discourse of the sex wars. From sex work to sexting, it could recognize the harms of sexual practices, without resorting to their criminalization.

Sex work is a site of both over- and underregulation and strong opinion. Those who advocate for decriminalizing sex work, and focus on the harms of criminal regulation, often leave sex work unregulated altogether in the aftermath. In an abolitionist criminal model that seeks to eliminate sex work completely,[90] sexual and other harms are left largely inactionable. While I will not go into a detailed analysis of the debates, they are clearly another instantiation of the sex wars, then and now, and could equally have been the focus of analysis in chapter 2. Indeed, feminist scholars cast contemporary debate around sex work as part of the "latter day feminist sex wars."[91] Alison Phipps reveals the extent to which "contemporary feminist opposition to the sex industry is shaped by a 'sex war' paradigm which relies on a binary opposition between radical feminists and 'sex positive' perspectives."[92] Sex workers, she argues, are seen as "either helpless victims or privileged promoters of the industry, which leaves little room for discussion of their diverse experiences or labour rights."[93]

A reparative approach could help in rethinking the regulation of sex work without resort to the criminal justice system. Feminists opposed to sex work use the asymmetrical criminalization of the Nordic model that, while only targeting clients and "traffickers," remains rooted in a carceral approach. The debate continues to play out; one side emphasizes the harms of sex work while the other focuses on the harms of regulating it. Holding both of these in view, we could seek to redress the risks of sex work while not exacerbating them through criminal regulation. The point of incommensurability not readily resolvable is whether the exchange of sex for money is inherently exploitative. But, a reparative reading could affirm that in specific circumstances, there is exploitative potential in the exchange, and moreover, that sex workers face many potential abuses. A reparative approach would again need to reject the reductive logic of victim versus agent, recognizing that sex workers exercise varying degrees of agency in circumstances that are potentially harmful.

Regulating sex work could address potential harms without criminalization. The regulatory alternative need not be an absence of law but simply a different modality more narrowly tailored to the nature of the harms, from police violence to occupational health and safety. There are a myriad of models for noncriminal regulation of sex work around the world, some more harmful than others. From public health models to restrictive zoning laws, many are based on surveillance, discipline, and control, often with an underlying carceral logic. A reparative approach would critically examine the potential harms of regulation, keeping them in view alongside the harms that sex workers encounter.

A reparative approach could similarly be brought to bear on the feminist debates surrounding sexting, "revenge porn," and the nonconsensual distribution of sexually intimate images. Although not as high-profile as the feminist flashpoints, it is another site of feminists lined up for and against criminalization of images and text. Some argue for criminal law to take on-line harassment and the nonconsensual distribution of sexual images more seriously. Others express concern that such regulation produces young women in particular as victims, devoid of agency, in need of the law's protection.[94] It is another area where a reparative reading could help disarticulate regulation from the criminal justice system and focus on the specific nature of the problem of on-line harassment, rather than risk the criminalization of sexual images more generally. Regulating reparatively keeps in view the potential harms both of nonconsensual sexual practices and of regulation.

My call for the decentering of the criminal law will undoubtedly raise questions of how to deal with serial sexual predators like Weinstein and Epstein, whose behavior seems antithetical to taking responsibility and who, in the absence of more severe consequences, are likely to reoffend. Mariame Kaba, a leading feminist abolitionist, addresses what she calls "the Ted Bundy problem": "I don't understand why we would build a system based on the exceptional when the vast majority of people are not Ted Bundy."[95] Kaba acknowledges that we will need to come up with solutions for people who "cause inordinate repetitive harm to people on a regular basis." But, she argues, it should not be a prison. Tarana Burke has similarly expressed frustration that #MeToo conversations dwell on individuals like Weinstein: "I don't want to keep talking about individuals. . . . You are all going to keep making boogeymen when we should be talking about systems. A person like Harvey Weinstein doesn't just exist in a vacuum."[96] Burke has said repeatedly that the stories of some individuals have been centered in the #MeToo narrative, while "the women of color, trans women, queer people—our stories get pushed aside and our pain is never prioritized."[97] Yet, Burke still expressed a sense of vindication when Weinstein was convicted. "Today, a jury confirmed what we all know: Harvey Weinstein committed sexual assault." After the verdict, Burke wrote on the MeToo website, "This wouldn't have been possible without the voices of the silence breakers in and outside of the courtroom, the survivors who courageously testified, and the jurors who, despite an unrelenting and unethical defense strategy, voted to find an unremorseful Harvey Weinstein guilty."[98]

Thinking alongside Burke is a deeply reparative exercise. She consistently keeps the tensions in view. In the context of high-profile criminal prosecutions that reinforce a problematic system, sideline the quotidian experiences of marginalized women, fail to focus on structural sexism and racism, and give short shrift to the challenge of healing, she never fails to ask what is included and what is left out—what is achieved and what is not. If we start and end with Weinstein, we miss much of what needs to be brought into view using a reparative approach. We need to start and end instead with Tarana Burke and the many others, some of whom have been canvassed in this chapter, who already advocate for alternative paradigms for thinking through sexual violence.

Finally, the focus on Weinstein, and indeed, my focus throughout this chapter on the possibilities of regulating reparatively risk obscuring an important feature of #MeToo—that it was very much about the limits of law. We need to keep in view how to move beyond legal definitions and avoid reinforcing law's exclusive jurisdiction over discussions of sexual harm. #MeToo challenged the idea that the law alone has the authority to decide if and when sexual harm exists. As Jessica Valenti argued, "#MeToo is not about what's legal, it's about what's right."[99] And Emma Gray flagged the need "to renegotiate the sexual narratives we've long accepted. And that involves having complicated conversations about sex that is violating but not criminal."[100] Regulating reparatively must recognize that law may not be the solution; not every harm calls for a legal remedy. Rather, some call for changing the narratives of sexual norms, behaviors, expectations, and ethicality. We need to return to the flashpoints of the sex wars and #MeToo, while anticipating those to come, with an ear to the nuanced voices, claims, experiences, and arguments too often overpowered by reductive narratives of generational conflict and feminist catfights. We might well be surprised if we do.

CONCLUSION

Beyond War, beside Anger

> It is long past time to move away from war metaphors, and more
> importantly, the kind of excessive polarization and "calling out"
> that seems to characterize too much feminist debate, particularly
> debate that takes place on the intimate and fraught space of the
> body, of desire, of pleasure, of violation.
> —Suzanna Danuta Walters, 2011

Walters is right. We need to retreat from the language of war. This may
seem an odd observation at the end of a book focused on tracking the
sex wars past and present. However, my consistent purpose has been to
highlight the traps and limitations of these intractably antagonistic feminist disagreements and the extent to which we remain involved, after
decades, in fundamentally similar disputes about sexuality, agency, and
law. I want to break away from the recursivity of this debate. As Walters
observes, "The language of war creates enemies rather than interlocutors."[1] We need more interlocutors. Feminist contestation is unlikely to
magically disappear, nor would that be good if it did, since contestation
reveals complex insights about the world we live in and the one that we
seek to bring about. To equate disagreement with harassment, betrayal,
and/or collaboration with misogyny is to lose an opportunity to put it to
productive use as a way to rethink controversies and alternative modalities of regulation. The reparative reading I advocate can begin to mend
the ongoing harm of the sex wars themselves, by finding new ways to
approach disagreement.

The escalation of feminist contestations to war rhetoric was in part the product of affect—of anger, shock, betrayal—by feminists on both sides of the sex wars. Disagreement, syphoned through these emotions, produced polarization. Feminists have always been understandably angry, but that anger easily turned inward and toward each other. Repair might begin by confronting the role of affect, and anger in particular, in this history of disagreement. In fact it could be said that anger is having a moment. Pankaj Mishra has called ours "the age of anger," characterized by deep resentment, manifested in the resurgence of reactionary nationalisms, racisms, and misogynies.[2] Feminism, too, seems to be sharing in this moment. Jilly Boyce Kay and Sarah Banet-Weiser argue that "we are witnessing an extraordinary new visibility of women's anger—we might even say feminist anger—in public discourse and popular culture."[3] There has been an explosion of writing. From Rebecca Traister's *Good and Mad* (2018) to Brittney Cooper's *Eloquent Rage: A Black Feminist Discovers Her Superpower* (2018) to Surraya Chemaly's *Rage Becomes Her* (2018), feminist authors are embracing women's anger and highlighting the deep racial and gender disparities of the moment that produced it.[4] Bitch Media published "The Future Is Furious," a series that zeroes in on women's anger.[5] As the story goes, women have long been denied anger: "Most of the time, female anger is discouraged, repressed, ignored, swallowed."[6] But women are now finding their anger and expressing it, as anger.

This is in fact not new. Black feminism has long understood anger as personally and politically useful in the struggle against racism. Audre Lorde famously wrote of the "Uses of Anger," "Every woman has a well-stocked arsenal of anger potentially useful against those oppressions, personal and institutional, which brought that anger into being."[7] Lorde spoke of anger as "loaded with information and energy," from which women must not recoil: "We cannot allow our fear of anger to deflect us nor seduce us into settling for anything else than the hard work of excavating honesty."[8] Amid the days of raging sex wars, Audre Lorde called for developing tools to face anger constructively. Brittany Cooper builds on this legacy of Black women's anger, exploring the legitimacy of their rage alongside caricatures that have long been politicized against them.

While anger may be gaining political traction, it is an affect that has accompanied feminism through its many instantiations and contestations. It is an affect, I would argue, that leaps off the pages of the stories told in this book. The sex wars are imbued with anger: anger at the injustices of sexual harms, and equally anger at other feminists for not seeing those injustices in the same ways—an all-too-easy misdirection. It is a challenging affect, riddled with destructive, explosive, violent potential. How might we think through the affective, the felt experience, and put anger to more productive uses? Putting anger aside is not the goal. Women have been asked to do that for too long.[9] As Traister argues in *Good and Mad*, quoting Sara Robinson, "'Women's rage has been sublimated for so long that there's simply no frame for what happens when it finally comes to the surface.'"[10] The sex wars, I would suggest, are partially a result of the absence of this frame—of a sense of what to do with anger, of its uses and abuses. It is part of the failure of feminists, as Lorde remarked long ago, to develop the tools we need to face anger constructively in the face of disagreement.[11] A reparative sensibility might help negotiate the terrain of disagreement, avoiding the inevitable fall from criticism to outrage to anger.

Judith Butler has explored the question of rage in her work on the force of nonviolence. Rage, Butler suggests, is entirely reasonable given the current state of our world: "We have every reason to be absolutely enraged by the systemic and local injustices in our world. Not a day goes by under the present regime when I'm not seized with rage of one kind or another."[12] But, for Butler, the question is, So what? "What can be done with rage? We don't always think about that, because we view rage as an uncontrollable impulse that needs to come out in unmediated forms. But people craft rage, they cultivate rage, and not just as individuals. Communities craft their rage."

Butler's query about how to craft our rage in ways that do not perpetuate patterns and structures of violence, alongside Lorde's advice to face anger constructively, can aid in a reparative reading of both women's anger about sexual violence and the anger that underlies our disagreements about it. While a catalyst, anger can also be destructive to the self and others. It can lead to eruptions of mass protest for change but equally it can lead us "to imagine scenes of destruction, and to even be overwhelmed with murderous feelings or impulse." Anger often produces a desire for revenge, a getting even. How might we think of crafting this anger in ways that are more productive, or at a minimum, less violent? To be angry, to affirm anger, is not to predetermine the actions that follow that anger.

The objects of anger range from those who commit sexual violence to those who condone it. In the context of the sex wars, the charge of condoning sexual violence is not restricted to state or corporate actors but is extended to other feminists. Disagreement about what is and is not sexual violence gets read as not taking it seriously and in its more extreme instantiations, as collaboration. Feminist dissent equals joining forces with the pornographers (Sex Wars 1.0) or with the sex offenders (Sex Wars 2.0). Anger at the individuals and institutions that have failed to take sexual violence seriously becomes inseparable from anger at feminist dissenters—not a productive way to craft it. We need instead to find ways to negotiate disagreement without burning down the house. Walters, in arguing that we withdraw the call to arms, recognizes the challenge anger presents: "We live in a political time already so toxic . . . and one in which self-righteous anger is made even more instantaneous with the advent of the Twitterati and blogger brigadistas."[13] Walters suggests that debates over how best to approach sexual violence could benefit from a little more "shared goodwill and intentions," recognizing that feminists who may profoundly disagree on strategies share "deep and abiding commitments to enabling women and girls to live lives free from violence and coercion." We might begin by approaching feminist disagreement with more generosity of spirit, recognizing that neither "side" of the sex wars is in favor of sexual violence. We can learn, Walters says, from the passion of the earlier debates in imagining a different feminist future, "by abjur[ing] the throwing down of gauntlets and the drawing of lines in the sand. Like sex itself, feminism is messy. And perhaps one lesson of those debates is that we would do well to revel in that messiness rather than to divide ourselves into neat and tidy categories of pro-sex and anti-sex feminists."

#MeToo/fourth-wave/anti-violence feminists of the Sex Wars 2.0 are not anti-sex; nor are the #MeToo detractors/sex-positive feminists pro-violence. Simplistic caricatures are cheap, easy, and unproductive. How much "closer" could the sides get if we abandoned the polemic and affect of outrage? Disagreement need not be synonymous with a callous disregard for the position of the other. What insights might we be afforded if we invested in understanding seemingly incompatible visions and avoided wasting time on accusations of betrayal or high feminist treason? What if, upon encountering a sharp difference of opinion, we said, "Maybe she has a point"? What if we deconstructed the argument, recognizing both the potential validity and the affect behind it?

Anger necessarily abounds. Beyond the interlocutors of the sex wars who spend years steeped in injustice are the victims themselves (and of course these are rarely two separate groupings), who are often asked, if not forced, to relinquish or hide their anger. In thinking through alternative reparative modes of regulation that emphasize restoration, restitution, and/or repair, we need to make space for it. Leigh Good-mark notes that

> victim advocate Mary Achilles asks, "Can we make room for victims in a restorative process when they are screaming out in pain or when they are vengeful, angry and full of rage? Can we make room for victims when they are not interested in what happens to the offender or, if they are interested in what happens, their interest does not fit with what some of us would refer to as a restorative response?" The criminal legal system is often

hostile to women's anger and pain. Anger is inconsistent with stereotypes of people subjected to abuse; judges and jurors use that anger to cast doubt on the credibility of women's accounts of violence. A restorative response should not make the same mistake.[14]

In crafting our anger, we might try to disarticulate it from its "logical" connection to vengeance and retribution and allow it to feed demands for accountability and responsibility. Anger could lead to calls for recognition, apology, and modes of repair beyond the retributive. When denied or repressed—as it so often is—the affect will recursively reappear in ways that do not help the victim and reinforce structures of violence. Restorative processes must be designed to center the victim's story, the harm they have suffered, and their emotional reactions. The more acutely attuned to emotion and affect, the more likely dispute resolution, and law more generally, will be to produce better, sustainable outcomes.

What has become clear to me in the process of writing this book is the need for the law and feminist debates equally to engage with affect, the affective nature of law and the possibilities of affective justice. The stories of the sex wars and the #MeToo controversies are deeply animated by affect. Anger, accompanied by frustration, regret, and disgust, lies on top of grief, sadness, fear, despair, and anxiety. Understanding feminist contestations and the potential of reparative regulation requires deeper attention to how structures of dominance *feel*—how sexual harm in the context of pervasive sexual and racist inequality feels, even how disagreement feels and how it gets easily tangled with negative affect. Bringing emotion to the discussion does not mean the wholesale relinquishing of analysis to experience and subjectivity; as American gender historian Joan Scott has argued about experience more generally, and Sara Ahmed about emotions, "Our emotional repertoires are also discursively and structurally shaped."[1]

However, interrogating and understanding our affective responses—to harm, to trauma, to disagreement—is crucial to breaking the recurrence of the sex wars.

Nor are the feelings entirely bad. While the sex wars appear to be overly imbued with the negative, a streak of hope, a belief that things could be better, supports and drives the work. Hope itself seems to be having its own feminist moment, as a kind of antidote to anger and despair. Author and activist Brittany Cooper's tribute to the eloquence of Black women's rage is equally a call for hope. Kay and Banet-Weiser speak of the possibility of feminist *respair*: "respair means fresh hope; a recovery from despair."[16] They argue for an embrace of anger and despair as a necessary part of feminist politics, but also for the "inextricability of hope and despair." Sedgwick spoke of reading with hope: "Hope, often a fracturing, even traumatic thing to experience, is among the energies by which the reparatively-positioned reader tries to organize the fragments and part-objects she encounters." Others, like Robin Wiegman, who has taken up the mantle of reparative reading, suggest that it would replace attachments produced by "correction, rejection and anger with those crafted by affection, gratitude, solidarity and love."[17] For Heather Love, the reparative "prefers acts of noticing, being affected, taking joy and making whole."[18]

Tarana Burke also speaks to the power of joy. Burke affirms anger but does not give it the last word: "I don't think there's anything wrong with the rage because it's a righteous rage. This is not people just angry to be angry. These are people who are hurt. One of the things I want to do at some point soon is to call for a healing."[19] Healing is a deeply hopeful practice, one that imagines transformation, personally and structurally. But, she argues, it is also about cultivating joy: "I want to teach people to not lean into their trauma. You can create the kind of joy in your life that allows you to lean into that instead."[20] According to Tarana Burke, "We must figure out how to curate joy in our own lives. I have to practice and work at it every day. I had previously decided that the trauma was my identity, but that isn't true. Joy can be my identity if I want. Once I realized that this was a necessary part of my healing process I wanted to share it with everyone: This thing isn't you. Your trauma isn't you."[21] Burke illuminates the possibility of reading joy and anger beside each other.

There is not a lot of joy in law. Nor is there joy in the seemingly endless feminist battles around sex and sexuality. Just as Burke argues that we need to cultivate joy in our lives, we need to cultivate joy in our reading practices, which may not come naturally to those of us schooled in criticism. We are paranoid, and have every reason to be. But beyond our individual healing from trauma, we must heal the schisms of the sex wars, the scars left by decades of bitter disagreement. Reading reparatively, with affection, gratitude, and solidarity, is a place to begin.

Jennifer Nash, in the context of a different set of feminist wars—the intersectionality wars within Black feminism—makes a plea for reading with love.[22] Nash argues that Black feminism as a political practice has long emphasized "the importance of love as a form of collectivity, a way of feeling, and a practice of ordering the self."[23] For her, that approach "encourages us to ask about our deep responsibilities to each other, and our enduring connections to each other, by virtue of our collective inhabitation of the social world."[24] Nash brings this practice back to law, arguing that it could help reorient law "around an ethics of vulnerability."[25] While speaking specifically to Black feminists, and the intersectionality wars, Nash argues for "a letting go" of a series of defensive positions that would allow, even require, dreaming of different ways of being and feeling.[26] Letting go, reading with love, and approaching law as a potential site for reimagining relationality are strategies from which we can all learn.

The stories of the sex wars and of #MeToo feminist flashpoints have been overwhelmingly white, reflecting political whiteness.[27] Abandoning the rigid sex-wars dynamic requires seeing what is in plain sight including the range of alternative political imaginaries proposed by

Black and other feminists of color. I have highlighted some of this work, which was developed concurrently but remained underrepresented within mainstream feminism. The silos limit our thinking, our imagination. At this moment of reckoning with racism and white supremacy, with the resurgence of #BlackLivesMatter, sexual violence can no longer be primarily examined through the feminist lens of the sex wars and #MeToo, with its lip service to intersectionality. Reading and regulating reparatively demands that #MeToo be read alongside #BlackLivesMatter, that the law's response to sexual harm be read beside mass incarceration. Tarana Burke's MeToo practice was doing this long before either became a hashtag.

A feminism that integrates the harm of sexual violence and the harm of the carceral state is on the rise. Although Black feminists have long been doing so, new books appearing almost daily call feminism (aka white feminism) to account: Judith Levine and Erica Meiners's *Feminist and the Sex Offender* (2020), Aya Gruber's *Feminist War on Crime* (2020), Alison Phipps's *Me Not You: The Trouble with Mainstream Feminism* (2020), Joann Wypijewski's *What We Don't Talk about When We Talk about #MeToo: Essays on Sex, Authority, and the Mess of Life* (2020). It is, thankfully, a sensibility now permeating the feminist zeitgeist and indeed my own project and thinking, without my being entirely aware that this was the company I was keeping.

If truly reimagining the regulation of sexual harm means unsticking ourselves from the sex-wars binary, and I believe it does, it requires new skills, new forms of knowledge, new reading practices, strategies previously unheeded, and a truckload of giving the benefit of the doubt to feminists who see things differently—assuming that *Maybe she has a point* stance and keeping that point in view. Enough with the same fights and affective antagonisms. #MeToo may have created new space to speak about sexual violence, but its legacy remains in our hands. We can reperform the sex wars, and keep getting mad at each other— because that was so much fun—or we can move beyond, learning from the successes and failures of our divisive history. What if, instead of wasting energy taking our anger from zero to sixty and getting to the same place yet again, we thought of how to craft and harness our rage for productive, game-changing ends? Then what if we threw some empathy and joy into the mix? We have much of what we need to work with, as we rethink what law can and cannot do. We can hold the insights of the sex wars, then and now, beside each other, as we reimagine the kind of reparative and affective justice that law could deliver.

ACKNOWLEDGMENTS

The New Sex Wars has been a long time coming. Ever since my interventions in the sex wars of the 1990s, I have been reflecting on the uncomfortable aspects of this legacy. While I remain steadfast in my criticism of anti-pornography law and activism in Canada and beyond, from time to time I have tried to complicate the theoretical underpinnings of my earlier work. Indeed, most of my scholarship on the legal regulation of sexuality has sought to challenge simple either/or dichotomies, and create instead a space for more ambivalence and nuance. Yet, my scholarly and activist work in the sex wars was just a little too definitive, a little too binary, and frankly a little too mean. The opportunity to rethink my approach arose when Ummni Khan invited me to speak at her wonderful conference Feminist Sex Wars: Sexual Representation as Threat and Empowerment at Carleton University in February 2017, where two things happened. First, I coined the term "sex wars 2.0" to capture the connections I started to see between the feminist debates of the past and the ones that were raging at the time. Second, in sharing the stage with a former interlocutor, Professor Karen Busby, I recognized how unnecessarily combative our history had been, notwithstanding Karen's repeated gracious attempts to save our engagements from deteriorating into another feminist catfight. The conference allowed me to thank her for her generosity of spirit. It also set me on a course of rethinking the sex wars, then and now. In October of the same year, #MeToo erupted. Admittedly, when you are a hammer, everything looks like a nail, but in the emerging feminist debates, I saw sex wars everywhere. *The New Sex Wars* was born.

I am indebted to my colleagues, near and far, who took the time to read parts of the manuscript and provide valuable feedback. Thank you to Joseph Fischel, David Rayside, Ratna Kapur, Michael Trebilcock, Daniel Del Gobbo, and Joshua Sealy-Harrington. A very special thanks to Ummni Khan both for getting me started and for her ongoing engagement with my work.

I was fortunate to present parts of my research at various conferences, including the Conference on Gender and Sexuality at the British Institute for International and Comparative Law; the American Law and Society Annual Conference in Washington, DC; the Law, Culture, and the Humanities Conference in Washington, DC; the joint Canadian/American Law and Society Conference in Ottawa; the Queer Legal Studies Symposium at Yale University; and the American Studies Association Conference. I benefited greatly from conversations with colleagues through presentations of my work at Osgoode Hall Law School, the Faculty of Law Seminar Series at the University of Toronto, and the Department of Law and Legal Studies at Carleton University. I was honored to present the work at the Patricia Allan Memorial Lecture at the Faculty of Law, McGill University. Audience feedback and informal chats in hallways have contributed to my thinking every step of the way. Writing can be isolating, but each of these forums provided the intellectual sustenance to keep me going.

Then came the pandemic. Classes, talks, conferences, and accidental exchanges of ideas evaporated overnight. It took a while to collectively find our way to what we could actually do on-line, admittedly without the alchemy of shared coffees and late-night drinks. Kudos to Penny Andrews, who as president of the Law and Society Association, pushed forward with our plenary session at the annual conference. Zoom will never replace being together, but Penny and my amazing copanelists seamlessly displayed that rigorous scholarly engagement was still possible.

For intellectual sustenance through the lockdown, I am especially grateful to my coterie of graduate students, current and former, who gathered virtually every week across a multitude of time zones, to share our work. Ido Katri, Megan Ross, Daniel Del Gobbo, Luke Taylor, Noy Namaan, Mercedes Cavallo, and Joshua Sealy-Harrington—I thank each of them for their engagement with my book.

I owe much to Clara Platter at NYU Press for believing in the project and supporting me throughout the process.

Thank you to Charlotte Bunch for her wonderful research assistance and infectious enthusiasm, all the more appreciated through pandemic times. The manuscript also benefited from the amazing editing of Aviva Rubin, who delved deep and made the ideas pop.

This book draws on research supported by the Social Sciences and Humanities Research Council. I am grateful for their support.

An earlier version of the concepts developed in this book appeared in "#MeToo, Sex Wars 2.0, and the Power of Law," *Asian Yearbook of Human Rights and Humanitarian Law* 3 (2019)

The last word goes to my daughters, Bao and Leah, who inspire everything in me. This book is for them.

NOTES

INTRODUCTION

1 Ali, "Dear Colleague Letter."

2 According to Tarana Burke's MeToo website, "The 'me too' movement was founded in 2006 to help survivors of sexual violence, particularly Black women and girls, and other young women of color from low wealth communities, find pathways to healing. Our vision from the beginning was to address both the dearth in resources for survivors of sexual violence and to build a community of advocates, driven by survivors, who will be at the forefront of creating solutions to interrupt sexual violence in their communities." "About: History and Vision," Me Too Movement, updated February 24, 2020, https://metoomvmt.org/; Sandra E. Garcia, "The Woman Who Created #MeToo Long before the Hashtag," *New York Times*, October 20, 2017, www.nytimes.com.

3 Bazelon, "The Return of the Sex Wars."

4 Abrams, "Sex Wars Redux"; Duggan and Hunter, *Sex Wars*; Lynn Comella, "Revisiting the Feminist Sex Wars"; Kipnis, *Bound and Gagged*; Ferguson, "Sex War."

5 Brownmiller, *Against Our Will*; Dworkin, *Pornography*; Dworkin and MacKinnon, *Pornography and Civil Rights*.

6 Rubin, "Thinking Sex"; Vance, *Danger and Pleasure*; Willis, "Feminism, Morality, and Pornography."

7 Rubin, *Deviations*.

8 Gessen, "When Does a Watershed Become a Sex Panic?"

9 See for example Bernstein, "Militarized Humanitarianism Meets Carceral Feminism."

10 Cossman et al., *Bad Attitudes on Trial*.

11 See the following articles from the special issue of *Signs* on the Sex Wars: Waters, "Introduction: The Dangers of a Metaphor"; Echols, "Retrospective"; Rubin, "Blood under the Bridge"; Phipps, "Sex Wars Revisited."

12 Sedgwick, "Paranoid Reading and Reparative Reading."

13 Sedgwick, "Paranoid Reading and Reparative Reading," 146.

14 Tweeden, "Senator Franken Kissed and Groped Me without My Consent."

15 Weiss, "Are others disturbed by the moral flattening going on?"

16 Way, "I Went on a Date with Aziz Ansari."

17 Dean, "Op-Ed: Who are You Calling a 'Second-Wave' Feminist?"

18 Gersen and Suk, "The Sex Bureaucracy."

19   Kipnis, *Unwanted Advances*; Halley, "Trading the Megaphone for the Gavel in Title IX Enforcement"; Suk Gersen, "Laura Kipnis's Endless Trial by Title IX"; Suk Gersen, "Betsy DeVos, Title IX, and the 'Both Sides' Approach to Sexual Assault."

20   Halley, "The Move to Affirmative Consent."

21   MacKinnon, "Feminism, Marxism, Method, and the State." MacKinnon wrote, "If sex is normally something men do to women, the issue is less whether there was force and more whether consent is a meaningful standard." See also MacKinnon, *Toward a Feminist Theory of the State*; more recently, MacKinnon, "Rape Redefined." MacKinnon maintains the position that "one does not meaningfully consent to the imposition of conditions of inequality." See also MacKinnon, *Butterfly Politics*. MacKinnon challenged the liberal legal definition of consent, in the context of systemic inequality against women. MacKinnon is often misattributed to have said that all heterosexual sex is rape. As Joseph Fischel notes, "Given the ubiquity of the misattribution, it bears repeating over and over and over that Catharine MacKinnon never said or wrote that all heterosexual sex is rape." See Fischel, *Screw Consent*, 13.

22   Nwanevu, "There Is No Rampaging #MeToo Mob."

23   Greenberg, "What Happens to #MeToo When a Feminist Is Accused?"

24   Mayer, "The Case of Al Franken."

25   Banet-Weiser, "Popular Feminism."

26   Banet-Weiser, "Popular Feminism."

27   Banet-Weiser, "Popular Feminism."

28   Phipps, "'Every Woman Knows a Weinstein'"; Phipps, *Me, Not You*; See also Phipps, "The Political Whiteness of #MeToo."

29   Martinez HoSang, *Racial Propositions*, 21.

30   Adetaba, "Tarana Burke Says #MeToo Should Center Marginalized Communities."

31   Phipps, "'Every Woman Knows a Weinstein,'" citing Michelle Rodino-Colocino, "Me Too, #MeToo: Countering Cruelty with Empathy," *Communications and Critical/Cultural Studies* 15, no. 1 (2018): 96–100.

32   Tambe, "Reckoning with the Silences of #MeToo."

33   Duggan and Hunter, *Sex War*.

34   *Lexico*, s.v. "2.0."

35   Waters, "Introduction: The Dangers of a Metaphor."

36   Waters, "Introduction: The Dangers of a Metaphor," 1.

37   Waters, "Introduction: The Dangers of Metaphor," 1.

1. #METOO FEMINIST DEBATES

1   Kantor and Twohey, "Harvey Weinstein Paid Off Sexual Harassment Accusers for Decades." The *New York Times* story was followed quickly by Farrow, "From Aggressive Overtures to Sexual Assault."

2   Barker and Gabler, "Charlie Rose Made Crude Sexual Advances, Multiple Women Say."

3   Gabler et al., "NBC Fires Matt Lauer, the Face of 'Today.'"

4   According to an October 2018 report from the *New York Times*, "Since the publishing of the exposé (followed days later by a *New Yorker* investigation), at least 200 prominent men have lost their jobs after public allegations of sexual assault." Carlsen et al., "#MeToo Brought Down 201 Powerful Men."

5   Bennett, "The 'Click' Movement."

6 The discourse of the witch hunt was first put forward by Woody Allen in the immediate aftermath of Harvey Weinstein's expulsion from the Academy of Motion Pictures. In an interview with the BBC, Allen said it would be important to avoid "a witch hunt atmosphere, a Salem atmosphere. . . . [E]very guy in an office who winks at a woman is suddenly having to call a lawyer to defend himself" (Mumford, "Woody Allen Was Forced to Clarify Comments about 'Sad' Harvey Weinstein"). While conservative critiques echoed the witch-hunt narrative (for example, William Sullivan, "#MeToo: From Salem to Now," *American Thinker*, December 12, 2017, described the #MeToo movement as having "an atmosphere of a looming, if not entirely underway, witch hunt"), the allegation seemed to spur many more articles arguing against the witch-hunt narrative, no doubt in part due to the fact that it was Woody Allen, who himself had been the subject of allegations of sexual abuse for years, who initiated the narrative. Filipovic, "Weinstein 'Witch Hunt'? Wrong, Woody Allen"; Lindy West, "Yes, This Is a Witch Hunt."

7 Tweeden, "Senator Al Franken Kissed and Groped Me without My Consent"; see also Whelan, "A Year of Sexual Unfreedom," where she argues that #MeToo feminism "denigrates the seriousness of rape by lumping together everything from cat calling to serious sexual violence."

8 The due process critique, discussed in greater detail below and in later chapters, was widespread from the inception of #MeToo. See for example Hernroth-Rothstein, "#MeToo and Trial by Mob"; Gessen, "Al Franken's Resignation and the Selective Force of #MeToo," in which she writes, "The force of the #MeToo moment leaves no room for due process"; Sullivan, "It's Time to Resist the Excesses of #MeToo."

9 See Tolentino, "The Rising Pressure of the #MeToo Backlash"; Wright, "The Backlash to Believing Women Has Begun."

10 Way, "I Went on a Date with Aziz Ansari."

11 Carmen and Brittain, "Eight Women Say Charlie Rose Sexually Harassed Them."

12 Setoodeh and Wagmeister, "Matt Lauer Accused of Sexual Harassment by Multiple Women." *Variety* described the gamut of sexual misconduct alleged against Matt Lauer.

13 Ryzik et al., "Louis CK Is Accused by Five Women of Sexual Misconduct."

14 Itzkoff, "Louis C.K. Admits to Sexual Misconduct as Media Companies Cut Ties."

15 Vary, "Kevin Spacey Made a Sexual Advance against Me When I Was 14."

16 Puente, "Kevin Spacey Complete List of 13 Accusers."

17 Rory Carroll, "Ridley Scott on Erasing Kevin Spacey from His New Film: 'He's a Very Good Actor. It's a Pity,'" *Guardian*, January 5, 2018, www.theguardian.com.

18 Gessen, "When Does a Watershed Become a Sex Panic?" Gessen would repeat these lumping concerns as #MeToo developed over the course of the next weeks and months; Gessen, "Al Franken's Resignation and the Selective Force of #MeToo"; Gessen "Sex, Consent, and the Dangers of Misplaced Scale."

19 Tweeden, "Senator Al Franken Kissed and Groped Me without My Consent."

20 Tweeden, "Senator Al Franken Kissed and Groped Me without My Consent."

21 "Read Al Franken's Apology Following Accusation of Groping and Kissing without Consent."

22 Fandos, "Al Franken Issues Apology after Accusation of Forcible Kissing and Groping."

23 Gambino, "Al Franken"; Lee, "Army Veteran Says Franken Groped Her during USO Tour."

24 See for example Dupuy, "I Believe Franken's Accusers Because He Groped Me, Too."

25 Alcindor and Fandos, "A Democratic Chorus Rises in the Senate."

26 Leach, "Bill Maher."
27 Peyser, "#MeToo Has Lumped Trivial in with Legitimate Sexual Assault."
28 Weiss, "Are others disturbed by the moral flattening going on?"
29 Harding, "I am a Feminist."
30 Harding, "I am a Feminist."
31 Teachout, "I'm Not Convinced Franken Should Quit."
32 Yoffe, "Why the #MeToo Movement Should Be Ready for a Backlash."
33 Yoffe, "Why the #MeToo Movement Should Be Ready for a Backlash."
34 Yoffe, "Why the #MeToo Movement Should Be Ready for a Backlash."
35 Merkin, "Publicly, We Say #MeToo, Privately, We Have Misgivings."
36 Merkin, "Publicly, We Say #MeToo, Privately, We Have Misgivings."
37 Merkin, "Publicly, We Say #MeToo, Privately, We Have Misgivings."
38 Safronova, "Catherine Deneuve and Others Denounce the #MeToo Movement." While the letter was cowritten by five French women—Sarah Chiche (writer/psychoanalyst), Catherine Millet (author/art critic), Catherine Robbe-Grillet (actress/writer), Peggy Sastre (author/journalist), and Abnousse Shalmani (writer/journalist), it came to be associated with its most famous signatory, Catherine Deneuve.
39 Safronova, "Catherine Deneuve and Others Denounce the #MeToo Movement."
40 Burrows-Taylor, "'Revolting.'"
41 "Les porcs et leurs allie.e.s. ont raison de s'inquiéter."
42 Osez le Féminisme, "Révoltant," as cited in Burrows-Taylor, "'Revolting.'"
43 Collins, "Why Did Catherine Deneuve and Other Prominent French Women Denounce #MeToo?"; Badham, "Catherine Deneuve, Let Me Explain Why #MeToo Is Nothing like a Witch-Hunt."
44 Argento, "Catherine Deneuve and other French women tell the world how their interiorized misogyny has lobotomized them to the point of no return," as cited in "Catherine Deneuve Clarifies #MeToo Views."
45 See for example Klein, "Rebecca Traister on the Coming #MeToo Backlash"; Wulfhorst, "Could Fear of #MeToo Backlash Silence Women's Voices?"; Wright, "The Backlash to Believing Women Has Begun."
46 Tolentino, "The Rising Pressure of the #MeToo Backlash."
47 Edwards, "The Backlash to #MeToo Is Second Wave Feminism."
48 See Shaffrir, "What to Do with 'Shitty Media Men'?"
49 Donegan "I Started the Shitty Men List."
50 Edwards, "The Backlash to #MeToo Is Second Wave Feminism."
51 Edwards, "The Backlash to #MeToo Is Second Wave Feminism."
52 Edwards, "The Backlash to #MeToo Is Second Wave Feminism."
53 Atwood, "Am I a Bad Feminist?"
54 "Open Counter-Letter about the Steven Galloway Case at UBC."
55 According to Atwood, "My position is that the UBC process is flawed and failed both sides and the rest of my position is that the model of the Salem witch trials is not a good one." Atwood, "Margaret Atwood on the Galloway Affair."
56 Atwood, "Am I a Bad Feminist?"
57 Atwood, "Am I a Bad Feminist?"
58 Atwood, "Am I a Bad Feminist?"
59 Atwood, "Am I a Bad Feminist?"

60 Kassam, "Margaret Atwood Faces Feminist Backlash on Social Media over #MeToo."

61 Jean, "Yes when you prioritize your powerful male friend over sexual assault/harassment victims you are in fact a bad feminist," cited in Grady, "Why *Handmaid's Tale* Author Margaret Atwood Is Facing #MeToo Backlash."

62 Lee Kong, "Yes, Margaret Atwood Is a Bad Feminist."

63 Lee Kong "Yes, Margaret Atwood Is a Bad Feminist.."

64 Thorkelson, "If @MargaretAtwood would like to stop warring amongst women, she should stop declaring war against younger, less powerful women and start listening."

65 Thorkelson, "If @MargaretAtwood would like to stop warring amongst women, she should stop declaring war against younger, less powerful women and start listening."

66 See for example "Is There a Generational Divide in the #MeToo Movement?"; McCartney, "The New Feminist War."

67 Way, "I Went on a Date with Aziz Ansari."

68 Swertlow, "Aziz Ansari Releases Statement after Being Accused of Sexual Misconduct."

69 Flanagan, "The Humiliation of Aziz Ansari."

70 Weiss, "Aziz Ansari Is Guilty—of Not Being a Mind Reader."

71 Flanagan, "The Humiliation of Aziz Ansari."

72 Weiss, "Aziz Ansari Is Guilty—of Not Being a Mind Reader."

73 Weiss, "'Aziz Ansari Is Guilty—of Not Being a Mind Reader." Weiss aligns with Atwood's warnings again in Bennett, "The #MeToo Moment."

74 Flanagan, "The Humiliation of Aziz Ansari."

75 Banfield, *Crime and Justice.*

76 Cited in Kilkenny, "Ashleigh Banfield Escalates Feud with Reporter of Aziz Ansari Story."

77 Bennett, "The #MeToo Moment"; Weller, "#MeToo's Generational Divide"; "Is There a Generational Divide in the #MeToo Movement?"; McCartney, "The New Feminist War."

78 Hudson, "Forget the Backlash."

79 Hudson, "I have great respect for the contributions that many older women made to the feminist movement, at times when it was harder than I have ever experienced."

80 Horton, "Germaine Greer Criticises Whingeing MeToo Movement."

81 "Germaine Greer Has Said 'It Is Too Late Now to Start Whingeing' for Women Who Have Made Allegations against Men, as She Questioned the #MeToo Movement," *News Corp Australia Network*, January 21, 2018, www.news.com.au.

82 "Catherine Deneuve Apologizes to Sex Assault Victims, Stands by Letter."

83 Harding, "The Intergenerational Feminist Divide over #MeToo Is Painful but Necessary."

84 Harding, "The Intergenerational Feminist Divide over #MeToo Is Painful but Necessary."

85 Fallon, "The Fake Feminism of the #MeToo Backlash."

86 Doyle, "It's Not (All) Second Generation Feminism's Fault."

87 Doyle, "It's Not (All) Second Generation Feminism's Fault."

88 Fallon, "The Fake Feminism of the #MeToo Backlash"; Grady, "The Waves of Feminism, and Why People Keep Fighting over Them, Explained."

89 Dean, "Op-Ed: Who Are You Calling a 'Second Wave Feminist'?"

90 Dean, "Op-Ed: Who Are You Calling a 'Second Wave Feminist'?"

91 Dean, "Op-Ed: Who Are You Calling a 'Second Wave Feminist'?"

92 Grady, "The Waves of Feminism and Why People Keep Fighting over Them, Explained."

93 Grady, "The Waves of Feminism and Why People Keep Fighting over Them, Explained."

94 Donegan, "How #MeToo Revealed the Central Rift within Feminism Today."

95 Bennett, "The #MeToo Moment"; Crary and Rush, "#MeToo Movement Starting to Show Generational Divides"; "Is There a Generational Divide in the #MeToo Movement?"; Weller, "#MeToo's Generational Divide."

96 Crary and Rush, "#MeToo Movement Starting to Show Generational Divides."

97 Martha Weinman Lear, "The Second Feminist Wave," *New York Times*, March 10, 1968, https://timesmachine.nytimes.com.

98 Rebecca Walker, "Becoming the Third Wave," *Ms. Magazine*, January/February 1992, 39–41.

99 Rebecca Walker, ed., *To Be Real: Telling the Truth and the Changing of Face of Feminism* (New York: Anchor Books, 1995); Baumgardner, *Manifesta*; Heywood and Drake, *Third Wave Agenda*; Piepmeier and Dicker, *Catching a Wave*.

100 Dean, "Who's Afraid of Third Wave Feminism?" Dean describes "third wave" as an "essentially contested signifier." Many scholars discussing third wave feminism begin routinely with the idea of its contestation.

101 Baumgardner, *Manifesta*, 17.

102 Johnson, *Jane Sexes It Up*.

103 Solomon, "Questions for Jessica Valenti."

104 Cochrane, "The Fourth Wave of Feminism."

105 "Project."

106 Valenti, "#YesAllWomen Reveals the Constant Barrage of Sexism That Women Face."

107 Baumgardner, *F'em*.

108 In their lecture "The Rebirth of Feminism? Situating Feminism in the Popular Imaginary," Erin Sanders McDonagh and Elena Vacchelli argue that the "concept of temporal 'waves' of feminism serves to create a version of feminist activity that is presented as monolithic, and neatly ensconced in a clearly defined and delineated period of time" (symposium at Middlesex University, October 30, 2013).

109 Nicholson, "Feminism in 'Waves.'"

110 Cott, *The Grounding of Modern Feminism*, cited in Nicholson, "Feminism in 'Waves.'"

111 Siibak and Vittadini, "Editorial."

112 Siibak and Vittadini, "Editorial."

113 Snyder, "What Is Third-Wave Feminism?"

114 Roiphe, *The Morning After*.

115 Sommers, *Who Stole Feminism?*

116 Denfeld, *The New Victorians*.

117 Wolf, *Fire with Fire*.

118 Wolf, *Fire with Fire*, 14, 15.

119 Faludi, "'I'm Not a Feminist but I Play One on TV.'"

120 Dean, "Op-Ed: Who Are You Calling a Second-Wave Feminist?"; Budgeon, *Third Wave Feminism and the Politics of Gender in Late Modernity*; Detloff, "Mean Spirits"; Henry, *Not My Mother's Sister*.

121 Lois Leveen, "Sex and the Scholarly Girl: Plugging the Feminist Generation Gap," *Women's Studies* 25, no. 6 (November 1996): 619–35. https://doi.org/10.1080/00497878.1996.9979142.

122 Leveen, "Sex and the Scholarly Girl."

123 Alison Winch, "Does Feminism Have a Generation Gap?" *Angelaki: Journal of the Theoretical Humanities* 22, no. 1 (January 2017): 207. https://doi.org/10.1080/0969725X.2017.1286005.

124 Bulbeck and Harris, "Feminism, Youth Politics, and Generational Change."

125 Douglas, *Where the Girls Are*.

126 Douglas, *Where the Girls Are*; Reinke, "Catfight." Relying on Douglas, Reinke argues, "Catfight, as a verb, is defined by the *Oxford English Dictionary* as 'To have a vicious fight or altercation; spec. (of women) to fight in a vicious, cat-like manner, esp. by scratching, pulling hair, and biting.' This definition particularly focuses on the nature of the actual physicality of catfighting, and notably includes such ineffectual motions as 'scratching, pulling hair, and biting,' which actually have little relation to the more physically aggressive and effective features of a typical fight—that is, a *male* fight."

127 Donegan, "I Started the Shitty Men List."

128 Donegan, "I Started the Shitty Men List."

129 Budgeon, *Third Wave Feminism and the Politics of Gender in Late Modernity*, 39.

130 See for example Jean Burgess, Elija Cassidy, Stefanie Duguay, "Making Digital Cultures of Gender and Sexuality with Social Media," *Social Media and Society* 2, no. 4 (October 2016); Shaw and Sender, "Queer Technologies"; DeNardis and Hackel, "Internet Control Points as LGBT Rights Mediation."

2. FEMINIST SEX WARS

1 See Bronstein and Strub, *Porno Chic and the Sex Wars*; Vance, *Pleasure and Danger*; Rubin, "Thinking Sex"; Duggan and Hunter, *Sex Wars*; Comella, "Revisiting the Feminist Sex Wars."

2 Gersen and Suk, "The Sex Bureaucracy."

3 Kipnis, *Unwanted Advances*; Halley, "Trading the Megaphone for the Gavel in Title IX Enforcement"; Suk Gersen, "Laura Kipnis's Endless Trial by Title IX"; Suk Gersen, "Betsy DeVos, Title IX, and the 'Both Sides' Approach to Sexual Assault."

4 Halley, "The Move to Affirmative Consent."

5 Morgan, "Theory and Practice"; Lederer, *Take Back the Night*.

6 Brownmiller, *Against Our Will*.

7 Bronstein and Strub, *Porno Chic and the Sex Wars*, 125, citing LA WAVAW, "Words and Phrases and Ideas for Emphasis," n.d., Organizing Principles file, Boston WAVAW Papers. Northeastern University Archives and Special Collections, Boston, Massachusetts.

8 Bronstein and Strub, *Porno Chic and the Sex Wars*, 83.

9 Bronstein and Strub, *Porno Chic and the Sex Wars*, 133. Provides the WAVA Statement of Principles, February 1977.

10 Boston WAVAW, "Proposal to Join the Women's Center as an Affiliated Project." Boston WAVAW Papers, Northeastern University Archives and Special Collections, Boston, Massachusetts.

11 Bronstein and Strub, *Porno Chic and the Sex Wars*, 103, citing Boston WAVAW Papers, Northeastern University Archives and Special Collections, Boston, Massachusetts.

12 Rubin, "Thinking Sex," 31.

13 Califia, "A Personal View of the History of S/M Sexuality Reader."

14 Califia, "A Personal View of the History of S/M Sexuality Reader"; Khan, *Vicarious Kinks*.

15 Russell, "Pornography and the Women's Liberation Movement," 304, cited in Bronstein and Strub, *Porno Chic and the Sex Wars*, 133.

16 Bronstein and Strub, *Porno Chic and the Sex Wars*, 133.

17 Bronstein and Strub, *Porno Chic and the Sex Wars*, 133.

18 Dworkin, *Pornography*.

19 Steinem, "Erotica and Pornography."

20 Steinem, "Erotica and Pornography," 37. It was a message she would repeat at the 1979 East Coast conference on pornography organized by the newly formed WAP, but this time picked up by the mainstream press: "Erotica is something quite different, portraying love as something chosen. Pornography is not sex, and sex need not be violent or aggressive at all. It is violence and domination that are pornographic." Bennetts, "Conference Examines Pornography as a Feminist Issue."

21 Bennetts, "Conference Examines Pornography as a Feminist Issue."

22 Kaminer, "Where We Stand on the First Amendment," 52–53.

23 Brownmiller, "Let's Put Pornography Back in the Closet," 41.

24 Willis, "Classical and Baroque Sex in Everyday Life."

25 Willis, "Classical and Baroque Sex in Everday Life."

26 Ellen Willis, qtd. in *Pornography, Sex Work, and Hate Speech*, edited by Karen J. Maschke (New York: Routledge, 1997).

27 Letter published in *Plexus* (May 1981), reproduced in *Heresies* 3, no. 4 (January 1981).

28 Letter published in *Plexus*.

29 See Califia, "Feminism and Sadomasochism"; Califia, "Among Us, against Us"; Califia, *Sapphistry*. *Sapphistry* described and defended a range of lesbian sexual practices, including butch/femme and S/M.

30 Webster, "Pornography and Pleasure."

31 Bronstein and Strub, *Porno Chic and the Sex Wars*, 318.

32 Bronstein and Strub, *Porno Chic and the Sex Wars*.

33 Kaminer, as cited in Bronstein and Strub, *Porno Chic and the Sex Wars*.

34 Vance, "Invitation Letter," 200.

35 "Dear Diary!"

36 Vance, "Conference Statement."

37 See Dejanikus, "Charges of Exclusion and McCarthyism at Barnard Conference"; see also Wilson, "The Context of 'Between Pleasure and Danger.'"

38 Vance, *Pleasure and Danger*, 431.

39 Vance, *Pleasure and Danger*, 432.

40 "Leaflet."

41 Vance, "Petition." The petition was first published in *Off Our Backs*, July 1982, with seventy-five signatures of prominent feminist academics, writers, and activists; by the time it was reprinted in *Feminist Studies* in 1983, it included over 190 signatories.

42 Vance, "Letter to the Editors."

43 Vance, "Petition."

44 Joan Nestle, qtd. in Dejanikus, "Charges of Exclusion and McCarthyism at Barnard Conference."

45 Willis, "Letter to the Editors."

46 For the editors' apology and letters of response from women named in the leaflet, see *Feminist Studies* 9, no. 3 (Fall 1983): 589–602.

47 Rubin, in "Blood under the Bridge," similarly observed that "the conference's reputation . . . bears almost no relationship to the substance of the event."

48 Comella, "Looking Backwards," 205.

49 Comella, "Looking Backwards."

50 MacKinnon, "Feminism, Marxism, Method, and the State."

51 For an in-depth discussion of the politics of the anti-pornography ordinance in Minneapolis, see Brest and Vandenberg, "Politics, Feminism, and the Constitution."

52 Brest and Vandenberg, "Politics, Feminism, and the Constitution."

53 Duggan and Hunter, *Sex Wars*. In relation to the coercion into pornographic performances offense, the remedy included "the elimination of the products of the performance(s) from the public view."

54 Brest and Vandenberg, "Politics, Feminism, and the Constitution."

55 Bronstein and Strub, *Porno Chic and the Sex*.

56 Bronstein and Strub, *Porno Chic and the Sex Wars*, citing Walter Goodman, "Battle on Pornography Spurred by New Tactics," *New York Times*, July 3, 1984, A8.

57 General Ordinances No. 24, 1984, and No. 35, 1984, amended the Code of Indianapolis and Marion County, Indiana, chapter 16, "Human Relations and Equal Opportunity."

58 Duggan, "Censorship in the Name of Feminism."

59 Downs, *The New Politics of Pornography*; Duggan and Hunter, *Sex Wars*; Bronstein and Strub, *Porno Chic and the Sex Wars*.

60 American Booksellers Association, Inc. v. Hudnut, 598 F. Supp. 1316 (S.D. Ind. 1984), aff'd, 771 F.2d 323 (7th Cir. 1985), aff'd, 475 U.S. 1001, 106 S. Ct. 1172, 89 L. Ed. 2d 291 (1986).

61 American Booksellers Association, 598 F. Supp. 1316, 1334.

62 Duggan, "Censorship in the Name of Feminism."

63 Irvine, "Interview with Carole Vance."

64 Irvine, "Interview with Carole Vance."

65 Hunter and Law, "Brief Amici Curiae of Feminist Anti-Censorship Taskforce, et al., in *American Booksellers Association v. Hudnut*."

66 Morgan and Barry, "Letter."

67 MacKinnon, "Liberalism and the Death of Feminism."

68 MacKinnon, "Liberalism and the Death of Feminism," 12.

69 MacKinnon, "Women and the Law."

70 Leidholdt, qtd. in Hunter, "Modern McCarthyism." Leidholdt was also defending comments she made to a television producer, resulting in FACT being disinvited from a televized debate. Nan Hunter wrote a letter to the editor of *OOB*, describing the event, but did not name Leidhold; Hunter, "Sex Baiting and Dangerous Bedfellows." Leidholdt responded with a letter to *OOB*, in which she identified herself. Carol Vance described that it "became common for FACT in New York to be disinvited to events and kicked off TV and radio shows" because anti-pornography feminists would tell media outlets and event organizers that the women of FACT were "not feminists, . . . we were pornographers; and . . . we were members of some deviant sexual group" (Vance, in Irvine, "Interview with Carole Vance").

71 Leidholdt, qtd. in Hunter, "Modern McCarthyism," 26.

72 Duggan et al., "False Promises."

73 Rich, "We Don't Have to Come Apart over Pornography."

74 American Booksellers Association, Inc. v. Hudnut, 771 F. 2d 323 (7th Cir. 1985). Rehearing and rehearing en banc denied Sept. 20, 1985.

75 American Booksellers Association, Inc. v. Hudnut, 771 F. 2d at 328.

76 American Booksellers Association, Inc. v. Hudnut, 771 F. 2d at 329.

77 American Booksellers Association, Inc. v. Hundut, 475 U.S. 1001, 106 S. Ct. 1172, 89 L. Ed. 2d 291 (1986).

78 Abrams, "Sex Wars Redux," 304.

79 MacKinnon, "Feminism, Marxism, Method, and the State," 650.

80 Bronstein and Strub, *Porno Chic and the Sex Wars.*

81 Butler, *Gender Trouble*, 30.

82 Duggan and Hunter, *Sex Wars*, 181.

83 Duggan and Hunt, *Sex Wars*, 7.

84 Abrams, "Sex Wars Redux," 308.

85 Abrams, "Sex Wars Redux," 314.

86 Duggan and Hunter, *Sex Wars*, 5.

87 Abrams, "Sex Wars Redux."

88 Ali, "Dear Colleague Letter."

89 Title IX of the Education Amendments of 1972, 20 U.S.C. §§ 1681–88 (2012).

90 Department of Education, *Sexual Harassment Guidance.*

91 Ali, "Dear Colleague Letter," 11.

92 Brodsky, "Working for Change, Learning from Work."

93 Pérez-Peña, "Student's Account Has Rape in Spotlight."

94 Pérez-Peña, "Student's Account Has Rape in Spotlight"; see also Choi, "Amherst Severely Mishandles Rape Charge."

95 Brodsky, "Working for Change, Learning from Work," 245.

96 Pérez-Peña, "College Groups Connect to Fight Sexual Assault."

97 Pérez-Peña and Taylor, "Fight against Sexual Assaults Holds Colleges to Account."

98 Sulkowicz, "My Rapist Is Still on Campus."

99 Smith, "In a Mattress, a Lever for Art and Political Protest."

100 Taylor, "Mattress Protest at Columbia University Continues into Graduation Event."

101 McDonald, "It's Hard to Ignore a Woman Toting a Mattress Everywhere"; McDonald, "Columbia Student Emma Sulkowicz Carried Mattress to Protest Campus Rape."

102 "Columbia Student Protests University's Response to Alleged Rape."

103 While campus activists against sexual violence are often referred to as "anti-rape" activists, the terminology itself is problematic, setting up their opponents as if they are "pro-rape." The language of the opponents, described as feminist critics, is similarly problematic, suggesting that the anti-rape activists were not engaged in feminist criticism. I deploy the terms because they are the commonly used ones, while noting the problematic binary that the terms themselves set up.

104 Harvard University, "Procedures for Handling Complaints Involving Students Pursuant to the Sexual and Gender-Based Harassment Policy."

105 Cole, "Reinstating Student Rights or Criminalizing Title IX?" provides an excellent overview of the Harvard sexual harassment policy controversy.

106 On the leading role of Halley, see Duehren, "A Call to Arms."

107 Halley, "A Call to Reform the New Harvard University Sexual Harassment Policy and Procedures."

108 Bartholet et al., "Rethink Harvard's Sexual Harassment Policy"; Duehren, "A Call to Arms."

109 Bidgood and Lewin, "Some Harvard Law Professors Oppose Policy on Assaults."

110 Cole, "Reinstating Student Rights or Criminalizing Title IX?"; Duerhen, "A Call to Arms."

111 Gertner, "Sex, Lies, and Justice."

112 Gertner, "Sex, Lies, and Justice"; Gertner, "Complicated Process."

113 Halley, "Trading the Megaphone for the Gavel in Title IX Enforcement," 117; see Duehren, "A Call to Arms," and Duehren, "Memo, Law Profs Pushed for Title IX Procedural Changes."

114 Kipnis, "Sexual Paranoia Strikes Academe."

115 Kipnis, "My Title IX Inquisition."

116 Suk Gersen, "Laura Kipnis's Endless Trial by Title IX."

117 Barnes, "An Unblinking Look at Sexual Assaults on Campus"; Hornaday, "Review."

118 Yoffe, "*The Hunting Ground*."

119 Yoffe, "How *The Hunting Ground* Blurs the Truth."

120 Bartholet et al., "Press Release Re: *The Hunting Ground*"; Singal, "*The Hunting Ground* Uses a Striking Statistic about Campus Rape That's Almost Certainly False"; see also Jess Singal, "*The Hunting Ground* Uses a Striking Statistic about Campus Rape," *New York Magazine*, November 23, 2015, www.thecut.com.

121 Harvard Law Professors, "Press Release Re: *The Hunting Ground*."

122 Harvard Law Professors, "Press Release Re: *The Hunting Ground*."

123 Duehren, "Website Continues Challenge of 'The Hunting Ground' Film."

124 Dick and Ziering, "How Harvard Law Professors Retaliated against an Assault Survivor."

125 Suk Gersen, "Shutting Down Conversations about Rape at Harvard Law."

126 Bazelon, "The Return of the Sex Wars."

127 See Daniel Del Gobbo's description of the Harvard Law School sexual harassment controversies.

128 Gersen and Suk, "The Sex Bureaucracy," 881.

129 Gersen and Suk, "The Sex Bureaucracy," 884.

130 Halley, "Trading the Megaphone for the Gavel in Title IX Enforcement," 117.

131 Bogdanich, "Reporting Rape, and Wishing She Hadn't."

132 Halley, "The Move to Affirmative Consent"; California Education Code (2015) s. 67386; New York Education Law (2015) s. 6441 (2015).

133 The California Education Code defines consent as "affirmative, conscious, and voluntary agreement to engage in sexual activity." The New York law defines "affirmative consent [as] a knowing, voluntary and mutual decision among all participants to engage in sexual activity."

134 Halley, "The Move to Affirmative Consent," 259, 270.

135 Halley here cites MacKinnon, *Women's Lives, Men's Laws*: "An equality standard . . . requires that sex be welcome. For the criminal law to change to this standard would require that sex be wanted for it not to be assaultive" (244).

136 Halley, "The Move to Affirmative Consent," 259.

137 For a critique of this claim, see Fischel, *Screw Consent*.

138 Kathryn Abrams famously coined "sex wars redux" in the 1990s. Her insight remains prescient.

139 These campaigns have been criticized from a number of different perspectives. For example, Joe Fischel in *Screw Consent* is critical of these campaigns because of the extent to which they can obscure rather than clarify what can be harmful about sex. Fischel takes on the scaffolding of consent, arguing that it is insufficient, inapposite, and often riddled with contradictions. Melanie Ann Beres in "The Proliferation of Consent-Focused Rape Prevention Social Marketing Materials" argues that these campaigns are inconsistent with current feminist understandings of the role of consent in sexual-violence prevention. "Feminist theorising . . . is increasingly orienting itself away from the concept of consent for

explaining sexual violence. At the same time, feminist activism is increasingly orienting itself toward the concept of consent as a mechanism of prevention."

140 Brock Turner, a student at Stanford, was convicted of three counts of felony sexual assault, in relation to the sexual assault of an unconscious woman. The case attracted international media attention, referring to Turner as "the Stanford rapist." Superior Court Judge Aaron Persky sentenced Turner to six months in jail followed by three years of probation. There was widespread criticism of the sentence given by Judge Persky, and he was recalled by county voters on June 5, 2018.

141 Brodsky and Simonich, "Helping Rape Victims after the Brock Turner Case."

142 MacKinnon, "Rape Redefined."

3. #METOO AS SEX WARS

1 They were also seeking to defend against a conservative vision of sexuality that had been highly restrictive for women. In Merkin's view, "We are witnessing the re-moralization of sex."

2 Safronova, "Catherine Deneuve and Others Denounce the #MeToo Movement."

3 Badham, "Catherine Deneuve, Let Me Explain Why MeToo Is Nothing like a Witch Hunt."

4 Badham, "Catherine Deneuve, Let Me Explain Why MeToo Is Nothing like a Witch Hunt."

5 Yoffe, "Why the #MeToo Movement Should be Ready for a Backlash."

6 Haneke, "Michael Haneke."

7 Gessen, "When Does a Watershed Moment Become a Sex Panic?"

8 Gessen, "When Does a Watershed Moment Become a Sex Panic?"

9 Levine, "Will Feminism's Past Mistakes Haunt #MeToo?"

10 Wypijewski, "What We Don't Talk about When We Talk about #MeToo." "Look squarely at the presumption of guilt in light of experience, at the bundling of diverse behaviors under the rubric of sexual abuse, at emboldened efforts to drop statutes of limitation, and the zeitgeist feels like sex panic."

11 Wypijewski, "What We Don't Talk about When We Talk about #MeToo."

12 Berlinski, "The Warlock Hunt."

13 Fox, "Its Not a Sex Panic"; Schulte, "The Myth of the #MeToo Panic."

14 Flanagan, "To Hell with the Witch Hunt."

15 Beck, "#MeToo Is Not a Witch Hunt." Richard Beck represents a group of male critics who have written on moral panics and specifically engaged with the moral panic claims. "To call something a moral panic today is to say that the social concern is in some sense unfounded or misplaced. These moral panics feature a number of characteristics, including implausible allegations, exaggerated victimization, excessive punishment." Beck notes that there have been plenty, from the Salem witch trials to the McCarthy hearings to the 1980s panic around child sexual abuse in daycare centers. He argues that #MeToo has none of the characteristics of moral panic.

16 Badham, "Catherine Deneuve, Let Me Explain Why MeToo Is Nothing like a Witch Hunt."

17 Gilbert, "No, #MeToo Isn't McCarthyism."

18 Gentile, "Give a Woman an Inch, She'll Take a Penis."

19 Gentile, "Give a Woman an Inch, She'll Take a Penis."

20 Gentile, "Give a Woman an Inch, She'll Take a Penis."

21 Traister, "This Moment Isn't (Just) about Sex.".

22 Traister, "This Moment Isn't (Just) about Sex."

23 Traister, "This Moment Isn't (Just) about Sex."
24 Merkin, "Publicly, We Say #MeToo."
25 Catherine Deneuve, quoted in Safronova, "Catherine Deneuve and Others Denounce the #MeToo Movement."
26 Gessen, "Sex, Consent, and the Dangers of Misplaced Scale."
27 Levine, "Will Feminism's Past Mistakes Haunt #MeToo?"
28 Weiss, "Aziz Ansari is Guilty."
29 Merkin, "Publicly, We Say #MeToo."
30 Halley et al., *Governance Feminism*; Bartholet et al., *Fairness for All under Title IX.*
31 Nwanevu, "There Is No Rampaging #MeToo Mob."
32 Nwanevu, "There Is No Rampaging #MeToo Mob."
33 Rebecca Traister, quoted in Gray, "On Aziz Ansari and Sex That Feels Violating Even When It's Not Criminal."
34 Silman, "Aziz Ansari, 'Cat Person,' and the #MeToo Backlash."
35 Gray, "On Aziz Ansari and Sex That Feels Violating Even When It's Not Criminal."
36 Vance, *Pleasure and Danger.*
37 Vance, *Pleasure and Danger.*
38 There are also important differences in the debate about consent—about legal definitions of consent and about moving beyond consent. Some of this disagreement is related to the role of law in defining sexual harm discussed in the section below; some is more fully explored in the next chapter.
39 Hudson, "Forget the Backlash."
40 Valenti, "MeToo Is about More Than Stopping Rape."
41 Silman, "Aziz Ansari, 'Cat Person,' and the #MeToo Backlash." My emphasis.
42 Darcy, "Five Women Accuse Journalist and 'Game Change' Co-Author Mark Halperin of Sexual Harassment."
43 Kaminer, "Beware Vigilante Feminism."
44 Teachout, "I'm Not Convinced Al Franken Should Quit."
45 Lindin, "Sorry. If some innocent men's reputations have to take a hit in the process of undoing the patriarchy, that is a price I am absolutely willing to pay."
46 Merkin, "Publicly, We Say #MeToo."
47 Stewart, "Trump Wants 'Due Process' for Abuse Allegations."
48 There is a context in which due process would be relevant—that is, when the allegations involve government in some way. This might have been the case with Senator Al Franken, and this was the moment when the due process critique exploded. Franken ultimately resigned, and in the absence of any state action taken against him, due process was not relevant. But, once again, it sounded as if it were; without due process there could be no harm, and there should not be any punishment or consequence.
49 See discussion, chapter 2.
50 Yoffe, "Why the #MeToo Movement Should Be Ready for a Backlash."
51 Levine, "Will Feminism's Past Mistakes Haunt MeToo?"
52 Levine, "Will Feminism's Past Mistakes Haunt MeToo?"
53 Peyser, "#MeToo Has Lumped Trivial in with Legitimate Sexual Assault."
54 Levine, "Will Feminism's Past Mistakes Haunt MeToo?"; Weiss, "Aziz Ansari Is Guilty."
55 Valenti, "Our standard for sexual behavior has to be more than what's legal or illegal."
56 Gray, "On Aziz Ansari and Sex That Feels Violating Even When It's Not Criminal."

57 Levine, "Will Feminism's Past Mistakes Haunt #MeToo?"
58 Abrams, "Sex Wars Redux"; Adrienne Davis, "Regulating Sex Work."
59 Pellegrini, "#MeToo."
60 Pellegrini, "#MeToo."

4. READING BESIDE THE QUEER/FEMINIST DIVIDE

1 Greenberg, "What Happens to #MeToo When a Feminist Is Accused?"
2 Greenberg, "What Happens to #MeToo When a Feminist Is Accused?"
3 Avital Ronell, statement to investigators, reported in Greenberg, "What Happens to #MeToo When a Feminist Is Accused?"
4 Avital Ronell, statement to investigators, reported in Greenberg, "What Happens to #MeToo When a Feminist Is Accused?" See also Mangan, "NYU Scholar Accused of Harassment Assails Rush to Judgment as Sign of Sexual Paranoia."
5 The letter was leaked through the *Leiter Reports, a Philosophy Blog*; see Leiter, "Blaming the Victim Is Apparently OK When the Accused in a Title IX Proceeding Is a Feminist Literary Theorist."
6 Leiter, "Blaming the Victim Is Apparently OK When the Accused in a Title IX Proceeding Is a Feminist Literary Theorist."
7 Leiter, "Blaming the Victim Is Apparently OK When the Accused in a Title IX Proceeding Is a Feminist Literary Theorist."
8 See Gluckman, "How a Letter Defending Avital Ronell Sparked Confusion and Condemnation"; Mangan, "Scholars' Defense of an Accused Colleague Feels Eerily Familiar except for One Thing."
9 Greenberg, "What Happens to #MeToo When a Feminist Is Accused?".
10 Mangan, "New Disclosures about NYU Professor Reignite a War over Gender and Harassment"; see Robinson, "On Power and Aporia in the Academy."
11 Mangan, "Battle over Alleged Harassment Escalates as Former Graduate Students Sues Profesor and NYU."
12 Gessen, "An NYU Sexual Harassment Case Has Spurred a New Conversation about #MeToo."
13 Severson, "Asia Argento, a #MeToo Leader, Made a Deal with Her Accuser."
14 "'Almost Relief'; "Harvey Weinstein's Attorney Blasts Asia Argento."
15 Weiss, "Are others disturbed by the moral flattening going on?"; Weiss elaborated on this tweet in her column "Asia Argento Proves, Once Again, That Women Are Human Beings."
16 Weiss, "Asia Argento Proves, Once Again, That Women Are Human Beings."
17 Burke, "I've said repeatedly that the #metooMVMT is for all of us, including these brave young men who are now coming forward."
18 Rose McGowan, qtd. in "Rose McGowan Reacts to Asia Argento Reportedly Paying Off Assault Accusers."
19 Leiter, "Blaming the Victim Is Apparently OK When the Accused in a Title IX Proceeding Is a Feminist Literary Theorist."
20 During the three days after the post, Leiter's blog saw a dramatic increase in visits. June 11 had twenty-four thousand visits, June 12 peaked at thirty-four thousand, and June 13, at twenty-four thousand. The daily average on the Leiter blog is approximately twelve thousand views (Statscounter, Leiter blog).
21 Leiter, "Blaming the Victim Is Apparently OK When the Accused in a Title IX Proceeding Is a Feminist Literary Theorist."

22 Gluckman, "How a Letter Defending Avital Ronell Sparked Confusion and Condemnation."

23 Gluckman, "How a Letter Defending Avital Ronell Sparked Confusion and Condemnation."

24 Gluckman, referencing the American Association of University Professors, *History, Uses, and Abuses of Title IX.*

25 Mangan, "Scholars' Defense of an Accused Colleague Feels Eerily Familiar except for One Thing."

26 As quoted in Mangan, "Scholars' Defense of an Accused Colleague Feels Eerily Familiar cxcept for One Thing."

27 Leiter, "Blaming the Victim Is Apparently OK When the Accused in a Title IX Proceeding Is a Feminist Literary Theorist."

28 Judith Butler, as quoted in Mangan, "Scholars' Defense of an Accused Colleague Feels Eerily Familiar except for One Thing."

29 Mangan, "Scholars' Defense of an Accused Colleague Feels Eerily Familiar except for One Thing."

30 Greenberg, "What Happens to #MeToo When a Feminist Is Accused?"

31 Reitman v. Ronell and New York University, Complaint (N.Y. 2018), pdf from *Simple Justice: A Criminal Defense Blog*, https://blog.simplejustice.us/wp-content/uploads/2018/08/FINAL-Complaint-Reitman-v.-Ronell-and-NYU.pdf. A few days later, the statement of claim filed by Reitman described each of the alleged encounters in even more vivid detail.

32 Greenberg, "What Happens to #MeToo When a Feminist Is Accused?"

33 Greenberg, "What Happens to #MeToo When a Feminist Is Accused?"

34 Greenberg, "What Happens to #MeToo When a Feminist Is Accused?"; also see Mangan, "Battle over Alleged Harassment Escalates." More details emerged when Reitman filed his lawsuit against Ronell and NYU a few days later, which were again reported in the media. The statement of claim described each of the alleged encounters in even more vivid detail.

35 "Press Release on Behalf of Avital Ronell," link provided in Mangan, "Battle over Alleged Harassment Escalates as Former Graduate Student Sues Professor and NYU."

36 Mangan, "NYU Scholar Accused of Harassment Assails Rush to Judgment as Sign of 'Sexual Paranoia.'"

37 Ronell, as quoted in Mangan. "Battle over Alleged Harassment Escalates."

38 Mangan, "Battle over Alleged Harassment Escalates."

39 Ronell, as quoted in Mangan, "Battle over Alleged Harassment Escalates."

40 Ronell, as quoted in Mangan, "Battle over Alleged Harassment Escalates."

41 Greenfield, "Prof. Avital Ronell and the Lie of the Feminist Academy."

42 Sommers, "Oh no!"

43 Dana Bolger, as quoted in Mangan, "New Disclosures about NYU Professor."

44 Louis, "Not in the Name of Feminism." Louis further writes, "There is *nothing* in feminist thought, activism, or belief that justifies this terrible overture of support to an accused person who seems to have been afforded due process. As a feminist, I vehemently reject any notion that this overreach is in any way connected to feminism, or women's rights, or the #metoo movement. If the allegations are found credible, that is another success for the #metoo movement."

45 Goldhill, "Feminist Scholars Argue a Title IX Case Is Unfair."

46 Louis, "Not in the Name of Feminism."

47 American Association of University Professors' Committee A on Academic Freedom and Tenure and Committee on Women in the Academic Profession, "The History, Uses, and Abuses of Title IX."

48 O'Hehir, "When a Woman Is Accused of Sexual Misconduct." O'Hehir describes the intra-feminist debate as one between liberal versus radical visions of justice, noting that the signatories like Davis were emphasizing the extent to which sexual harassment "is not just individualized, but part of structural subordination."

49 Duggan, "The Full Catastrophe."

50 Duggan, "The Full Catastrophe."

51 Duggan, "The Full Catastrophe."

52 Halberstam, "This is a clear, politically savvy take on the Ronell case by Lisa Duggan," as quoted in Arnold, "What's Going On with Avital Ronell, the Prominent Theorist Accused of Harassment?" Halberstam also posed a highly satirical piece on *Bully Bloggers* entitled "The DeVos University Online Sexual Harassment Training Course," in which he highlighted the differential treatment of people accused of sexual harassment, from white men to queer people of color; Chris Kraus, writer and filmmaker, also weighed in, with a more personal defense, in "Dialing: Back: Darkness." She writes, "Beyond my empathy with Avital and my horror at the destructive power of these accusations couched in the disingenuous sentiments of #MeToo, I'm depressed that this seems like the end of all but the most technocratic pedagogy.... Those outside this world don't seem to realize that Reitman—or any Ph.D. student at NYU—is hardly an innocent" (link no longer available on-line).

53 Gessen, "An NYU Sexual Harassment Case Has Spurred a New Conversation about #MeToo."

54 Gessen, "An NYU Sexual Harassment Case Has Spurred a New Conversation about #MeToo."

55 Butler, "Judith Butler Explains Letter in Support of Avital Ronell."

56 See for example Wong, "What Are We to Make of the Case of Scholar Avital Ronell?"; Robinson, "On Power and Aporia in the Academy."

57 Livingstone, "Asia Argento, Avital Ronell, and the Integrity of #MeToo."

58 Long Chu, "I Worked with Avital Ronell."

59 Long Chu, "I Worked with Avital Ronell."

60 Corey Robin, "The Unsexy Truth about the Avital Ronell Scandal," *Chronicle of Higher Education*, August 20, 2018, www.chronicle.com; for a good review of the argument that the Ronell case was all about the power of senior academics, see Flaherty, "Harassment and Power."

61 Robin, "The Unsexy Truth about the Avital Ronell Scandal."

62 "Hold NYU Accountable: Terminate Avital Ronell's Employment and Implement Institutional Reform #NYUtoo" (no date, but prior to her return to classroom in September 2019), https://docs.google.com.

63 Zach Rivers, GSOC steward for the Graduate School of Arts, quoted in Lisa Cochrane and Victor Porcelli, "Some Students Welcome Ronell's Return, Others Denounce It," *Washington Square News*, September 9, 2019, https://nyunews.com.

64 Cochrane, "Ronell Takes Leave of Absence after Contentious Return Last Semester." "Professor Ronell is not teaching this semester simply because she is on leave for the term," NYU Graduate School of Arts and Science dean Brian Harper told *Washington Square News*: "This is a normal circumstance, and it has nothing to do with the case involving Professor Ronell and Nimrod Reitman."

65 Robin, "The Unsexy Truth about the Avital Ronell Scandal." See quotation at note 61.
66 See for example Rubin, "Thinking Sex."
67 Rubin, "Thinking Sex," 308.
68 Rubin, "Thinking Sex," 308.
69 Sedgwick, *Epistemology of the Closet*, 27. She adds, "The question of gender and the question of sexuality, inextricable from one another though they are . . . are nonetheless not the same question, . . . [I]n twentieth-century Western culture, gender and sexuality represent two analytic axes that may productively be imagined as being distinct from one another."
70 Halperin, *Saint Foucault*, 62. Halperin writes, "Queer . . . does not designate a class of already objectified pathologies or perversions. . . . [R]ather, it describes a horizon of possibility whose precise extent and heterogeneous scope cannot in principle be limited in advance."
71 Berlant and Warner, "Guest Column."
72 Butler, *Gender Trouble*; Butler, *Bodies That Matter*; Rubin, "Thinking Sex." I am cognizant of the fetishization of certain foundational texts; Berlant and Warner have argued that "no particular project is metonymic of queer commentary," including the texts of Sedgwick and Butler. See Berlant and Warner, "Sex in Public."
73 Foucault, *The History of Sexuality*, vol. 1.
74 Teresa de Lauretis, "Special Issue: Queer Theory; Lesbian and Gay Sexualities." *differences: A Journal of Feminist Critical Studies* 3, no. 2 (1991).
75 Crimp, "Right on, Girlfriend," 214.
76 Halperin, *Saint Foucault*, 62.
77 Halperin, *Saint Foucault*, 62.
78 Stockton Bond, "Queer Theory."
79 This critique put queer studies in a fraught relationship with sexual violence. Its defenses of nonnormative sexualities such as BDSM and of sexual desires as unpredictable and self-sabotaging, and its critique of sexuality as overburdend with significance have meant that it could not in good faith categorically condemn sexual misconduct with the same assuredness as some strands of feminist thought.
80 See for example Edelman, *No Future*; Halberstam, *In a Queer Time and Place*; Esteban Muñoz, *Cruising Utopia*; Freeman, *Time Binds*; Rodríguez, *Sexual Futures*.
81 Sedgwick, *Touching Feeling*.
82 See for example Cvetkovich, *An Archive of Feeling*; Love, *Feeling Backwards*.
83 Robyn Wiegman and Elizabeth A. Wilson, in "Introduction: Anti-Normativity Queer's Conventions," argue that "antinormativity not only collectivizes the diverse work of such foundational figures as Leo Bersani, Judith Butler, Michel Foucault, Gayle Rubin, Eve Kosofsky Sedgwick, and Michael Warner, but it also underwrites the critical analyses and political activisms of the field's most important interlocutors."
84 See Duggan, "Queer Complacency without Empire"; see also Halberstam, "Straight Eye for the Queer Theorist"; see also Tremblay, "'I'm Just Normal,'" noting that "by formulating the complex study of norms as *anti*-antinormativity, Wiegman and Wilson reproduce the logic of simplification via opposition that they accuse queer theorists of perpetrating."
85 Duggan, "Queer Complacency without Empire."
86 Duggan, "Queer Complacency without Empire."
87 Halperin, "Introduction," 4.
88 See also Joseph Fischel, *Sodomitical Justic: A Solicitation* (Philadelphia: Temple University Press, forthcoming). Fischel has argued that Halperin's is an overly simplistic approach to

sex law—one in which "a few sex laws are simply and summarily good (harm prevention), most are bad (sex repressive) [and] harm is a self-evident category."

89 Halperin, "Introduction," 4.

90 Judith Levine, in Halperin and Hoppe, *The War on Sex*, 48.

91 Halperin and Hoppe, *The War on Sex*, 48.

92 For discussions of the points of convergence and divergence between feminist and queer theory, see Lynn Huffer, *Are the Lips a Grave? A Queer Feminist on the Ethics of Sex* (New York: Columbia University Press, 2013); Schor and Weed, *Feminism Meets Queer Theory*; Martha Albertson Fineman, Jack Jackson, and Adam Romero, *Feminist and Queer Legal Theory: Intimate Encounters, Uncomfortable Conversations* (New York: Routledge, 2009).

93 Aya Gruber, "Sex Wars as Proxy Wars," *Critical Analysis of Law* 6, no. 1 (2019): 102–34.

94 Gruber, "Sex Wars as Proxy Wars," 134.

95 See Rubin, "The Unsexy Truth about the Avital Ronell Scandal"; see also Long Chu, "I Worked with Avital Ronell."

96 Bersani, "Is the Rectum a Grave?" 97, cited in Halley, "Take a Break from Feminism?"

97 I say "so-called" because so many of those writing about the Ronell controversy offered what could be framed as a queer critique without specifically defending the conduct of Ronell.

98 Duggan, "The Full Catastrophe."

99 Duggan, "The Full Catastrophe."

100 Duggan, "The Full Catastrophe."

101 Duggan, "The Full Catastrophe."

102 Sedgwick, "Paranoid Reading and Reparative Reading," 124.

103 The problem, according to Sedgwick, occurs when paranoid inquiry comes to be "co-extensive with critical theoretical inquiry rather than being viewed as one kind of cognitive/affective theoretical practice among other, alternative kinds." Sedgwick, "Paranoid Reading and Reparative Reading," 126.

104 Sedgwick, "Paranoid Reading and Reparative Reading," 130.

105 Sedgwick, "Paranoid Reading and Reparative Reading," 146.

106 Sedgwick, "Introduction."

107 Sedgwick, "Introduction," 8.

108 Weed, "The Way We Read Now," 95; see also Hansen, "The Future's Eve"; Wiegman, "The Times We're In."

109 Love, "Truth and Consequences," 237.

110 Love, "Truth and Consequences," 238.

111 Wiegman, "The Times We're In," 7.

112 Wiegman, "The Times We're In," 7. McCallum and Bradway, "Introduction." McCallum and Bradway argue, "Insofar as queer is a mode of thinking, it is a mode of thinking sideways, of turning around a question in unexpected ways."

113 Seitler, *Reading Sideways*. Dana Seitler has explored the idea of reading sideways, or "lateral reading," in her analysis of the role of art in American literary fiction, teasing out the politics of gender and sexuality. For Seitler, lateral reading is "a mode of interpretation that moves horizontally through various historical entanglements and across the fields of the arts to make sense of, and see in a new light, their connections, challenges, and productive frictions."

114 Seitler, *Reading Sideways*.

115 Sedgwick, "Paranoid Reading and Reparative Reading," 150.
116 Nyong'o, "Trapped in the Closet with Eve."
117 Sedgwick, "Paranoid Reading and Reparative Reading," 147.
118 As I argue in chapter 3, #MeToo feminism has also focused its energy on sexual conduct that is not illegal, but is ethically problematic, challenging law's hegemony to define sexual harm.
119 Noa Ben-Asher, "Of Trauma and Power: Celebrity Sexual Misconduct Tribunals," *Critical Analysis of Law Journal* 6, no. 1 (2019).
120 Butler, "Judith Butler Explains Letter in Support of Avital Ronell."
121 Fischel, *Screw Consent.*
122 Mayer, "The Case of Al Franken."
123 Quoted in Mayer, "The Case of Al Franken."
124 Mayer writes,

> Bill Nelson, the former Florida senator, said, "I realized almost right away I'd made a mistake. I felt terrible. I should have stood up for due process to render what it's supposed to—the truth." Tom Udall, the senior Democratic senator from New Mexico, said, "I made a mistake. I started having second thoughts shortly after he stepped down. He had the right to be heard by an independent investigative body. I've heard from people around my state, and around the country, saying that they think he got railroaded. It doesn't seem fair. I'm a lawyer. I really believe in due process.

125 For example Donegan, "The War on #MeToo Will Fail." Donegan framed the article as feeding into a backlash against #MeToo, which she describes "as a return to familiar social and intellectual habits . . . of depicting women as incompetent and untrustworthy, of thinking of men as honorable and incapable of meaning any harm, of thinking of feminists as unreasonable, and their calls for men to think more about the emotions, rights and desires of women as unreasonable, even totalitarian."
126 Filipovic, "Did Al Franken Get 'Railroaded'?"
127 Filipovic, "Did Al Franken Get 'Railroaded'?"
128 Marcotte, "What Drove the *New Yorker*'s Jane Mayer into Al Franken Denialism?"
129 Marcotte, "What Drove the *New Yorker*'s Jane Mayer into Al Franken Denialism?"
130 Filipovic, "Did Al Franken Get 'Railroaded'?" She says, "Just look at the blame heaped on Sen. Kirsten Gillibrand for saying Franken should resign. She didn't force him out; he left voluntarily, if—certainly—under pressure. And yet she shoulders the burden of his decisions, without the excuse of 'undermining due process wasn't her intent.'"
131 Sontag, *On Photography.*
132 Fiske, *Introduction to Communication Studies*; Tagg, *The Burden of Representation*; Tagg, *Grounds of Dispute*; Victor Burgin, ed., *Thinking Photography* (New York: Red Globe Press, 1984); Krauss, "Photography's Discursive Spaces."
133 Barthes, "The Photographic Message." Barthes's later work explored the more subjective elements of photography; see Barthes, *Camera Lucida.*
134 Tagg, *The Burden of Representation.*
135 Tagg, "Mindless Photography," 25.
136 Sontag, *On Photography*, 23.
137 Brown and Phu, *Feeling Photography.*
138 Brown and Phu, *Feeling Photography.*
139 Christine Zander, quoted in Mayer, "The Case of Al Franken."
140 Berlant, "The Predator and the Jokester."

141 Berlant, "The Predator and the Jokester."
142 Berlant, "The Predator and the Jokester." Berlant argues that this power works "by control over time and space and the framing of consequences in domains of capital, labor, institutional belonging," and speech situations where the structurally vulnerable are forced to "'choose their battles' or just act like a good sport."
143 Berlant, "The Predator and the Jokester."
144 Berlant, "The Predator and the Jokester."
145 Berlant, "The Predator and the Jokester."
146 DeBonis, "Rep. Tim Murphy Resigns from Congress after Allegedly Asking Woman to Have Abortion."
147 Mayer, "The Case of Al Franken."
148 Price, *A Theory of Regret*, 128.
149 See for example Goktepe, "Review."
150 Love, *Feeling Backwards*.
151 Sara Ahmed speaks of the stickiness of emotions, exploring the ways in which signs, objects, and surfaces become "sticky or saturated with affect." Ahmed, "The Cultural Politics of Emotion," 194–95.
152 Fischel, "How Calling Kevin Spacey a Pedophile Hurts the Gay Community."
153 Duggan, "The Full Catastrophe."

5. REGULATING REPARATIVELY

1 Kantor et al., "'Finally'": Debra Katz captured the sentiment when she said, "When we got to the first count of guilty, there was a feeling of extraordinary relief."
2 Jane Manning, Women's Equal Justice Project, qtd. in Kantor et al., "'Finally.'"
3 Jessica Valenti, "It says a lot about rape culture and how accustomed women are to losing that nearly every female friend I have was expecting a 'not guilty' verdict in the Weinstein trial." Twitter, February 24, 2020, 12:20 p.m. https://twitter.com.
4 Roxanna Gay, Twitter, February 24, 2020.
5 Roxanna Gay, Twitter, February 24, 2020.
6 Kantor et al., "'Finally.'"
7 Nolan, "I'm Relieved Harvey Weinstein Is Going to Prison."
8 Bazelon and Gruber, "#MeToo Doesn't Always Have to Mean Prison."
9 Grant, "No Justice for Harvey Weinstein's Victims."
10 In no way do I suggest that there was a "right" feminist reaction to the conviction; victims/survivors in particular and women more generally have enough pent-up anger, trauma, and frustration that no one should judge an appropriate response. I return below to discuss the question of feminist anger and its uses. My sole point here is that there *were* different reactions, and that differing emphases gestured towards some of the underlying tensions of the sex wars.
11 Kim, "The Carceral Creep."
12 Davis, *Are Prisons Obsolete?*; Richie and Gilmore, *Golden Gulag*.
13 Major abolition works include Davis and Richie, *Golden Gulag*; Forman, *Locking Up Our Own*; Gottschalk, *The Prison and the Gallows*; Abolition Collective, *Abolishing Carceral Society*; Kushner, "Is Prison Necessary?"
14 Richie and Martenson, "Resisting Carcerality, Embracing Abolition"; Kim, "The Carceral Creep"; Kim, "From Carceral Feminism to Transformative Justice"; Richie, "Reimagining the Movement to End Gender Violence."

15 Critical Resistance and INCITE!, "Statement on Gender Violence and the Prison-Industrial Complex."

16 Richie, *Arrested Justice.*

17 Davis, "Feminism and Abolition." Angela Davis coined "abolition feminism."

18 Bernstein, "The Sexual Politics of the 'New Abolitionism'"; see also Bernstein, "Militarized Humanitarianism Meets Carceral Feminism."

19 Kim, "From Carceral Feminism to Transformative Justice."

20 Bumiller, *In an Abusive State.*

21 Gruber, *The Feminist War on Crime*; see also Gruber, "The Feminist War on Crime."

22 Gruber, *The Feminist War on Crime*, 192.

23 Murphy, "The Ethics of Diversity in Transitional Settings."

24 Webber, "Forms of Transitional Justice."

25 Braithwaite, "Restorative Justice and De-Professionalization," 28.

26 Wenzel et al., "Retributive and Restorative Justice."

27 Kohn, "#MeToo, Wrongs against Women, and Restorative Justice."

28 Boesten, "Transformative Gender Justice."

29 Wexler et al., "#MeToo, Time's Up, and Theories of Justice."

30 Donna Coker, "Transformative Justice." Coker argues that "restorative justice" and "transformative justice" are often used interchangeably in the literature. Coker echoes Kathleen Daly in "Restorative Justice." Daly argues against the false dichotomy between retributive- and restorative-justice models.

31 Kathleen Daly, Barbara Hudson, Leigh Goodmark, and Donna Coker are among those who have done work in this area.

32 Hudson, "Restorative Justice and the Challenge of Sexual and Racial Violence"; Hudson, "Restorative Justice and Gendered Violence."

33 Goodmark, *Decriminalizing Domestic Violence.*

34 Goodmark, *Decriminalizing Domestic Violence.*

35 Goodmark, *Decriminalizing Domestic Violence.*

36 Goodmark, *Decriminalizing Domestic Violence.*

37 Goodmark writes,

> Voice involves both the opportunity to actively participate in a justice process and the ability to speak out. . . . Validation—an acknowledgement of the harm done—is a second concern of some people subjected to abuse. Women subjected to abuse seek a mechanism to communicate loudly and clearly that they were serious, and a public record of the abuse and their effort to stop it. If validation is an acknowledgment of harm, vindication is a clear and unequivocal stand in condemnation of the offense. . . . Vindication requires the community to publicly stand with the victim of harm and to hold offenders accountable for their actions.

38 Goodmark, *Decriminalizing Domestic Violence.*

39 Wexler and Robbenolt, "#MeToo and Restorative Justice."

40 Kohn, "#MeToo, Wrongs against Women, and Restorative Justice."

41 Kohn, "#MeToo, Wrongs against Women, and Restorative Justice," citing Howard Kehr, *The Little Book of Restorative Justice*, 28–29.

42 Kohn, "#MeToo, Wrongs against Women, and Restorative Justice."

43 Rojas et al., "Introduction."

44 Coker, "Transformative Justice," 143.

45 Davis, *Are Prisons Obsolete?* 106.

46 Reparative justice is generally associated with material restitution through the payment of financial reparations. It seeks to centralize the harm done to the victim(s) rather than the more abstract harm done to the community of criminal law; victim reparation rather than offender punishment is prioritized. There are many elements ascribed to reparative justice that go beyond the payment of money. They might include "acts of atonement and apology." McCarthy, "Reparations under the Rome Statute of the International Criminal Court and Reparative Justice Theory," 250. Others emphasize the expressive or communicative nature of reparative justice (Walker, *What Is Reparative Justice?*). Reparations is about a recognition of a wrong, and related lawsuits are also "about the process: telling the true story of setting the record straight has itself acquired a type of reparative currency" (Joseph, "The Verdict from the Porch"). Reparative justice has to date received the least feminist interrogation.

47 Taylor, "Anti-Carceral Feminism and Sexual Assault."

48 INCITE!, "About."

49 Ruth Wilson Gilmore, quoted in Kushner, "Is Prison Necessary?" This is not to say that Gilmore and other abolitionists are opposed to all reforms: "It's obvious that the system won't disappear overnight," Gilmore has said. "No abolitionist thinks that will be the case."

50 Terwiel, "What Is Carceral Feminism?"

51 Terwiel, "What Is Carceral Feminism?"

52 Rather than judge feminist practices as "carceral" or "anti-carceral" on the basis of their degree of separation from state institutions and the law, we might ask how they enable a rethinking of punishment, justice, and citizenship in their gendered and racialized complexity.

53 Roberts, "Abolition Constitutionalism."

54 Serisier, *Feminism, Rape, and Narrative Politics.*

55 On the role of remorse in criminal sentencing, and the controversies around it, see, e.g., Hannah Maslen, *Remorse, Penal Theory, and Sentencing* (Oxford: Hart Publishing, 2015); Steven Keith Tudor, "Why Should Remorse Be a Mitigating Factor in Sentencing?" *Criminal Law and Philosophy* 2, no. 3 (2008): 241; Susan A. Bandes, "Remorse and Criminal Justice." *Emotion Review* 8, no. 1 (2015): 14. The interrogation of remorse for both offenders and victims holds important potential in a noncriminal reconceptualization of justice.

56 Del Gobbo, "Queer Dispute Resolution."

57 Brown, "Wounded Attachments"; Brown, *States of Injury*; Halley, *Split Decisions.*

58 Stringer, "Vulnerability after Wounding"; see also Stringer, *Knowing Victims.*

59 On the shift to responsibilization in neoliberalism, see generally Lemke, "'The Birth of Bio-Politics'"; Rose and Miller, *Governing the Present*; Rose, *Powers of Freedom*; Trnka and Trundle, *Competing Responsibilities.* On feminism and the rise of neoliberal governance, see generally Cossman and Fudge, *Privatization, Law, and the Challenge to Feminism.*

60 Mardorossian, "Towards a New Theory of Rape."

61 Mardorossian, "Towards a New Theory of Rape," 771.

62 Halley, *Split Decisions*, 345.

63 Michelle Anderson, "Campus Sexual Assault Adjudication and Resistance to Reform."

64 Marcus, "Fighting Bodies, Fighting Words." Marcus used the term "rape scripts" to critique feminist anti-rape politics as overly rooted in narratives of inevitable victimization. My deployment of the term "victim script," although indebted to Marcus, is more closely

aligned with those scholars who refuse the either/or of the victim/agency binary; see also Stringer, "Vulnerability after Wounding."

65 Stringer, "Vulnerability after Wounding," 164.

66 Stringer, *Knowing Victims*.

67 Stringer, "Vulnerability after Wounding," 148. Stringer here relies on Lyotard's concept of the "differend" and his theory of the victim "as one who has suffered a wrong that is not presently recognized in law and exists instead as a differend or a form of suffering that cannot be phrased in a shared idiom."

68 Goodmark, "Restorative Justice as Feminist Practice."

69 Goodmark, "Restorative Justice as Feminist Practice."

70 Goodmark, "Restorative Justice as Feminist Practice," 378, quoting C. Q. Hopkins, M. P. Koss, and K. J. Bachar, "Applying Restorative Justice to Ongoing Intimate Partner Violence: Problems and Possibilities." *St. Louis University Public Law Review* 23, no. 1 (2004): 298.

71 Del Gobbo, "Negotiating Feminism."

72 Delwiche and Duehren, "New Law School Sexual Harassment Procedures Break from University Framework"; see also Cole, "Reinstating Student Rights or Criminalizing Title IX?"

73 Harvard Law School, *HLS Sexual Harassment Resources and Procedures for Students*.

74 Delwiche and Duehren, "New Law School Sexual Harassment Procedures Break from University Framework."

75 Bartholet et al., *Fairness for All under Title IX*.

76 Sexual harassment is narrowly defined in this context as "any unwelcome conduct that a reasonable person would find so severe, pervasive and objectively offensive that it denies a person equal educational access." Reports of sexual assault, dating violence, domestic violence, and stalking do not need to meet the description of "severe, pervasive and objectively offensive," as they are now included as examples of sexual harassment under Title IX. Colleges will be able to determine whether to use a "preponderance of the evidence" or "clear and convincing" standard as a burden of proof and must use the same standard for all complaints, no matter whether they involve student or faculty misconduct. See Office for Civil Rights, "Summary of the Major Provisions of the Department of Education's Title IX Final Rule."

77 Office of Civil Rights, "Summary of Major Provisions of the Department of Education's Title IX Final Rule."

78 Ted Mitchell, ACE's president, quoted in Anderson, "U.S. Publishes New Regulations on Campus Sexual Assault."

79 Anderson, "U.S. Publishes New Regulations on Campus Sexual Assault."

80 Janet Halley, quoted in Powell, "Trump Overhaul of Campus Sexual Assault Rule Wins Surprising Support."

81 Know Your IX v. Devos (4th Circuit, May 4, 2020), www.aclu.org.

82 Commonwealth of Pennsylvania et al. v. Devos 1:2020cv01468 (U.S. Court of Appeals, 2020). www.courtlistener.com.

83 "The Biden Plan to End Violence against Women." https://joebiden.com/vawa.

84 Anderson, "A Long and Complicated Road Ahead."

85 For a more detailed discussion of how such a restorative model could be brought to bear on campus sexual violence dispute resolution, see Del Gobbo, "Feminism in Conversation"; Del Gobbo, "The Return of the Sex Wars."

86 Consent is defined in Canada's *Criminal Code* in s. 273.1(1) as the voluntary agreement to engage in the sexual activity in question. Section 273.1 (3) elaborates on circumstances of forced submission that do not constitute consent:

No consent is obtained, for the purposes of [this section], where (a) the agreement is expressed by the words or conduct of a person other than the complainant; (b) the complainant is incapable of consenting to the activity; (c) the accused induces the complainant to engage in the activity by abusing a position of trust, power or authority; (d) the complainant expresses, by words or conduct, a lack of agreement to engage in the activity; or (e) the complainant, having consented to engage in sexual activity, expresses, by words or conduct, a lack of agreement to continue to engage in the activity.

The criminal law also limits the defense of mistaken belief. Section 273.2 states, "It is not a defence . . . that the accused believed that the complainant consented . . . where (a) the accused's belief arose from the accused's: (i) self-induced intoxication, or (ii) recklessness or willful blindness; or (b) the accused did not take reasonable steps, in the circumstances known to the accused at the time, to ascertain that the complainant was consenting."

87 Pierson, "Increasing Returns, Path Dependence, and the Study of Politics." Pierson defines path dependency, citing Levi, "A Model, a Method, and a Map," 19.

88 Muñoz, *Cruising Utopia*.

89 Sedgwick, "Paranoid Reading and Reparative Reading," 146.

90 In the context of sex work, "abolitionism" has an entirely different meaning than the feminist abolitionism of feminists of color. Here, "abolition" refers to the movement to abolish sex work.

91 Heath et al., "Judging Women's Sexual Agency."

92 Phipps, "Sex Wars Revisited"; see also Barton, "Dancing on the Möbius Strip," 585, arguing that the participants of the sex wars "characterize sex work in univocal terms. . . . [that] ignore the multilayered nature of human experience"; Comella, "Revisiting the Feminist Sex Wars," 437. Comella similarly observes that the positions of anti-pornography and sex-positive feminists from the sex wars "continue to occupy a domain space in public conversations and academic research" on issues such as sex work.

93 Phipps, "Sex Wars Revisited."

94 See for example Karaian, "Lolita Speaks"; Karaian, "Policing 'sexting.'" Karaian argues, from a sex-positive lens, against denying agency to young women in criminal responses to sexting.

95 Hayes and Kaba, "Prison Abolition with Mariame Kaba."

96 Burke, "What's Next in Healing and Activism?"

97 Tarana Burke, qtd. in "'Our Pain Is Never Prioritized.'"

98 Tarana Burke, quoted in Arthur, "#MeToo Founder Tarana Burke on Weinstein Verdict."

99 Valenti, "MeToo Is about More Than Stopping Rape."

100 Gray, "On Aziz Ansari and Sex That Feels Violating Even When It's Not Criminal."

CONCLUSION. BEYOND WAR, BESIDE ANGER

1 Waters, "Introduction."

2 Mishra, *The Age of Anger*.

3 Jilly Boyce Kay and Sarah Banet-Weiser, "Feminist Anger and Feminist Respair." *Feminist Media Studies* 19, no. 4 (2019): 603–9.

4 Traister, *Good and Mad*; Cooper, *Eloquent Rage*; Chemaly, *Rage Becomes Her*.

5 Dionne and Membreno, "The Future Is Furious."

6 Traister, "Fury Is a Political Weapon." Traister focuses on what the testimonies of Christine Blasey Ford and Brett Kavanaugh tell us about the gendered nature of anger.

7 Lorde, "The Uses of Anger."

8 Lorde, "The Uses of Anger."

9 Traister, *Good and Mad.*

10 Sara Robinson, quoted in Traister, *Good and Mad.*

11 Lorde, "The Uses of Anger."

12 Judith Butler, quoted in Terry and Butler, "The Radical Equality of Lives."

13 Waters, "Introduction," 3.

14 Goodmark, "Restorative Justice as Feminist Practice," 381.

15 Ahmed, *The Cultural Politics of Emotion.*

16 Kay and Banet-Weiser, "Feminist Anger and Feminist Respair."

17 Wiegman, "The Times We're In," 7.

18 Love, "Truth and Consequences."

19 Tarana Burke, quoted in Aisha Harris, "She Founded Me Too. Now She Wants to Move Past the Trauma," *New York Times,* October 15, 2018, www.nytimes.com.

20 Tarana Burke, quoted in Harris, "She Founded Me Too."

21 Anderson, "#MeToo Founder Tarana Burke on Working through Trauma to Create Joy."

22 Nash, *Black Feminism Reimagined.*

23 Nash, *Black Feminism Reimagined,* 115.

24 Nash, *Black Feminism Reimagined,* 117.

25 Nash, *Black Feminism Reimagined,* 126.

26 Nash, *Black Feminism Reimagined,* 131

27 Phipps, *Me, Not You.*

BIBLIOGRAPHY

Abolition Collective. *Abolishing Carceral Society*. Brooklyn, NY: Common Notions, 2018.

Abrams, Kathryn. "Sex Wars Redux: Agency and Coercion in Feminist Legal Theory." *Columbia Law Review* 95, no. 2 (1995): 304.

Adetaba, Elizabeth. "Tarana Burke Says #MeToo Should Center Marginalized Communities: An Interview with the Woman Who Launched the Me Too Campaign over a Decade Ago." *Nation*, November 17, 2017. www.thenation.com.

Ahmed, Sara. *The Cultural Politics of Emotion*. Edinburgh: Edinburgh University Press, 2004.

Albertson Fineman, Martha, Jack Jackson, and Adam Romero. *Feminist and Queer Legal Theory: Intimate Encounters, Uncomfortable Conversations*. New York: Routledge, 2009.

Alcindor, Yamiche, and Nicholas Fandos. "A Democratic Chorus Rises in the Senate: 'Franken Should Resign.'" *New York Times*, December 6, 2017. www.nytimes.com.

Ali, Russlynn. "Dear Colleague Letter," April 4, 2011. Office of the Assistant Secretary, US Department of Education. Last updated January 1, 2020. www2.ed.gov.

"'Almost Relief': Lawyer Describes Harvey Weinstein's Reaction to Asia Argento Report." *CBS This Morning*, August 20, 2018. www.cbsnews.com.

American Association of University Professors' Committee A on Academic Freedom and Tenure and Committee on Women in the Academic Profession, "The History, Uses, and Abuses of Title IX" (report adopted by the American Association of University Professors, June 16, 2016). https://www.aaup.org.

Anderson, Greta. "A Long and Complicated Road Ahead." *Inside Higher Ed*, January 22, 2021. www.insidehighered.com.

———. "U.S. Publishes New Regulations on Campus Sexual Assault." *Inside Higher Ed*, May 7, 2020. www.insidehighered.com.

Anderson, Kenya. "#MeToo Founder Tarana Burke on Working through Trauma to Create Joy." *Vice*, September 11, 2018. www.vice.com.

Anderson, Michelle. "Campus Sexual Assault Adjudication and Resistance to Reform." *Yale Law Journal* 125, no. 7 (May 2016).

Argento, Asia (@AsiaArgento). "Catherine Deneuve and other French women tell the world how their interiorized misogyny has lobotomized them to the point of no return." Twitter. January 9, 2018.

Arnold, Amanda. "What's Going on with Avital Ronnell, the Prominent Theorist Accused of Harassment?" *The Cut*, August 21, 2018. www.thecut.com.

Arthur, Kate. "#MeToo Founder Tarana Burke on Weinstein Verdict: 'Implications Reverberate Far beyond Hollywood.'" *Variety*, February 24, 2020. https://variety.com.

Atwood, Margaret. "Am I a Bad Feminist?" *Globe and Mail*, January 13, 2018. www.theglobeand-mail.com.

———. "Margaret Atwood on the Galloway Affair." *Walrus*, November 17, 2016. https://thewalrus.ca.

Badham, Van. "Catherine Deneuve, Let Me Explain Why #Metoo Is Nothing like a Witch-Hunt." *Guardian*, January 10, 2018. www.theguardian.com.

Banet-Weiser, Sarah. "Popular Feminism: Feminist Flashpoints." *LA Review of Books*, October 5, 2018. https://lareviewofbooks.org.

Banfield, Ashleigh. *Crime and Justice*. CNN, aired January 15, 2018.

Barker, Kim, and Ellen Gabler. "Charlie Rose Made Crude Sexual Advances, Multiple Women Say." *New York Times*, November 20, 2017. www.nytimes.com.

Barnes, Brooks. "An Unblinking Look at Sexual Assaults on Campus." *New York Times*, January 25, 2015.

Barthes, Roland. *Camera Lucida: Reflections on Photography*. Translated by Richard Howard. New York: Hill and Wang/Farrar, Strauss & Giroux, 1981.

———. "The Photographic Message" (1961). In *Barthes Reader*. Edited by Susan Sontag. New York: Hill and Wang, 1975.

Bartholet, Elizabeth, Scott Brewer, Robert Clark, et al. "Rethink Harvard's Sexual Harassment Policy." *Boston Globe*, October 15, 2014. www.bostonglobe.com.

Bartholet, Elizabeth, Scott Brewer, Charles Donahue, et al. "Press Release Re: *The Hunting Ground*." Harvard Law School, November 11, 2015. https://kcjohnson.files.wordpress.com/2013/08/hls-pressrelease.pdf.

Bartholet, Elizabeth, Nancy Gertner, Janet Halley, and Jeannie Suk Gersen. *Fairness for All under Title IX*. Harvard Law School, August 21, 2017. https://dash.harvard.edu.

Barton, Bernadette. "Dancing on the Möbius Strip: Challenge the Sex War Paradigm." *Gender and Society* 16, no. 5 (2002).

Baumgardner, Jennifer. *Fem: Goo Goo, Gaga, and Some Thoughts on Balls*. Berkeley, CA: Seal Press, 2011.

———. *Manifesta: Young Women, Feminism, and the Future*. New York: Farrar, Straus and Giroux, 2000.

Bazelon, Emily. "The Return of the Sex Wars." *New York Times Magazine*, September 10, 2015. www.nytimes.com.

Bazelon, Laura, and Aya Gruber. "#MeToo Doesn't Always Have to Mean Prison: Restorative Justice Is an Alternative We Should Also Consider." *New York Times*, March 2, 2020. www.nytimes.com.

Beck, Richard. "#MeToo Is Not a Witch Hunt." *Vox*, January 11, 2018. www.vox.com.

Bennett, Jessica. "The 'Click' Movement: How the Weinstein Scandal Unleashed a Tsunami." *New York Times*, November 5, 2017. www.nytimes.com.

———. "The #MeToo Moment: Parsing the Generational Divide." *New York Times*, January 17, 2018. www.nytimes.com.

Bennetts, Leslie. "Conference Examines Pornography as a Feminist Issue." *New York Times*, September 17, 1979. www.nytimes.com.

Beres, Melanie Ann. "The Proliferation of Consent-Focused Rape Prevention Social Marketing Materials." In *Orienting Feminism: Media, Activism, and Cultural Representation*. Edited by Catherine Dale and Rosemary Overell. London: Palgrave MacMillan, 2018.

Berlant, Lauren. "The Predator and the Jokester." *New Inquiry*, December 13, 2017. https://thenewinquiry.com.

Berlant, Lauren, and Michael Warner. "Guest Column: What Does Queer Theory Teach Us about X?" *PMLA* 110 (1995): 343–49.

———. "Sex in Public." *Critical Inquiry* 24, no. 2 (Winter 1998): 547–56.

Berlinski, Claire. "The Warlock Hunt." *American Interest*, December 6, 2017. www.the-american-interest.com.

Bernstein, Elizabeth. "Militarized Humanitarianism Meets Carceral Feminism: The Politics of Sex, Rights, and Freedom in Contemporary Antitrafficking Campaigns." *Signs* 45 (Autumn 2010): 45–71. https://doi.org/10.1086/652918.

———. "The Sexual Politics of the 'New Abolitionism.'" *differences: A Journal of Feminist Cultural Studies* 18, no. 3 (2007): 128–51.

Bersani, Leo. "Is the Rectum a Grave?" In *AIDS: Cultural Analysis, Cultural Activism*. Edited by Douglas Crimp. Cambridge, MA: MIT Press, 1998.

Bidgood, Jess, and Tamar Lewin. "Some Harvard Law Professors Oppose Policy on Assaults." *New York Times*, October 15, 2014. www.nytimes.com.

Boesten, Jelke. "Transformative Gender Justice: Setting an Agenda." *Women's Studies International Forum* 51 (2014).

Bogdanich, Walt. "Reporting Rape, and Wishing She Hadn't." *New York Times*, July 12, 2014. www.nytimes.com.

Boston WAVAW. "Proposal to Join the Women's Center as an Affiliated Project." N.d. History: Cambridge Women's Center file, Women Against Violence Against Women, Papers, 1977–1984. Northeastern University Archives and Special Collections, Boston, Massachusetts.

Boyce Kay, Jilly, and Sarah Banet-Weiser. "Feminist Anger and Feminist Respair." *Feminist Media Studies* 19, no. 4 (2019): 603–9.

Braithwaite, John. "Restorative Justice and De-Professionalization." *Good Society* 13, no. 1 (2004).

Brest, Paul, and Ann Vandenberg. "Politics, Feminism, and the Constitution: The Anti-Pornography Movement in Minneapolis." *Stanford Law Review* 39, no. 3 (February 1987): 607–61. https://doi.org/10.2307/1228761.

Brodsky, Alexandra. "Working for Change, Learning from Work: Student Empowerment and Challenges in the Movement to End Campus Gender Violence." In *Contemporary Youth Activism: Advancing Social Justice in the United States*, 245–60. Edited by Jerusha Conner and Sonia M. Rosen. Westport, CT: Praeger, 2016.

Brodsky, Alexandra, and Claire Simonich. "Helping Rape Victims after the Brock Turner Case." *New York Times*, August 11, 2016. www.nytimes.com.

Bronstein, Carolyn, and Whitney Strub, eds. *Porno Chic and the Sex Wars: American Sexual Representations in the 1970s*. Amherst: University of Massachusetts Press, 2016.

Brown, Elspeth, and Thy Phu, eds. *Feeling Photography*. Durham, NC: Duke University Press, 2014.

Brown, Wendy. *States of Injury*. Princeton, NJ: Princeton University Press, 1995.

———. "Wounded Attachments." *Political Theory* 21, no. 3 (August 1993): 390–410.

Brownmiller, Susan. *Against Our Will*. New York: Simon & Schuster, 1975.

———. "Let's Put Pornography Back in the Closet." *Newsday*, July 17, 1979.

———. *Phil Donahue Show* appearance, July 18, 1979, as reported in Bronstein and Strub, *Porno Chic and the Sex Wars*.

Budgeon, Shelley. *Third Wave Feminism and the Politics of Gender in Late Modernity*. London: Palgrave MacMillan, 2011.

Bulbeck, Chilla, and Anita Harris. "Feminism, Youth Politics, and Generational Change." In *Next Wave Cultures: Feminism, Subcultures, Activism*, 221–41. Edited by Anita Harris. London: Routledge, 2008.

Bumiller, Kristen. *In an Abusive State: How Neoliberalism Appropriated the Feminist Movement against Sexual Violence*. Durham, NC: Duke University Press, 2008.

Burgess, Jean, Elija Cassidy, and Stefanie Duguay. "Making Digital Cultures of Gender and Sexuality with Social Media." *Social Media and Society* 2, no. 4 (October 2016). Victor Burgin, ed. *Thinking Photography*. New York: Red Globe Press, 1984.

Burgin, Victor, ed. *Thinking Photography*. New York: Red Globe Press, 1984.

Burke, Tarana (@TaranaBurke). "I've said repeatedly that the #metooMVMT is for all of us, including these brave young men who are now coming forward." Twitter, August 20, 2018, 7:08 a.m. https://twitter.com/TaranaBurke/status/1031498206260150272.

———. "What's Next in Healing and Activism?" Lecture, Brown University, February 14, 2018. https://www.youtube.com/watch?v=AKZsXuag_DU&feature=emb_title.

Burrows-Taylor, Evie. "'Revolting': French Feminists Hit Back at Actress Catherine Deneuve over Defense of Sleazy Men." *Local*, January 10, 2018. www.thelocal.fr.

Butler, Judith. *Bodies That Matter: On the Discursive Limits of "Sex."* New York: Routledge, 1993.

———. *Gender Trouble: Feminism and the Subversion of Identity*, 2nd ed. Boston: Routledge, 1999.

———. "Judith Butler Explains Letter in Support of Avital Ronell." *Chronicle of Higher Education*, August 19, 2018. www.chronicle.com.

Califia, Pat. "Among Us, against Us: The New Puritans." *Advocate*, April 17, 1980.

———. "Feminism and Sadomasochism." *Heresies* 3, no. 4 (1981): 30–34.

———. "A Personal View of the History of S/M Sexuality Reader" (1981). In *Coming to Power: Writings and Graphics on Lesbian S/M*. Edited by Samois. New York: Alyson Books, 1983.

———. *Sapphistry: The Book of Lesbian Sexuality*. Tallahassee, FL: Naiad Press, 1980.

Carlsen, Audrey, Maya Salam, Claire Cain Miller, Denise Lu, Ash Ngu, Jugal K. Patel, and Zach Wichter. "#MeToo Brought Down 201 Powerful Men: Nearly Half of Their Replacements Are Women." *New York Times*, updated October 29, 2018. www.nytimes.com.

Carmen, Irin, and Amy Brittain. "Eight Women Say Charlie Rose Sexually Harassed Them—with Nudity, Groping, and Lewd Calls." *Washington Post*, November 20, 2017. www.washingtonpost.com.

"Catherine Deneuve Apologizes to Sex Assault Victims, Stands by Letter." *Sydney Morning Herald*, January 16, 2018. www.smh.com.au.

"Catherine Deneuve Clarifies #MeToo Views." *Associated Press*, January 16, 2018. https://apnews.com.

Chemaly, Surraya. *Rage Becomes Her*. New York: Atria Books, 2018.

Choi, Vivian. "Amherst Severely Mishandles Rape Charge: Amherst's Female Students Are Not Surprised." *Slate*, October 25, 2012. www.slate.com.

Cochrane, Kira. "The Fourth Wave of Feminism: Meet the Rebel Women." *Guardian*, December 10, 2013. www.theguardian.com.

Cochrane, Lisa. "Ronell Takes Leave of Absence after Contentious Return Last Semester." *Washington Square News*, February 4, 2020. https://nyunews.com.

Cochrane, Lisa, and Victor Porcelli. "Some Students Welcome Ronell's Return, Others Denounce It." *Washington Square News*, September 9, 2019. https://nyunews.com.

Coker, Donna. "Transformative Justice: Anti-Subordination Processes in Cases of Domestic Violence." In *Restorative Justice and Family Violence*. Edited by Heather Strang and John Braithwaite. Cambridge: Cambridge University Press, 2002.

Cole, Cory. "Reinstating Student Rights or Criminalizing Title IX? The Struggle to Define Sexual Harassment at Harvard Law School." *Women Leading Change* 2, no. 1 (2017).

Collins, Lauren. "Why Did Catherine Deneuve and Other Prominent French Women Denounce #MeToo?" *New Yorker*, January 10, 2018. www.newyorker.com.

"Columbia Student Protests University's Response to Alleged Rape." *NBC News*, September 5, 2014. www.nbcnews.com.

Comella, Lynn. "Looking Backwards: Barnard and Its Legacies." *Communication Review* 11, no. 3 (October 2008): 202–11 at 205.

———. "Revisiting the Feminist Sex Wars" (1992). *Feminist Studies* 41, no. 2 (Summer 2015): 267–93.

Cooper, Brittney. *Eloquent Rage: A Black Feminist Discovers Her Superpower.* New York: St. Martin's Press, 2018.

Cossman, Brenda, Shannon Bell, Lise Gotell, and Becki L. Ross. *Bad Attitude/s on Trial: Pornography, Feminism, and the Butler Decision.* Toronto: University of Toronto Press, 1997.

Cossman, Brenda, and Judy Fudge. *Privatization, Law, and the Challenge to Feminism.* Toronto: University of Toronto Press, 2002.

Cott, Nancy. *The Grounding of Modern Feminism.* New Haven, CT: Yale University Press, 1987.

Crary, David, and Tamara Rush. "#MeToo Movement Starting to Show Generational Divides." *Associated Press*, January 28, 2018. www.apnews.com.

Crimp, Douglas. "Right On, Girlfriend." In *Fear of a Queer Planet: Queer Politics and Social Theory.* Edited by Michael Warner. Minneapolis: University of Minnesota Press, 1993.

Critical Resistance and INCITE! "Statement on Gender Violence and the Prison-Industrial Complex." *Social Justice* 30, no. 3 (2003): 141–50.

Cvetkovich, Ann. *An Archive of Feeling: Trauma, Sexuality, and Lesbian Public Cultures.* Durham, NC: Duke University Press, 2003.

Daly, Kathleen. "Restorative Justice: The Real Story." *Punishment and Society* 4, no. 1 (2002).

Darcy, Oliver. "Five Women Accuse Journalist and 'Game Change' Co-Author Mark Halperin of Sexual Harassment." CNN, October 26, 2017. https://money.cnn.com.

Davis, Adrienne. "Regulating Sex Work: Assimilation, Erotic Exceptionalism, and Beyond." *California Law Review* 103 (1995).

Davis, Angela. *Are Prisons Obsolete?* New York: Seven Stories Press, 2003.

———. "Feminism and Abolition: Theories and Practices for the Twenty-first Century." Lecture delivered May 2013, University of Chicago. Available on YouTube, www.youtube.com/.

de Lauretis, Teresa. "Special Issue: Queer Theory; Lesbian and Gay Sexualities." *differences: A Journal of Feminist Critical Studies* 3, no. 2 (1991).

Dean, Jonathan. "Who's Afraid of Third Wave Feminism?" *International Feminist Journal of Politics* 11, no. 3 (2009). https://doi.org/10.1080/14616740903017711.

Dean, Michelle. "Op-Ed: Who Are You Calling a 'Second Wave Feminist'?" *Los Angeles Times*, January 24, 2018. www.latimes.com.

"Dear Colleague Letter." Office for Civil Rights, US Department of Education, last modified January 10, 2020. www2.ed.gov/.

"Dear Diary!" September 16, 1981. In *Diary of a Conference*, 4–5. Edited by Hannah Alderfer, Beth Jaker, and Marybeth Nelson. New York: Faculty Press, 1981.

DeBonis, Mike. "Rep. Tim Murphy Resigns from Congress after Allegedly Asking Woman to Have Abortion." *Washington Post*, October 5, 2017. www.washingtonpost.com.

Dejanikus, Tacie. "Charges of Exclusion and McCarthyism at Barnard Conference." *Off Our Backs* 12, no. 6. (June 1982): 19–20.

Del Gobbo, Daniel. "Feminism in Conversation: Campus Sexual Violence and the Negotiation Within." *University of British Columbia Law Review* 53, no. 3 (forthcoming).

———. Negotiating Feminism: Campus Sexual Violence and the Politics of Settlement (unpublished manuscript, 2020; manuscript on file with the author, who is an SJD at the University of Toronto).

———. "Queer Dispute Resolution." *Cardozo Journal of Conflict Resolution* 20, no. 2 (Winter 2019). https://ssrn.com.

———. "The Return of the Sex Wars: Contesting Rights and Interests in Campus Sexual Violence Reform." In *Violence Interrupted: Confronting Sexual Violence on University Campuses.* Edited by Diane Crocker, Joanne Minaker, and Amanda Nelund. Montreal-Kingston: McGill-Queen's University Press, 2020.

Delwiche, Theodore, and Andrew Duehren. "New Law School Sexual Harassment Procedures Break from University Framework." *Harvard Crimson*, Janaury 3, 2015.

DeNardis, Laura, and Andrea M. Hackel. "Internet Control Points as LGBT Rights Mediation." *Information, Communication, and Society* 19 (2016): 753–70. https://doi.org/10.1080/13691 18X.2016.1153123.

Denfeld, Rene. *The New Victorians: A Young Woman's Challenge to the Old Feminist Order.* New York: Grand Central Publishing, 1995.

Department of Education. *Sexual Harassment Guidance: Harassment of Students by School Employees, Other Students, or Third Parties,* 62 Fed. Reg. 12,034 (Mar. 13, 1997).

Detloff, Madelyn. "Mean Spirits: The Politics of Contempt between Feminist Generations." *Hypatia: A Journal of Feminist Philosophy* 12, no. 3 (1997): 76–99. www.jstor.org/stable/3810223.

Dick, Kirby, and Amy Ziering. "How Harvard Law Professors Retaliated against an Assault Survivor." *Huffington Post*, January 5, 2016. www.huffpost.com.

Dionne, Evette, and Soraya Membreno. "The Future Is Furious." *Bitch Media*, October 2018, 2018. www.bitchmedia.org.

"Disgraced Representative Ruben Kihuen Tries to Alter His Sexual Harassment Record." *Rollcall*, February 26, 2019. www.rollcall.com.

Donegan, Moira. "How #MeToo Revealed the Central Rift within Feminism Today." *Guardian*, May 11, 2018. www.theguardian.com.

———. "I Started the Shitty Men List." *The Cut*, January 10, 2018. www.thecut.com.

———. "The War on #MeToo Will Fail: Women Cannot Be Un-Radicalized." *Guardian*, September 6, 2019. www.theguardian.com.

Douglas, Susan. *Where the Girls Are: Growing Up Female with the Mass Media.* New York: Random House, 1994.

Downs, Donald Alexander. *The New Politics of Pornography.* Chicago: University of Chicago Press, 1992.

Doyle, Sady. "It's Not (All) Second-Generation Feminism's Fault." *Elle Magazine*, January 22, 2018. www.elle.com.

Duehren, Andrew. "A Call to Arms: Law School Professor Janet Halley Is Pushing Back against Harvard and the Government's Approach to Title IX." *Harvard Crimson*, May 28, 2015. www.thecrimson.com.

———. "Memo, Law Profs Pushed for Title IX Procedural Changes." *Harvard Crimson*, February 13, 2015. www.thecrimson.com.

———. "Website Continues Challenge of 'The Hunting Ground' Film." *Harvard Crimson*, December 3, 2015. https://www.thecrimson.com.

Duggan, Lisa. "Censorship in the Name of Feminism." *Village Voice*, October 16, 1984.

———. "The Full Catastrophe." *Bully Bloggers*, August 18, 2018. https://bullybloggers.wordpress.com/2018/08/18/the-full-catastrophe/.

———. "Queer Complacency without Empire." *Bully Bloggers*, September 22, 2016. https://bully-bloggers.wordpress.com/2015/09/22/queer-complacency-without-empire/.

Duggan, Lisa, and Nan Hunter. *Sex Wars: Sexual Dissent and Political Culture*. New York: Routledge, 2006.

Duggan, Lisa, Nan Hunter, and Carole Vance. "False Promises: Feminist Antipornography Legislation." In *Sex Wars: Sexual Dissent and Political Culture*, 61. Edited by Lisa Duggan and Nan Hunter. New York: Routledge, 2014.

Dupuy, Tina. "I Believe Franken's Accusers Because He Groped Me, Too." *Atlantic*, December 6, 2017. www.theatlantic.com.

Dworkin, Andrea. *Pornography: Men Possessing Women*. New York: Dutton, 1979.

Dworkin, Andrea, and Catharine MacKinnon. *Pornography and Civil Rights: A New Day for Women's Equality*. Minneapolis, MN: Organizing Against Pornography, 1988.

Echols, Alice. "Retrospective: Tangled Up in Pleasure and Danger." *Signs* 42, no. 1 (2016).

Edelman, Lee. *No Future: Queer Theory and the Death Drive*. Edited by Eve Kosofsky Sedgwick and Michael Moon. Durham, NC: Duke University Press, 2004.

Edwards, Stassa. "The Backlash to #MeToo Is Second Wave Feminism." *Jezebel*, January 11, 2018. https://jezebel.com.

Fallon, Claire. "The Fake Feminism of the #MeToo Backlash." *Huffington Post*, January 19, 2018. www.huffingtonpost.ca.

Faludi, Susan. "'I'm Not a Feminist but I Play One on TV': Susan Faludi Exposes the Newest Crop of Media Darlings." *Ms. Magazine*, March/April, 1995.

Fandos, Nicholas. "Al Franken Issues Apology after Accusation of Forcible Kissing and Groping." *New York Times*, November 16, 2017. www.nytimes.com.

Farrow, Ronan. "From Aggressive Overtures to Sexual Assault: Harvey Weinstein's Accusers Tell Their Stories." *New Yorker*, October 10, 2017. www.newyorker.com.

Ferguson, Ann. "Sex War: The Debate between Radical and Libertarian Feminists." *Signs* 10, no. 1 (Autumn 1984): 106–12. www.jstor.org/stable/3174240.

Filipovic, Jill. "Did Al Franken Get 'Railroaded'?" CNN, July 24, 2019. www.cnn.com.

———. "Weinstein 'Witch Hunt'? Wrong, Woody Allen." CNN, October 18, 2017. www.cnn.com.

Fischel, Joseph. "How Calling Kevin Spacey a Pedophile Hurts the Gay Community." *Slate*, November 1, 2017. Slate.com.

———. *Screw Consent: A Better Politics of Sexual Justice*. Berkeley: University of California Press, 2019.

Fiske, John. *Introduction to Communication Studies*. New York: Routledge, 1990.

Flaherty, Collen. "Harassment and Power." *Inside Higher Ed*, August 20, 2018. www.insidehighered.com.

Flanagan, Caitlin. "The Humiliation of Aziz Ansari." *Atlantic*, January 14, 2018. www.theatlantic.com.

———. "To Hell with the Witch Hunt." *Atlantic*, November 22, 2017. www.theatlantic.com.

Forman, James Jr. *Locking Up Our Own: Crime and Punishment in Black America*. New York: Farrar, Straus & Giroux, 2017.

Foucault, Michel. *The History of Sexuality*. Volume 1, *An Introduction*. Translated by Robert Hurley. New York: Pantheon Books, 1978.

Fox, Faulkner. "It's Not a Sex Panic: Approaching Women in the Age of #MeToo." *Salon*, January 14, 2018. www.salon.com.

Freeman, Elizabeth. *Time Binds: Queer Temporalities, Queer Histories*. Durham, NC: Duke University Press, 2010.

Gabler, Ellen, Jim Rutenberg, Michael M. Grynbaum, and Rachel Abrams. "NBC Fires Matt Lauer, the Face of 'Today.'" *New York Times*, November 29, 2017. www.nytimes.com.

Gambino, Lauren. "Al Franken: Two More Women Accuse Senator of Sexual Misconduct." *Guardian*, November 30, 2017. www.theguardian.com.

Gentile, Katie. "Give a Woman an Inch, She'll Take a Penis." *Studies in Gender and Sexuality* 19, no. 4 (November 2018): 241–45.https://doi-org.myaccess.library.utoronto.ca/.

Gersen, Jacob, and Jeannie Suk. "The Sex Bureaucracy." *California Law Review* 104, no. 4 (August 2016): 881–948. https://www.jstor.org/stable/24758740.

Gertner, Nancy. "Complicated Process." *Yale Law Journal Forum* 125 (2016). www.yalelawjournal. org.

———. "Sex, Lies, and Justice." *America Prospect*, January 12, 2015. https://prospect.org/.

Gessen, Masha. "Al Franken's Resignation and the Selective Force of #MeToo." *New Yorker*, December 7, 2017. www.newyorker.com.

———. "An NYU Sexual Harassment Case Has Spurred a New Conversation about #MeToo." *New Yorker*, August 25, 2018. www.newyorker.com.

———. "Sex, Consent, and the Dangers of Misplaced Scale." *New Yorker*, November 27, 2017. www. newyorker.com.

———. "When Does a Watershed Become a Sex Panic?" *New Yorker*, November 14, 2018.

Gilbert, Sophie. "No, #MeToo Isn't McCarthyism." *Atlantic*, January 13, 2018. www.theatlantic. com.

Gluckman, Nell. "How a Letter Defending Avital Ronell Sparked Confusion and Condemnation." *Chronicle of Higher Education*, June 12, 2018.

Goktepe, Katherine. "Review: A Theory of Regret." *Contemporary Political Theory* 18 (2019): 202–5.

Goldhill, Olivia. "Feminist Scholars Argue a Title IX Case Is Unfair." *Authory*, June 12, 2018. www. authory.com.

Goodmark, Leigh. *Decriminalizing Domestic Violence*. Berkeley: University of California Press, 2018.

———. "Restorative Justice as Feminist Practice." *International Journal of Restorative Justice* 1, no. 3 (October 2018): 372–84.

Gottschalk, Marie. *The Prison and the Gallows: The Politics of Mass Incarceration in America*. Philadelphia: University of Pennsylvania Press, 2012.

Grady, Constance. "The Waves of Feminism, and Why People Keep Fighting over Them, Explained." *Vox*, July 20, 2018. www.vox.com.

———. "Why *Handmaid's Tale* Author Margaret Atwood Is Facing #MeToo Backlash." *Vox*, January 17, 2018. www.vox.com.

Grant, Melissa Gira. "No Justice for Harvey Weinstein's Victims." *New Republic*, March 10, 2020. https://newrepublic.com.

Gray, Emma. "On Aziz Ansari and Sex That Feels Violating Even When It's Not Criminal." *Huffington Post*, January 1, 2016. www.huffingtonpost.com.

Greenberg, Zoe. "What Happens to #MeToo When a Feminist Is Accused?" *New York Times*, August 13, 2018. www.nytimes.com.

Greenfield, Scott. "Prof. Avital Ronell and the Lie of the Feminist Academy." *Simple Justice: A Criminal Law Defense Blog*. August 14, 2018. https://blog.simplejustice.us/2018/08/14/ prof-avital-ronell-and-the-lie-of-the-feminist-academy/.

Gruber, Aya. "The Feminist War on Crime." *Iowa Law Review* 92 (2007): 742.

———. *The Feminist War on Crime: The Unexpected Role of Women's Liberation in Mass Incarceration*. Berkeley: University of California Press, 2020.

———. "Sex Wars as Proxy Wars." *Critical Analysis of Law* 6, no. 1 (2019): 102–34.

Halberstam, Jack (@Jhalberstam). *In a Queer Time and Place: Transgender Bodies, Subcultural Lives*. New York: NYU Press, 2005.

———. "Straight Eye for the Queer Theorist: A Review of Queer Theory without Normativity." *Bully Bloggers*, September 12, 2016. https://bullybloggers.wordpress.com.

———. "This is a clear, politically savvy take on the Ronell case by Lisa Duggan. Enough of the he said/she said, let's move to the analysis. Enough twitter outrage, and facebook high horse, read this, circulate and get real!!" Twitter, August 18, 2018. Screen shot available at. https:// www.thecut.com/2018/08/avital-ronell-professor-accused-of-harassment-what-to-know.html.

Halley, Janet. "A Call to Reform the New Harvard University Sexual Harassment Policy and Procedures." Harvard Law School Student Organizations, October 28, 2014. https://orgs.law. harvard.edu.

———. "Harvard's New Sexual Harassment Policy Must Change." *Cognoscenti*, November 14, 2014. Wbur.org.cognoscenti.

———. "The Move to Affirmative Consent." *Signs: Journal of Women in Culture and Society* 42 (2016): 257–79.

———. *Split Decisions: How and Why to Take a Break from Feminism*. Princeton, NJ: Princeton University Press, 2006.

———. "Trading the Megaphone for the Gavel in Title IX Enforcement." *Harvard Law Review Forum* 128 (2015): 103–17.

Halley, Janet, Prabha Kotiswaran, Rachel Rebouché, and Hila Shamir. *Governance Feminism: An Introduction*. Minneapolis: University of Minnesota Press, 2018.

Halperin, David. "Introduction." In *The War on Sex*. Edited by David Halperin and Trevor Hoppe. Durham, NC: Duke University Press, 2017.

———. *Saint Foucault: Towards a Gay Hagiography*. Oxford: Oxford University Press, 1995.

Halperin, David, and Trevor Hoppe, eds. *The War on Sex*. Durham, NC: Duke University Press, 2017.

Haneke, Michael. "Michael Haneke: #MeToo Has Led to a Witch Hunt Coloured by a Hatred of Men." *Guardian*, February 12, 2018. www.theguardian.com.

Hansen, Ellis. "The Future's Eve: Reparative Reading after Sedgewick." *South Atlantic Quarterly* 110, no. 1 (2011): 101–19.

Harding, Kate. "I Am a Feminist. I Study Rape. And I Don't Want Al Franken to Resign." *Washington Post*, November 17, 2017. www.washingtonpost.com.

———. "The Intergenerational Feminist Divide over #MeToo Is Painful but Necessary." *NBC News*, January 20, 2018. www.nbcnews.com.

Harris, Aisha. "She Founded Me Too: Now She Wants to Move Past the Trauma." *New York Times*, October 15, 2018. www.nytimes.com.

Harvard Law Professors. "Press Release Re: *The Hunting Ground*." November 23, 2015.

Harvard Law School. *HLS Sexual Harassment Resources and Procedures for Students* (December 18, 2014).

Harvard University. "Procedures for Handling Complaints involving Students Pursuant to the Sexual and Gender-Based Harassment Policy." July 1, 2014. https://perma.cc.

"Harvey Weinstein's Attorney Blasts Asia Argento: You're a Hypocrite." *TMZ*, August 20, 2018. www.tmz.com.

Hayes, Chris, and Mariame Kaba. "Prison Abolition with Mariame Kaba." *Justice in America Podcast*. March 20, 2019.

Heath, Melanie, Julia Gouweloos, and Jessica Braimoh. "Judging Women's Sexual Agency: Contemporary Sex Wars in the Legal Terrain of Prostitution and Polygamy." *Sings* 42, no. 1 (Autumn 2016).

Henry, Astrid. *Not My Mother's Sister: Generational Conflict and Third-Wave Feminism*. Bloomington: Indiana University Press, 2004. https://doi.org/10.1080/00497878.1996.9979142.

Hernroth-Rothstein, Annika. "#MeToo and Trial by Mob." *National Review*, October 27, 2017. www.nationalreview.com.

Heywood, Leslie, and Jennifer Drake, eds. *Third Wave Agenda: Being Feminist, Doing Feminism*. Minneapolis: University of Minnesota Press, 1997.

Hornaday, Ann. "Review: *The Hunting Ground* Lucidly Investigates the Issue of Campus Rape." *Washington Post*, March 12, 2015. www.washingtonpost.com.

Horton, Helena. "Germaine Greer Criticises Whingeing MeToo Movement." *Guardian*, January 23, 2018. www.telegraph.co.uk.

H.R. Report of the Committee on Ethics: In the Matter of Allegations Relating to Representative Ruben Kihuen, 115th Cong., 2nd sess. (November 16, 2018).

Hudson, Barbara. "Restorative Justice and the Challenge of Sexual and Racial Violence." *Journal of Law and Society* 25, no. 2 (June 1998): 237–56.

———. "Restorative Justice and Gendered Violence: Diversion or Effective Justice." *British Journal of Criminology* 42, no. 3 (Summer 2002): 616–34.

Hudson, Laura (@laura_hudson). "Forget the Backlash: We Need #MeToo Now More Than Ever." *Verge*, January 15, 2018. www.theverge.com.

———. "I have great respect for the contributions that many older women made to the feminist movement, at times when it was harder than I have ever experienced. It is also time for them to listen, to learn, to step aside." Twitter. January 17, 2018.

Hunter, Nan, and Sylvia A. Law. "Brief Amici Curiae of Feminist Anti-Censorship Taskforce, et al., in *American Booksellers Association v. Hudnut*." *University of Michigan Journal of Law Reform* 21, no. 1 (1988): 6.

———. "Sex Baiting and Dangerous Bedfellows." *Off Our Backs* 15, no. 7 (July 1985). www.jstor.org/stable/25794670.

INCITE! "About: Principles of Unity." https://incite-national.org. Accessed August 1, 2020.

Irvine, Janice. "Interview with Carole Vance." *Sojourner*, December 1985, 18.

"Is There a Generational Divide in the #MeToo Movement?" *Current*. CBC, January 16, 2018.

Itzkoff, David. "Louis C.K. Admits to Sexual Misconduct as Media Companies Cut Ties." *New York Times*, November 10, 2017. www.nytimes.com.

Jagose, Annamarie. "The Trouble with Anti-Normativity." *differences: A Journal of Feminist Critical Studies* 26, no. 1 (2015): 26–47. doi.org/10.1215/10407391-2880591.

Jean, Alison (@jalison100). "Yes when you prioritize your powerful male friend over sexual assault/harassment victims you are in fact a bad feminist." Twitter, January 13, 2018.

Johnson, Merri Lisa, ed. *Jane Sexes It Up: True Confessions of Feminist Desire*. New York: Four Walls, Eight Windows, 2002.

Joseph, Paul. "The Verdict from the Porch: Zora Neale Hurston and Reparative Justice." *American Literature* 74, no. 3 (September 2002): 455–83.

Kaminer, Wendy. "Beware Vigilante Feminism." *Boston Globe*, October 27, 2017. www.bostonglobe.com.

———. "Where We Stand on the First Amendment: Women against Pornography." *Aegis: Magazine on Ending Violence against Women*, September/October 1979, 52–53.

Kantor, Jodie, and Megan Twohey. "Harvey Weinstein Paid Off Sexual Harassment Accusers for Decades." *New York Times*, October 5, 2017. www.nytimes.com.

Kantor, Jodi, Megan Twohey, Grace Ashford, Catrin Einhorn, and Ellen Gabler. "'Finally': Ashley Judd and Other Weinstein Accusers Respond to the Verdict." *New York Times*, February 24, 2020. www.nytimes.com.

Karaian, Lara. "Lolita Speaks: 'Sexting,' Teenage Girls, and the Law." *Crime, Media, Culture* 8, no. 1 (2012): 57–73.

———. "Policing 'Sexting': Responsibilization, Respectability, and Sexual Subjectivity in Child Protection/Crime Prevention Responses to Teenagers' Digital Sexual Expression." *Criminology and Criminal Justice* 18, no. 3 (2013).

Kassam, Ashifa. "Margaret Atwood Faces Feminist Backlash on Social Media over #MeToo." *Guardian*, January 15, 2018. www.theguardian.com.

Khan, Ummni. *Vicarious Kinks: S/M in the Socio Legal Imaginary*. Toronto: University of Toronto Press, 2014.

Kilkenny, Katie. "Ashleigh Banfield Escalates Feud with Reporter of Aziz Ansari Story." *Hollywood Reporter*, January 17, 2018. www.hollywoodreporter.com.

Kim, Mimi E. "The Carceral Creep: Gender-Based Violence, Race, and the Expansion of the Punitive State, 1973–1983." *Social Problems* 67, no. 2 (May 2020): 251–69.

———. "From Carceral Feminism to Transformative Justice: Women of Color Feminism and Alternatives to Incarceration." *Journal of Ethnic & Cultural Diversity in Social Work* 27 (2018): 219–33.

Kipnis, Laura. *Bound and Gagged: Pornography and the Politics of Fantasy in America*. Durham, NC: Duke University Press, 1999.

———. "My Title IX Inquisition." *Chronicle of Higher Education*, May 29, 2015. www.chronicle.com.

———. "Sexual Paranoia Strikes Academe." *Chronicle of Higher Education*, February 27, 2015. www.chronicle.com.

———. *Unwanted Advances: Sexual Paranoia Comes to Campus*. New York: HarperCollins, 2017.

Klein, Ezra. "Rebecca Traister on the Coming #MeToo Backlash." *Vox*, December 20, 2017. www.vox.com.

Kohn, Laurie S. "#MeToo, Wrongs against Women, and Restorative Justice." *Kansas Journal of Law & Public Policy* 28, no. 3 (Summer 2019): 561–86.

Kraus, Chris. "Dialing: Back: Darkness." *Theory Illuminati*, August 19, 2018. https://theoryilluminati.com/.

Krauss, Rosalind. "Photography's Discursive Spaces: Landscape/View." *Art Journal* 42, no. 4 (1982): 311–19.

Kushner, Rachel. "Is Prison Necessary? Ruth Wilson Gilmore Might Change Your Mind." *New York Times*, April 17, 2019. www.nytimes.com.

Leach, Katie. "Bill Maher: Al Franken Doesn't Deserve to Be 'Lumped In' with Roy Moore, Harvey Weinstein." *Washington Examiner*, November 18, 2017. www.washingtonexaminer.com.

"Leaflet," in "Notes and Letters." *Feminist Studies* 9, no. 1 (Spring 1983): 180–82.

Lederer, Laura, ed. *Take Back the Night: Women on Pornography.* New York: William Morrow, 1980.

Lee, M. J. "Army Veteran Says Franken Groped Her during USO Tour." CNN, November 30, 2017. www.cnn.com.

Lee Kong, Stacey. "Yes, Margaret Atwood Is a Bad Feminist: Here's Why." *Flare Magazine,* January 15, 2018. www.flare.com.

Leidholdt, Dorchen. Quoted in Nan Hunter, "Modern McCarthyism." *Off Our Backs* 15, no. 11 (December 1985): 26. www.jstor.org/stable/i25775675.

Leiter, Brian. "Blaming the Victim Is Apparently OK When the Accused in a Title IX Proceeding Is a Feminist Literary Theorist." *Leiter Reports, a Philosophy Blog.* June 10, 2018. https://leiter-reports.typepad.com/blog/2018/06/blaming-the-victim-is-apparently-ok-when-the-accused-is-a-feminist-literary-theorist.html.

Lemke, Thomas. "'The Birth of Bio-politics': Michel Foucault's Lecture at the Collège de France on Neo-liberal Governmentality." *Economy and Society* 190 (2001): 201.

Levi, Margaret. "A Model, a Method, and a Map: The Model of Rational Choice." In *Comparative Politics: Rationality, Culture, and Structure.* Edited by Mark Lichbach and Alan Zuckerman. Cambridge: Cambridge University Press, 1997.

Levine, Judith. "Sympathy for the Devil: Why Progressives Haven't Helped the Sex Offender, Why They Should, and How They Can." In *The War on Sex.* Edited by David Halperin and Trevor Hoppe. Durham, NC: Duke University Press, 2017.

———. "Will Feminism's Past Mistakes Haunt #MeToo?" *Boston Review,* December 8, 2017. http://bostonreview.net.

Lexico: Oxford English and Spanish Dictionary, online edition, s.v. "2.0.," accessed August 1, 2020. https://en.oxforddictionaries.com.

Linden, Emily (@EmilyLindin). "Sorry. If some innocent men's reputations have to take a hit in the process of undoing the patriarchy, that is a price I am absolutely willing to pay." Twitter, November 21, 2017. https://twitter.com/EmilyLindin/status/933074980627030016.

Livingstone, Josephine. "Asia Argento, Avital Ronell, and the Integrity of #MeToo." *New Republic,* August 21, 2018. https://newrepublic.com.

Long Chu, Andrea. "I Worked with Avital Ronell: I Believe Her Accuser." *Chronicle of Higher Education,* August 30, 2018. www.chronicle.com.

Lorde, Audre. "The Uses of Anger." Lecture, National Women's Studies Association Conference, 1981.

Louis, Beatrice. "Not in the Name of Feminism: Nothing about the Defense of Professor Avital Ronell Is Feminist." *Uncommon Ground Media,* August 15, 2018. https://conatusnews.com/.

Love, Heather. *Feeling Backwards: Loss and the Politics of Queer History.* Cambridge, MA: Harvard University Press, 2007.

———. "Truth and Consequences: On Paranoid and Reparative Reading." *Criticism* 52, no. 1 (2010): 235–41.

Luciano, Dana, and Mel Y. Chen. "Queer Inhumanisms." *GLQ, A Journal of Gay and Lesbian Studies* 25, no. 1 (January 2019): 113–17.

MacKinnon, Catharine A. *Butterfly Politics.* Berkeley: University of California Press, 2017.

———. "Feminism, Marxism, Method, and the State: Toward Feminist Jurisprudence." *Signs* 8, no. 4 (Summer 1983): 635–58. www.jstor.org/stable/3173687.

———. "Liberalism and the Death of Feminism" (1990). In *The Sexual Liberals and the Attack on Feminism (Athene Series),* 3–13. Edited by Dorchen Leidholdt and Janice G. Raymond. Oxford: Pergamon Press, 1990.

———. "Rape Redefined." *Harvard Law and Policy Review* 10 (2016): 431–77.

———. *Toward a Feminist Theory of the State*. Cambridge, MA: Harvard University Press, 1989.

———. "Women and the Law: Omissions." *Off Our Backs* 15, no. 8 (August–September 1985): 32.

———. *Women's Lives, Men's Laws*. Cambridge, MA: Belknap Press of Harvard University Press. 2005.

MacKinnon, Catharine, and Andrea Dworkin, eds. *In Harm's Way: The Pornography Civil Rights Hearings*. Cambridge, MA: Harvard University Press, 1998.

Mangan, Katherine. "Battle over Alleged Harassment Escalates as Former Graduate Student Sues Profesor and NYU." *Chronicle of Higher Education*, August 16, 2018. www.chronicle.com.

———. "New Disclosures about NYU Professor Reignite a War over Gender and Harassment." *Chronicle of Higher Education*, August 15, 2018. www.chronicle.com.

———. "NYU Scholar Accused of Harassment Assails Rush to Judgment as Sign of 'Sexual Paranoia.'" *Chronicle of Higher Education*, August 17, 2018. www.chronicle.com.

———. "Scholars' Defense of an Accused Colleague Feels Eerily Familiar Except for One Thing: Her Gender." *Chronicle of Higher Education*, June 19, 2018. www.chronicle.com.

Manning, Jane. Women's Equal Justice Project, qtd. in Kantor et al., "'Finally': Ashley Judd and Other Weinstein Accusers Respond to the Verdict." *New York Times*, February 24, 2020. www.nytimes.com.

Marcotte, Amanda. "What Drove the *New Yorker*'s Jane Mayer into Al Franken Denialism?" *Salon*, July 22, 2019. www.salon.com.

Marcus, Sharon. "Fighting Bodies, Fighting Words." In *Feminists Theorize the Political*. Edited by Judith Butler and Joan W. Scott. New York: Routledge, 1992.

Mardorossian, Carine. "Towards a New Theory of Rape." *Signs* 27, no. 3 (Spring 2002): 743–75.

Martinez HoSang, Daniel. *Racial Propositions: Ballot Initiatives and the Making of Postwar California*. Berkeley: University of California Press, 2010.

Mayer, Jane. "The Case of Al Franken." *New Yorker*, July 29, 2019. www.newyorker.com.

McCallum, E. L., and Tyler Bradway. "Introduction: Thinking Sideways; or, An Untoward Genealogy of Queer Reading." In *After Queer Studies: Literature, Theory, and Sexuality in the 21st Century*. Cambridge: Cambridge University Press, 2019.

McCarthy, Connor. "Reparations under the Rome Statute of the International Criminal Court and Reparative Justice Theory." *International Journal of Transitional Justice* 3, no. 2 (2009): 250.

McCartney, Jenny. "The New Feminist War: Young Women vs Old Women." *Spectator*, January 27, 2018. www.spectator.co.uk.

McDonald, Sonya Nadia. "Columbia Student Emma Sulkowicz Carried Mattress to Protest Campus Rape: Now She's Attending the State of the Union." *Washington Post*, January 20, 2015. www.washingtonpost.com.

———. "It's Hard to Ignore a Woman Toting a Mattress Everywhere, Which Is Why Emma Sulkowicz Is Still Doing It." *Washington Post*, October 29, 2014. www.washingtonpost.com.

McElroy, Wendy. *XXX: A Woman's Right to Pornography*. New York: St. Martin's Press, 1997.

Me Too Movement. "About: History and Vision." Updated February 24, 2020. https://metoomvmt.org.

Merkin, Daphne. "Publicly, We Say #MeToo: Privately, We Have Misgivings." *New York Times*, January 5, 2018. www.nytimes.com.

Minow, Martha. "Chapter 1: The Dilemma of Difference." *Making All the Difference: Inclusion, Exclusion, and American Law*. Ithaca, NY: Cornell University Press, 1990.

Mishra, Pankaj. *The Age of Anger: A History of the Present*. New York: Farrar, Strauss, and Giroux, 2017.

Morgan, Robin. "Theory and Practice: Pornography and Rape." *Going Too Far: The Personal Chronicle of a Feminist.* New York: Random House, 1978.

Morgan, Robin, and Kathleen Barry. "Letter." In "Politics, Feminism, and the Constitution: The Anti-Pornography Movement in Minneapolis." Edited by Paul Brest and Ann Vandenberg. *Stanford Law Review* 39, no. 3 (February 1987): 607–61.

Mumford, Gwilym. "Woody Allen Forced to Clarify Comments about 'Sad' Harvey Weinstein." *New York Times*, October 16, 2017. www.theguardian.com.

Muñoz, José Esteban. *Cruising Utopia: The Then and There of Queer Futurity.* New York: NYU Press, 2009.

Murphy, Colleen. "The Ethics of Diversity in Transitional Settings." *Georgetown Journal of Law and Public Policy* 16 (Fall 2018).

Nash, Jennifer. *Black Feminism Reimagined: After Intersectionality.* Durham, NC: Duke University Press, 2019.

Nestle, Joan. Quoted in Tacie Dejanikus, "Charges of Exclusion and McCarthyism at Barnard Conference." *Off Our Backs* 12, no. 6 (June 1982).

Nicholson, Linda. "Feminism in 'Waves': Useful Metaphor or Not." *New Politics* 12, no. 4 (Winter 2010).

Nolan, Megan. "I'm Relieved Harvey Weinstein Is Going to Prison—but I Can't Bring Myself to Be Happy about It." *New Statesman*, March 4, 2020. www.newstatesman.com.

Nwanevu, Osita. "There Is No Rampaging #MeToo Mob." *Slate*, January 16, 2018. https://slate.com.

Nyong'o, Tavia. "Trapped in the Closet with Eve." *Criticism* 52, no. 2, Honoring Eve (Spring 2010): 243–51.

O'Hehir, Andrew. "When a Woman Is Accused of Sexual Misconduct: The Strange Case of Avital Ronell." *Salon*, August 18, 2018. www.salon.com.

"Open Counter-Letter about the Steven Galloway Case at UBC." Petition Update, Change.org, updated January 16, 2018. www.change.org.

Osez le Féminisme (@osezlefeminisme). "Révoltant. À rebours de la prise de conscience actuelle, des femmes défendent l'impunité des agresseurs et attaquent les féministes," Twitter. January 9, 2018, 7:23 a.m.

"'Our Pain Is Never Prioritized': #MeToo Founder Tarana Burke Says We Must Listen to 'Untold' Stories of Minority Women." *Time*, April 23, 2019. https://time.com.

Pellegrini, Ann. "#MeToo: Before and After." *Studies in Gender and Sexuality* 19, no. 4 (2018): 262–64.

Pérez-Peña, Richard. "College Groups Connect to Fight Sexual Assault." *New York Times*, March 19, 2013. www.nytimes.com.

———. "Student's Account Has Rape in Spotlight." *New York Times*, October 26, 2012. www.nytimes.com.

Pérez-Peña, Richard, and Kate Taylor. "Fight against Sexual Assaults Holds Colleges to Account." *New York Times*, May 3, 2014. www.nytimes.com.

Peyser, Andrea. "#MeToo Has Lumped Trivial In with Legitimate Sexual Assault." *New York Post*, November 17, 2017. https://nypost.com.

Phipps, Alison. "'Every Woman Knows a Weinstein': Political Whiteness and White Woundedness in #MeToo and Public Feminisms around Sexual Violence." *Feminist Formations* 31, no. 2 (2019): 1–25.

———. *Me, Not You: The Trouble with Mainstream Feminism.* Mancheste, UK: Manchester University Press, 2020.

———. "The Political Whiteness of #MeToo." *Red Pepper*, June 4, 2019. www.redpepper.org.

———. "Sex Wars Revisited: A Rhetorical Economy of Sex Industry Opposition." *Journal of International Women's Studies* 18, no. 4 (August 2017).

Piepmeier, Alison, and Rory Cooke Dicker, eds. *Catching a Wave: Reclaiming Feminism for the 21st Century*. Boston: Northeastern University Press, 2003.

Pierson, Paul. "Increasing Returns, Path Dependence, and the Study of Politics." *American Political Science Review* 94, no. 2 (2000): 251–52.

"'Les porcs et leurs allie.e.s. ont raison de s'inquiéter': Caroline de Haas et des militantes féministes répondent à la tribune publiée dans 'Le Monde.'" *Franceinfo*, January 10, 2018. www.francetvinfo.fr.

Powell, Michael. "Trump Overhaul of Campus Sexual Assault Rule Wins Surprising Support." *New York Times*, June 25, 2020. www.nytimes.com.

Price, Brian. *A Theory of Regret*. Durham, NC: Duke University Press, 2017.

"Project." Everyday Sexism Project. https://everydaysexism.com. Updated May 6, 2020.

Puente, Maria. "Kevin Spacey Complete List of 13 Accusers." *USA Today*, November 7, 2017. www.usatoday.com.

"Read Al Franken's Apology Following Accusation of Groping and Kissing without Consent." CNN, November 17, 2017. www.cnn.com.

Reinke, Rachel. "Catfight: A Feminist Analysis." *Chrestomathy* 9 (2010): 162–85. http://chrestomathy.cofc.edu.

Rich, Adrienne. "We Don't Have to Come Apart over Pornography." *Off Our Backs* 15, no. 7 (July 1985): 30, 32.

Richie, Beth. *Arrested Justice: Black Women, Violence, and America's Prison Nation*. New York: NYU Press, 2012.

———. "Reimagining the Movement to End Gender Violence: Anti-Racism, Prison Abolition, Women of Color Feminisms, and Other Radical Visions of Justice." *University of Miami Race & Social Justice Review* (2015).

Richie, Beth, and Ruth Gilmore. *Golden Gulag: Prisons, Surplus, Crisis, and Opposition in Globalizing California*. Berkeley: University of California Press, 2006.

Richie, Beth, and Kayla Martenson. "Resisting Carcerality, Embracing Abolition: Implications for Feminist Social Work Practice." *Affilia: Journal of Women and Social Work* 35, no. 1 (January 2020): 12–16.

Roberts, Dorothy. "Abolition Constitutionalism." *Harvard Law Review* 133 (2019).

Robinson, Amy Elizabeth. "On Power and Aporia in the Academy: A Response in Three Parts." *Medium*, August 19, 2018. https://medium.com.

Rodríguez, Juana María. *Sexual Futures, Queer Gestures, and Other Latina Longings*. New York: NYU Press, 2014.

Roiphe, Katie. *The Morning After: Sex, Fear, and Feminism on Campus*. Boston: Little, Brown, 1993.

Rojas, Clarissa, Mimi Kim, and Alissa Bierra. "Introduction: Community Accountability; Emerging Movements to Transform Violence." *Social Justice* 37, no. 4 (2011): 1–11.

"Rose McGowan Reacts to Asia Argento Reportedly Paying Off Assault Accusers." *Hollywood Reporter*, August 20, 2018. www.hollywoodreporter.com.

Rose, Nikolas. *Powers of Freedom*. Cambridge: Cambridge University Press, 1999.

Rose, Nikolas, and Peter Miller. *Governing the Present: Administering Economic, Social, and Personal Life*. New York: Wiley, 2008.

Rubin, Corey. "The Unsexy Truth about the Avital Ronell Scandal." *Chronicle of Higher Education*, August 20, 2018. www.chronicle.com.

Rubin, Gayle. "'Blood under the Bridge': Reflections on Thinking Sex." *GLQ* 17, no. 1 (2011): 15–48.

———. *Deviations: A Gayle Rubin Reader*. Durham, NC: Duke University Press, 2011.

———. *Social Perspectives in Lesbian and Gay Studies*. New York: Routledge, 1998.

———. "Thinking Sex: Notes for a Radical Theory of the Politics of Sexuality." In *Pleasure and Danger: Toward a Politics of Sexuality*. Edited by Carole Vance. Boston: Routledge and K. Paul, 1984.

Russell, Diana E. H. "Pornography and the Women's Liberation Movement." In *Take Back the Night*, 304. Edited by Laura Lederer. New York: William Morrow, 1980.

Ryzik, Melena, Cara Buckley, and Jodi Kantor. "Louis CK Is Accused by Five Women of Sexual Misconduct." *New York Times*, November 9, 2017. www.nytimes.com.

Safronova, Valeriya. "Catherine Deneuve and Others Denounce the #MeToo Movement." *New York Times*, January 9, 2018. www.nytimes.com.

Sanders McDonagh, Erin, and Elena Vacchelli. "The Rebirth of Feminism? Situating Feminism in the Popular Imaginary." Lecture presented at Middlesex University Symposium, October 2013.

Schor, Naomi, and Elizabeth Weed, eds. *Feminism Meets Queer Theory*. Bloomington: Indiana University Press, 1997.

Schulte, Elizabeth. "The Myth of the #MeToo Panic." *Socialist Worker*, April 19, 2018. https://socialistworker.org.

Sedgwick, Eve Kosofsky. *Epistemology of the Closet*. Berkeley: University of California Press, 1990.

———. "Introduction." In *Touching Feeling: Affect, Pedagogy, Performativity*. Durham, NC: Duke University Press, 2003.

———. "Paranoid Reading and Reparative Reading; or, You Are So Paranoid You Probably Think This Introduction Is about You" (1995). In *Touching Feeling: Affect, Pedagogy, Performativity*. Durham, NC: Duke University Press, 2003.

———. *Touching Feeling: Affect, Pedagogy, Performativity*. Durham, NC: Duke University Press, 2003.

Seitler, Dana. *Reading Sideways*. New York: Fordham University Press, 2019.

Serisier, Tanya. *Feminism, Rape, and Narrative Politics*. London: Palgrave MacMillan, 2018.

Setoodeh, Ramin, and Elizabeth Wagmeister. "Matt Lauer Accused of Sexual Harassment by Multiple Women." *Variety*, November 29, 2017. https://variety.com.

Severson, Kim. "Asia Argento, a #MeToo Leader, Made a Deal with Her Accuser." *New York Times*, August 19, 2018. www.nytimes.com.

Shaffrir, Doree. "What to Do with 'Shitty Media Men?'" *Buzzfeed News*, October 12, 2017. www.buzzfeed.com.

Shaw, Adrienne, and Katherine Sender. "Queer Technologies: Affordances, Affect, and Ambivalence." *Critical Studies in Media Communication* 33, no. 1 (2016): 1–5. https://doi.org/10.1080/15295036.2015.1129429.

Siibak, Andra, and Nicoletta Vittadini. "Editorial: Introducing Four Empirical Examples of the 'Generationing' Process." *Cyberpsychology: Journal of Psychosocial Research on Cyberspace* 6, no. 2 (2012). https://doi.org/10.5817/CP2012-2-1.

Silman, Ann. "Aziz Ansari, 'Cat Person,' and the #MeToo Backlash." *The Cut*, January 16, 2018. www.thecut.com.

Singal, Jess. "*The Hunting Ground* Uses a Striking Statistic about Campus Rape That's Almost Certainly False." *New York Magazine*, November 23, 2015. www.thecut.com.

Smith, Roberta. "In a Mattress, a Lever for Art and Political Protest." *New York Times*, September 21, 2014. www.nytimes.com.

Snyder, Claire R. "What Is Third-Wave Feminism? A New Directions Essay." *Signs* 34, no. 1 (2008). https://doi:10.1086/588436.

Solomon, Deborah. "Questions for Jessica Valenti: Fourth-Wave Feminism." *New York Times*, November 15, 2009. www.nytimes.com.

Sommers, Christina Hoff (@ChristinaHoffSommers). "Oh no! Mr. Reitman accused his former N.Y.U. grad school adviser, Avital Ronell, of sexually harassing him, & NYU found her responsible. But some leading feminist scholars have supported her in ways that echo the defenses of male harassers. #metoo." Twitter, August 13, 2018, 11:18 p.m. https://twitter.com/CHSommers/status/1029205529707667458.

———. *Who Stole Feminism? How Women Have Betrayed Women*. New York: Simon & Schuster, 1994.

Sontag, Susan. *On Photography*. New York: Farrar, Strauss, and Giroux, 1977.

Steinem, Gloria. "Erotica and Pornography: A Clear and Present Difference." In *Take Back the Night*. Edited by Laura Lederer. New York: William Morrow, 1980.

Stewart, Emily. "Trump Wants 'Due Process' for Abuse Allegations: I Asked 8 Legal Experts What That Means." *Vox*, February 12, 2018. www.vox.com.

Stockton Bond, Kathryn. "Queer Theory." *The Year's Work in Critical and Cultural Theory* 24, no. 1 (May 2016): 85–106. https://doi.org/10.1093/ywcct/mbw005.

Stringer, Rebecca. *Knowing Victims: Feminism, Agency, and Victim Politics in Neo-Liberal Times*. New York: Routledge, 2014.

———. "Vulnerability after Wounding: Feminism, Rape Law, and the Differend." *SubStance* 42, no. 3 (2013): 148–68.

Strossen, Nadine. *Defending Pornography: Free Speech, Sex, and the Fight for Women's Rights*. New York: Scribner's, 1995.

Suk Gersen, Jeannie. "Betsy DeVos, Title IX, and the 'Both Sides' Approach to Sexual Assault." *New Yorker Magazine*, September 8, 2017.

———. "Laura Kipnis's Endless Trial by Title IX." *New Yorker*, September 20, 2017. www.newyorker.com.

———. "Shutting Down Conversations about Rape at Harvard Law." *New Yorker*, December 11, 2015. www.newyorker.com.

Sulkowicz, Emma. "My Rapist Is Still on Campus." *Time Magazine*, May 15, 2014. www.times.com.

Sullivan, Andrew. "It's Time to Resist the Excesses of #MeToo." *New York Magazine*, January 12, 2018. https://nymag.com.

"Summary of Major Provisions of the Department of Education's Title IX Final Rule." Office for Civil Rights. https://www2.ed.gov.

Swertlow, Meg. "Aziz Ansari Releases Statement after Being Accused of Sexual Misconduct." *ENews*, January 14, 2018. www.eonline.com.

Tagg, John. *The Burden of Representation: Essays on Photographies and Histories*. Minneapolis: University of Minnesota Press, 1988.

———. "The Currency of the Photography." In *Thinking Photography*. Edited by Victor Burgin. London: MacMillan, 1982.

———. *Grounds of Dispute: Art History, Cultural Politics, and the Discursive Field*. Minneapolis: University of Minnesota Press, 1992.

———. "Mindless Photography." In *Photography: Theoretical Snapshots*. Edited by J. J. Long, Andrea Noble, and Edward Welch. New York: Routledge 2009.

Tambe, Ashwini. "Reckoning with the Silences of #MeToo." *Feminist Studies* 44, no. 1 (2018): 197–203.

Taylor, Chloë. "Anti-Carceral Feminism and Sexual Assault—a Defense: A Critique of the Critique of the Critique of Carceral Feminism." *Social Philosophy Today* 34 (2018): 29–49.

Taylor, Kate. "Mattress Protest at Columbia University Continues into Graduation Event." *New York Times*, May 19, 2015. www.nytimes.com.

Teachout, Zephyr. "I'm Not Convinced Al Franken Should Quit." *New York Times*, December 11, 2017. www.nytimes.com.

Terry, Brandon M., and Judith Butler. "The Radical Equality of Lives." *Boston Review*, January 7, 2020. www.bostonreview.net.

Terwiel, Anna. "What Is Carceral Feminism?" *Political Theory* 48, no. 4 (2020). https://doi.org/10.1177/0090591719889946.

Thorkelson, Erika (@ethorkel). "If @MargaretAtwood would like to stop warring amongst women, she should stop declaring war against younger, less powerful women and start listening." Twitter, January 13, 2018, 12:11 p.m. https://twitter.com/ethorkel/status/.

Tolentino, Jia. "The Rising Pressure of the #MeToo Backlash." *New Yorker*, January 24, 2018. www.newyorker.com.

Traister, Rebecca. "Fury Is a Political Weapon: And Women Need to Wield It." *New York Times*, September 29, 2018. www.nytimes.com.

———. *Good and Mad; The Revolutionary Power of Women's Anger*. New York: Simon & Schuster, 2018.

———. "This Moment Isn't (Just) about Sex." *New York Magazine*, December 11, 2017. www.thecut.com.

Tremblay, Jean-Thomas. "I'm Just Normal." *Arcade: Literature, Humanities, and the World*. Accessed May 15, 2020. https://arcade.stanford.edu.

Trnka, Susanna, and Catherine Trundle. *Competing Responsibilities: The Politics and Ethics of Contemporary Life*. Durham, NC: Duke University Press, 2017.

Tweeden, Leann. "Senator Al Franken Kissed and Groped Me without My Consent, and There's Nothing Funny about It." Interview by Doug McIntyre, *McIntyre in the Morning*. TalkRadio 790 KABC. November 16, 2017.

Valenti, Jessica (@JessicaValenti). "MeToo Is About More Than Stopping Rape: We Want More." *Guardian*, January 31, 2018. www.theguardian.com.

———. "Our standard for sexual behavior has to be more than what's legal or illegal." Twitter, January 31, 2018.

———. "That cheering you hear is the sound of female journalists finally being able to drop the 'alleged' before 'rapist Harvey Weinstein' in their columns." Twitter, February 24, 2020, 12:01 p.m. https://twitter.com/JessicaValenti/status/1231987599616729089.

———. "#YesAllWomen Reveals the Constant Barrage of Sexism That Women Face." *Guardian*, May 28, 2014. www.theguardian.com.

Vance, Carole S. "Conference Statement: The Scholar and the Feminist IX; Towards a Politics of Sexuality." Conference Paper, 1982 Barnard Conference on Sexuality. New York, NY, April 24, 1982. Reproduced in Jane S. Goul, *Juggling: A Memoir of Work, Family, and Feminism*, 236. New York: Feminist Press at CUNY, 1997.

———. "Invitation Letter." September 2, 1981. In *Diary of a Conference*. Edited by Hannah Alderfer, Beth Jaker, and Marybeth Nelson. New York: Faculty Press, 1981. Reproduced in Gayle Rubin, *Deviations: A Gayle Rubin Reader*, 200. Durham, NC: Duke University Press, 2011.

———. "Letter to the Editors." *Feminist Studies* 9, no. 3 (Fall 1983): 590.

———. "More Danger, More Pleasure: Ten Years after the Barnard Sexuality Conference." In *Pleasure and Danger: Exploring Female Sexuality*. Edited by Carole Vance. Baltimore, MD: Pandora Press, 1992.

———. "Petition." *Feminist Studies* 9, no. 3 (Fall 1983): 590.

———, ed. *Pleasure and Danger: Exploring Female Sexuality*. Boston: Routledge and Kegan Paul, 1984.

Vary, Adam B., "Kevin Spacey Made a Sexual Advance against Me When I Was 14." *Buzzfeed News*, October 29, 2017. www.buzzfeednews.com.

Walker, Margaret Urban. *What Is Restorative Justice?* Milwaukee: Marquette University Press, 2010.

Waters, Suzanna Danuta. "Introduction: The Dangers of a Metaphor; Beyond the Battlefield in the Sex Wars." *Signs* 42, no. 1 (Autumn 2011): 1–9. https://doi.org/10.1086/686750.

Way, Katie. "I Went on a Date with Aziz Ansari: It Turned into the Worst Night of My Life." *Babe. net*, January 13, 2018. https://babe.net.

Webber, J. "Forms of Transitional Justice." In *Transitional Justice*. Edited by M. S. Williams, R. Nagy, and J. Elster. New York: NYU Press, 2012.

Webster, Paula. "Pornography and Pleasure." *Heresies: A Feminist Publication on Art and Politics* 12, no. 3 (1981): 48–51.

Weed, Elizabeth. "The Way We Read Now." *History of the Present* 2, no. 1 (2012): 95–106.

Weiss, Bari (@bariweiss). "Are others disturbed by the moral flattening going on? Glenn Thrush/Al Franken should not be mentioned in the same breath as Harvey Weinstein/ Kevin Spacey." Twitter, November 21, 2017, 12:05 p.m. https://twitter.com/bariweiss/ status/933018615347073029.

———. "Asia Argento Proves, Once Again, That Women Are Human Beings: No Gender Has a Monopoly on Hypocrisy or Harm." *New York Times*, August 21, 2018. www.nytimes.com.

———. "Aziz Ansari Is Guilty—of Not Being a Mind Reader." *New York Times*, January 15, 2018. www.nytimes.com.

Weller, Sheila. "#MeToo's Generational Divide." *Time Magazine*, March 12, 2018. https://time.com.

Wenzel, Michael, Tyler G. Okimoto, et al. "Retributive and Restorative Justice." *Law and Human Behavior* 32, no. 5 (2008): 375–89.

West, Lindy. "Yes, This Is a Witch Hunt: I'm a Witch and I'm Hunting You." *New York Times*, October 17, 2017. www.nytimes.com.

Wexler, Lesley, and Jennifer K. Robbenolt. "#MeToo and Restorative Justice." *American Bar Association: Dispute Resolution Magazine*, Winter 2019.

Wexler, Lesley, Jennifer K. Robbenolt, and Colleen Murphy. "#MeToo, Time's Up, and Theories of Justice." *University of Illinois College of Law Legal Studies Research Paper No. 18–14*. University of Illinois College of Law. March 6, 2018. http://doi.org/10.2139/ssrn/3135442.

Whelan, Ella. "A Year of Sexual Unfreedom." *Spiked*, December 22, 2017. www.spiked-online.com.

Wiegman, Robyn. "The Times We're In: Queer Feminist Criticism and the Reparative Turn." *Feminist Theory* 15, no.1 (2014): 4–25.

Wiegman, Robyn, and Elizabeth A. Wilson. "Introduction: Anti-Normativity Queer's Conventions." *differences: A Journal of Feminist Critical Studies* 26, no. 1 (2015): 1–25.

Willis, Ellen. "Classical and Baroque Sex in Everyday Life." *Village Voice*, May 1979.

———. "Feminism, Mortality, and Pornography." In *Powers of Desire: The Politics of Sexuality*. Edited by Ann Snitow, Christine Stansell, and Sharon Thompson. New York: Monthly Review, 1983.

———. "Letter to the Editors." *Feminist Studies* 9, no. 3 (Fall 1983): 594.

Wilson, Elizabeth. "The Context of 'Between Pleasure and Danger': The Barnard Conference on Sexuality." *Feminist Review* 13 (Spring 1983): 35–41.

Wolf, Naomi. *Fire with Fire: The New Female Power and How It Will Change the 21st Century.* New York: Random House, 1994.

Wong, Ester. "What Are We to Make of the Case of Scholar Avital Ronell?" *Jezebel*, August 17, 2018. https://jezebel.com.

Wright, Jennifer. "The Backlash to Believing Women Has Begun." *Bazaar Magazine*, November 30, 2017. www.harpersbazaar.com.

Wulfhorst, Ellen. "Could Fear of #MeToo Backlash Silence Women's Voices?" *Reuters*, December 12, 2017. www.reuters.com.

Wypijewski, Joann. "What We Don't Talk about When We talk about #MeToo." *Nation*, February 22, 2018. www.thenation.com.

Yoffe, Emily. "How *The Hunting Ground* Blurs the Truth." *Slate*, June 1, 2015. https://slate.com.

———. "*The Hunting Ground*: The Failures of a New Documentary about Rape on College Campuses." *Slate*, February 27, 2015. https://slate.com.

———. "Why the #MeToo Movement Should be Ready for a Backlash." *Politico*, December 10, 2017. www.politico.com.

Zehr, Howard. *The Little Book of Restorative Justice.* New York: Good Books, 2002.

INDEX

Aberrations in Black (Ferguson), 131
abolition feminism, 168–70
abolition politics, 176, 232n49, 234n90
Abrams, Kathryn, 68, 70, 221n138
abuse: child sexual, 93, 132–33; of power, 12, 23; sexual, 93, 125, 132–33; sex worker, 193
accountability, 12, 95, 160–61, 164, 170, 179; anger and, 202; community, 174; offender, 171–72, 173, 178; UBC accountability letter, 25–26
accusations, 108; public, 17
Achilles, Mary, 201
acknowledgement, for victims, 178–79
activism: anti-rape, 84–85, 187, 220n103; anti-trafficking, 168–69; gender, 42; queer, 15
affect, law and, 202
affirmative consent, 81–82, 189–90, 221n113
African American men, incarceration of, 108, 168
age hierarchy, 146, 160
agency, 1, 53, 64, 65–69, 79, 81–86; sexual, 9, 48, 50, 55, 60–62; victimization and, 97–102, 183
"age of anger," 198
agism, 41
Ahmed, Sara, 202, 230n151
AIDS crisis, 130
Alexander, Michelle, 167
Allen, Woody, 213n6

American Civil Liberties Union, 187–88
American Council on Education, 187
"Am I a Bad Feminist?" (Atwood), 25, 26–27
Anderson, Kenya, 203–4
Anderson, Michelle, 182
anger, 34, 42, 204; accountability and, 202; "age of anger," 198; feminist, 12, 198; paranoia and, 147; rage, 199–200, 201–2, 203; reparative regulation and, 202; revenge and, 200; survivors and, 230n10; victims and, 201–2
Ansari, Aziz, 18, 25, 27–28, 96, 100, 191; gender hierarchy and, 160; sexual misconduct and, 109–10
anti-censorship, 67–68
antinormativity, 227n83
anti-pornography feminism, 46–47, 48, 51, 52–54, 66; Civil Rights Ordinance and, 56–65; FACT and, 60–63; Minneapolis ordinance for, 57–58, 219n51
anti-rape activism, 84–85, 187, 220n103
anti-rape movement, 38, 73, 82, 84–85
anti-trafficking activism, 168–69
Are the Lips a Grave? (Huffer), 228n92
Argento, Asia, 119–20
Arrested Justice (Richie), 168
assault. *See* sexual assault
attachments, wounded, 180
Atwood, Margaret, 25, 26–27, 214n55

backlash, against #MeToo, 25, 28, 32
Badham, Van, 91
#BalanceTonPorc, 23
Bandes, Susan A., 232n55
Banet-Weiser, Sarah, 12–13, 198
Banfield, Ashleigh, 28–29
Barnard College, 52, 72
Barnard Conference, 52–56, 62; Vance and, 144
Barthes, Roland, 152–53
Bartholet, Elizabeth, 74, 186
Barton, Joe, 158
battered women, 174–75
Battle of Cambridge, 184–85
Baumgardner, Jennifer, 36
Bazelon, Emily, 2–3, 79
BDSM, 67, 227n79
Bennett, Jimmy, 119
Beres, Melanie Ann, 221n139
Berlant, Lauren, 155, 230n142
Berlinski, Claire, 94, 95
Bernstein, Elizabeth, 134, 168–69
Biden, Joe, 188
Bitch Media, 198
Black feminism, 204–5
#BlackLivesMatter, 205
Black Lives Matter movement, 167
Black people, mass incarceration of, 168, 169
Black women, 2, 17, 199, 203, 211n2
"Blaming the victim is apparently OK when the accused in a Title IX proceeding is a feminist literary theorist" (Leiter), 121, 224n20
Bolger, Dana, 125
Bond, Kathryn Stockton, 131
Boomers, 18
Brodsky, Alexandra, 71, 79, 84–85
Brown, Elspeth, 153–54
Bumiller, Kristen, 169
Burke, James (judge), 163
Burke, Tarana, 2, 13–14, 17, 119–20, 194; on anger, 203–4; on #MeToo beginnings, 211n2
butch/femme, 55

Butler, Judith, 10, 130–31, 147–48, 227n72; on rage, 199; Ronell letter and, 119, 122–23, 127; on sex-radical movement, 66–67
Butterfly Politics (MacKinnon), 212n21

Califia, Pat, 46–47, 51
California Education Code, 221n113
campuses, University, 146; anti-rape movement on, 38; *The Hunting Grounds* (film), 76; sexual harassment on, 3, 21–22, 71, 233n76; sexual violence on, 70–72. *See also* Title IX
Canada *Criminal Code*, 234n86
carceral feminism, 113–14, 168–69, 176, 232n52
carceral state, 165, 166–67, 169, 205
Carson, Sage, 187
catfights, 39–40, 97, 195, 217n126
censorship, 43–44, 49, 50, 60; anti-, 67; battles around, 67–68
Central Park 5, 169
Chemaly, Surraya, 198
children, sexual abuse of, 93, 132–33
Chu, Andrea Long, 127
Civil Rights Ordinances, 43–44, 56–65, 66, 67
C.K., Louis, 19
Coker, Donna, 174, 231n30
Cole, Cory, 186
Columbia University, 72
comedy, pleasure and aggression in, 155–56
Comella, Lynn, 55
community accountability, 174
Comstock laws, 56
congress, members of, 157–59
consent, 2, 44, 51, 83, 97, 99–100; affirmative, 81–82, 189–90, 221n113; definition of, 189, 221n113, 223n38, 234n86; laws on, 189–90; MacKinnon on, 82, 212n21; policies and, 75; regulation and, 148; *Screw Consent* (Fischel), 221n39; sexual harm and, 140; sexual misconduct and,

110–11. *See also* nonconsensual behavior
"consent is sexy" campaigns, 83
contestation, feminist, 197–98
control, of women, 95–96
Cooper, Brittney, 198–99, 203
Cosby, Bill, 1
Coughenour, Beulah, 58–59
Criminal Code, Canada, 234n86
criminalization, of sexuality, 4, 165–66, 192
criminal justice system, 84–85, 103, 109, 161, 164, 166; abolition politics and, 176; critique of, 167–75; power of, 165; remorse and, 232n55; validation from, 178
criminal law, 165, 166–67
Critical Resistance, 168, 176
critics: feminist, 30, 31, 83–85, 110, 111; of #MeToo, 17–18, 23–24
critique: of criminal justice system, 167–75; of due process, 108, 213n8; queer, 131, 136, 140, 160–61, 227n79, 228n97. *See also* feminist critique
culture: digital, 42; rape, 163–64, 230n3

danger, 134, 136; pleasure and, 91, 95, 144–45, 180
date rape, 99
Davis, Angela, 167, 168, 175
Davis, Dianne, 125–26
DCL. *See* Dear Colleague Letter
Dean, Michelle, 31–32, 40, 216n100
Dear Colleague Letter (DCL), 70–71, 73, 186
decarceration, 177
decriminalization, of sex work, 192
de Hass, Caroline, 23
Democrats, 150, 151, 157
Deneuve, Catherine, 23–24, 94, 214n44
Denfeld, Rene, 38
Department of Education, US, 186, 187, 190
Derrida, Jacques, 122

detractors, #MeToo, 41, 89–90, 92, 97, 98
DeVos, Betsy, 187, 188
Diary of a Conference on Sexuality leaflet, 53–55
"Did Al Franken Get 'Railroaded'?" (Filipovic), 229n130
digital cultures, 42
disadvantaged communities, 84
discrimination, sex, 71
domestic violence, 176
dominance feminism, 64–65, 79–80, 87, 182–83
Donegan, Moira, 24, 32, 40–41, 229n125
Douglas, Susan, 40, 217n216
Doyle, Sady, 31, 40
Duckworth, Tammy, 150
due process, 26, 88, 105, 106–7, 109; absence of, 22; critique of, 108, 213n8; Franken and, 21, 152, 223n48; government and, 223n48; Kavanaugh and, 157; Weinstein and, 165
Duggan, Lisa, 60, 69, 126–27, 129, 137–39; on consent, 68; on ordinances, 62; on Ronell, 161
DuVernay, Ava, 167
Dworkin, Andrea, 48, 57, 61

Edwards, Stassa, 24–25
Eloquent Rage (Cooper), 198
emotions, 154, 202, 230n151
empathy, 27, 173, 206
empowerment, 9, 25, 33; women's, 86, 98, 173
End Rape on Campus, 72
Epistemology of the Closet (Sedgwick), 129
"Erotica and Pornography" (Steinem), 218n20
eroticism, 48, 50, 65, 218n20
ethics, 111, 204. *See also* Senate Ethics Committee
Etsy, Elizabeth, 158
Everyday Sexism (website), 36

evidence, 154; #MeToo and, 152, 155; visual, 158
exposé, of sexual violence, 17, 212n4

FACT. *See* Feminist Anti-Censorship Taskforce
FACT brief, 63
fairness, 107–8
Fallon, Claire, 31
Faludi, Susan, 38
feminism, 1, 12–13, 21–22; abolition, 168–70; anti-violence, 169; Black, 204–5; carceral, 113–14, 168–69, 176, 232n52; divide within, 32–33; dominance, 64–65, 79–80, 87, 182–83; fourth-wave, 35–36, 40, 201; history and, 115–16; laws and, 84; pro-sexuality, 67; queer/feminist divide, 129, 136, 144; queer theory and, 135–36, 228n92; radical, 3, 43, 87; second-wave, 2, 18, 24, 27, 28–32, 37–39; sex-positive, 14, 79, 129, 137, 177, 182–83; third-wave, 33–35, 37–39, 216n100; Title IX and, 126, 191; victim, 181; vigilante, 105; waves of, 33–37, 216n108; Weinstein and, 165; white, 205. *See also* anti-pornography feminism
"Feminism, Marxism, Method, and the State" (MacKinnon), 212n21
Feminism Meets Queer Theory (Schor and Weed), 228n92
Feminist and Queer Legal Theory (Fineman, Jackson, Romero), 228n92
Feminist and the Sex Offender (Levine and Meiners), 205
feminist anger, 12, 198
Feminist Anti-Censorship Taskforce (FACT), 56–65, 66, 68, 219n70
feminist contestation, 197–98
feminist critics, 30, 31, 83–85; on sexual misconduct, 110, 111
feminist critique, 44, 48, 111–12, 180; of consent, 9; of due process, 108,

213n8; of Ronell, 136; of victim politics, 181
feminist flashpoints, 12, 13, 18, 38, 43–44, 184–91, 193, 195, 204
feminist hypocrisy, 121, 124
feminist legal scholarship, 174
feminist *respair*, 203
feminists, 27; of color, 14; as critics of #MeToo, 18; #MeToo, 89–92, 97, 99–102
Feminist War on Crime (Gruber), 205
feminist writings, 33–34, 198
Ferguson, Roderick, 131
"Fighting Bodies, Fighting Words" (Marcus), 232n64
Filipovic, Jill, 150–51, 229n130
Fineman, Martha Albertson, 228n92
Fischel, Joseph, 148, 212n21, 221n139
Flanagan, Caitlin, 28
flashpoints, feminist, 184–91
fourth-wave feminism, 35–36, 40, 201
Franken, Al, 17, 18, 20–22, 105, 149–52, 154–60; due process and, 21, 223n48; resignation and, 229n130
freedom, sexual, 23, 91, 133–34
French women, #MeToo and, 23–24
Futter, Ellen, 53
"The Future Is Furious" (series), 198
futurity, queer, 191

Galloway, Steven, 25
gaslighting, 178–79, 183
Gay, Roxanne, 164
gender, 130; hierarchies of, 146, 160; inequalities of, 189; justice and, 184; #MeToo and, 120; sexual abuse and, 125; sexuality and, 129, 131, 227n69
gendered violence, 172–73
gender neutrality, 125, 126
Gender Violence Clinic, at University of Maryland, 173
generational power, 128
generation gap, 39, 42, 89; intergenerational feuds, 24, 27, 30–31, 32–33, 41; narrative of, 18, 28, 31, 40–41;

power and, 127. *See also* waves: of feminism
generationing, 37
generation war, 29–30, 32, 39–40
Generation X, 35, 42
Generation Y, 42
Gersen, Jeannie Suk, 74, 76, 78, 186
Gertner, Nancy, 74, 186
Gessen, Masha, 4, 19–20, 92–93, 213n18; on consent, 99–100; on victimization, 98
Ghomeshi, Jian, 1
Gillibrand, Kirsten, 151
Gilmore, Ruth Wilson, 168
Goldhill, Olivia, 125
Good and Mad (Traister), 198, 199
Goodmark, Leigh, 173, 184, 201–2, 231n37
Grace (accuser alias), 27–28, 92, 98, 110
Grady, Constance, 32, 40
Grant, Melissa, 164
Gray, Emma, 100, 195
"gray area," of sexuality, 100
Greenfield, Scott, 124
Greer, Germaine, 29
Gruber, Aya, 136, 137, 169, 205
guilt, 54, 61, 105, 222n10

Halberstam, Jack, 126, 127, 132, 226n52
Haley, Miriam, 163
Halley, Janet, 73–74, 79–82, 136, 186, 187
Halperin, David, 4, 131, 132–33, 134, 227n70
Halperin, Mark, 105
The Handmaid's Tale (tv series), 27
harassment, on-line, 193. *See also* sexual harassment
Harding, Kate, 21, 30
harm, validation of, 184, 231n37. *See also* sexual harm
Harvard Four, 186
Harvard Law School, 73–78, 79–80, 81; faculty committee at, 185–86; Title IX and, 184–86

healing, victim, 171–72
Heitkamp, Heidi, 150
heteronormative, 138
heterosexuality, 65, 130, 131
heterosexual masculinity, 95
hierarchies: age, 146, 160; gender, 146, 160; sexuality, 129–30
History, Uses, and Abuses of Title IX (report), 122
HIV, 132
Hobart and William Smith College, 80–81
homophobia, 130, 141
hope, 203
Hoppe, Trevor, 4, 132–33
HoSang, Daniel Martinez, 13
House of Representatives, 158
Hudnut, William, III, 58
Hudson, Barbara, 172
Hudson, Laura, 29
Huffer, Lynn, 228n92
human rights violations, 170
Hunter, Nan, 61, 68, 69, 219n53, 219n70
The Hunting Grounds (film), 76–78
hypersexualization, 137
hypocrisy, feminist, 121, 124

In an Abusive State (Bumiller), 169
incarceration, 162, 166, 173; of African American men, 108, 168; Black people, 168, 169; decarceration, 177; of people of color, 167
INCITE!, 168, 170, 174, 176
Indianapolis ordinance, 58–59, 60, 64
inequalities, 65, 174; gender, 189; social, 86; workplace, 96
innocence, presumption of, 106, 107
intergenerational feuds, 24, 27, 30–31, 32–33, 41
intimacy, queer, 138
intoxication, voluntary, 81
"It's Not (All) the Second Generation's Fault," (Doyle), 31

Jackson, Jack, 228n92
joke, sexual harm as, 155–56

"jokester," versus predator, 155–56, 230n142
joy, power of, 203–4
Judd, Ashley, 164
justice: gender and, 184; restorative, 171–75, 188, 231n30; retributive, 171, 177; transformative, 175, 176–77, 231n30; transitional, 170–73; for victims, 173, 174, 177; vigilante, 26. *See also* reparative justice
justice system, criminal, 84–85, 103, 109

Kaba, Mariame, 193–94
Kaminer, Wendy, 49, 52, 105
Karvonides, Mia, 185
Kavanaugh, Brett, 151, 157
Kay, Jilly Boyce, 198
Kim, Mimi, 169
Kipnis, Laura, 74–76, 78, 79, 91, 111
Know Your IX, 72, 125, 187–88
Kohn, Laurie, 174
Kraus, Chris, 226n52
Kujundzic, Dragan, 122

Lauer, Matt, 19
de Lauretis, Teresa, 130
law-and-order agenda, 169
laws, 3–4, 6, 43–44, 82–86, 165; affect and, 202; Civil Rights Ordinance, 56–65; Comstock, 56; consent, 189–90; criminal, 165, 166–67; due process, 21, 22, 26, 88, 105, 106–9; feminism and, 84; #MeToo and, 87–88, 102–6, 195; obscenity law, 5; pornography, 47, 50, 52, 54, 58–62, 104; power of, 9–10, 88, 102–6, 108, 111–14; rape, 183; reparative regulation and, 177, 195; sex radicals and, 67–69; sexual harassment, 32, 183; sexual harm and, 88, 106–9, 116, 223n28, 229n118; sexual misconduct and, 111–13
Leahy, Patrick, 150
LeGrand, Camille, 47
Leidholdt, Dorchen, 61, 219n70

Leiter, Brian, 121–22, 224n20
letter, of support for Ronell, 118–19, 122–27, 148
Levi, Margaret, 190–91
Levine, Judith, 93, 133, 205
LGBT community, 130, 134–35
Linden, Emily, 106–7
Lippitt, Jill, 52
Lorde, Audre, 198, 199–200
Louis, Beatrice, 125, 225n44
Love, Heather, 203
Ludlow, Peter, 75–76
lumping together, sexual misconduct, 112

MacKinnon, Catharine, 32, 56–57, 61–63, 65, 79; on consent, 82, 212n21; queer theory and, 136
male sexual violence, 44
male supremacy, 50
Mann, Jessica, 163
Marcotte, Amanda, 151
Marcus, Sharon, 183, 232n64
Mardorossian, Carine, 181
marginalized women, 194
masculinity, heterosexual, 95
Maslen, Hannah, 232n55
mass incarceration, of Black people, 168, 169
Mattress Performance (Sulkowicz), 72–73
Mayer, Jane, 149, 154–55, 156, 158, 229n124
McDonagh, Erin Sanders, 216n108
McGowan, Rose, 120
Meiners, Erica, 205
Me Not You (Phipps), 205
Merkin, Daphne, 22, 107
Merkley, Jeff, 150
#MeToo, 1, 2, 4, 19–21, 33, 211n2; backlash against, 25, 28, 32; #BlackLivesMatter and, 205; critics of, 17–18, 23–24; disagreement within, 92; due process and, 106–9; evidence and, 152, 154; exposé of sexual violence for, 17, 212n4;

French women and, 23–24; gender and, 120; laws and, 87–88, 102–6, 113, 195; paranoia and, 143–44; political whiteness of, 14; queer claims and, 146; reparative reading and, 160; restorative justice and, 174; sexual harm and, 89; sex wars and, 97; transitional justice and, 172; Weinstein and, 163–64; witch hunt claims and, 92, 94–95
Me Too campaign, 17
#MeToo detractors, 41, 89–90, 92, 97; on victimization, 98, 101–2
#MeToo feminists, 89–92, 97, 99–102
"#MeToo Is Not a Witch Hunt" (Beck), 222n15
Milano, Alyssa, 2, 17
millennials, 2, 18, 29, 42
Minneapolis ordinance, anti-pornography, 57–58, 219n51
minorities, sexual, 137
Minow, Martha, 185
misconduct, sexual, 89, 109–14
Mishra, Pankaj, 198
"Modern McCarthyism" (Hunter), 219n70
Moore, Roy, 150
Morning After (Riophe), 37–38
Muller, Sandra, 23
Muñoz, José Esteban, 141, 191
Murphy, Colleen, 170
"My Rapist Is Still on Campus" (Sulkowicz), 72

Nash, Jennifer, 204
National Organization of Women (NOW), 51
Nelson, Bill, 229n124
neoliberalism, 181, 232n59
New Jim Crow (Alexander), 167
New York University (NYU), 117, 128
Nicholson, Linda, 36
No More Nice Girls, 54
nonconsensual behavior, 123, 139–40, 151, 193; prevention of, 11, 165–66; victimization and, 83

nonviolence, 199
Nordic model, 192
Northwestern, 75–76
"Not in the Name of Feminism" (Louis), 225n44
NOW. *See* National Organization of Women
Nwanevu, Osita, 100
NYU. *See* New York University

Obama, Barack, 1, 186
obscenity law, 5, 46
offender accountability, 171–72, 173, 178
Office for Civil Rights (OCR), 70–71, 186
Off Our Backs, 54, 218n41
"Ok Boomer" retort, 18
Oncale, Joseph, 79
on-line harassment, 193
opposition, to sexual harassment policies, 185
ordinances. *See* Civil Rights Ordinances
overcriminalization, of sex, 145
overregulation, of sexuality, 148, 165
over-/under surveillance axis, 148

pandemic, 187
panic, sex, 93–95, 222n10
paranoia, 147; sexual, 124
paranoid reading, 141–43, 148, 228n103
"Paranoid Reading and Reparative Reading" (Sedgwick), 141–43
"paranoid temporality," 143
patriarchy, 53, 65, 95, 102
Pellegrini, Ann, 114
Persky, Aaron, 222n140
petition, feminist, 53, 54, 218n41
Phipps, Alison, 13, 192, 205, 234n92
photographs, 153; of Tweeden and Franken, 152, 154–56, 158
photography: photoshop and, 154; queer theory and, 153–54; theory of, 153, 154

Phu, Thy, 153–54
pleasure, 53, 89; in comedy, 155–56;
    danger and, 91, 95, 144–45, 180
policies, 1, 22, 73, 99, 112; consent and,
    75; at Harvard, 74–76, 79, 81; of in-
    dustry, 46; sexual harassment, 122,
    185; Title IX, 80, 186, 190
political movements, waves of, 41
political resignations, 157–59
political sex scandals, 157–58
political whiteness, 13, 204–5; of
    #MeToo, 14
politics: abolition, 176, 232n49,
    234n90; queer, 130–31; sexual harm
    in, 157–58; victim, 181
pornography, 5, 7, 14, 32, 43, 44,
    218n20; Civil Rights Ordinances
    and, 57–65; laws for, 47, 50, 52, 56,
    58–60, 104; rape and, 45, 46, 48, 50;
    revenge, 70, 193; sexual violence
    and, 45–46, 49, 52–53, 65; S/M, 46–
    47, 61. See also anti-pornography
    feminism; Women Against Por-
    nography (WAP)
Pornography (Dworkin), 48
"Pornography and Pleasure" (Webster),
    51
positivity, sex, 48
power, 29, 127–29, 138, 155; abuse
    of, 12, 23; back to victims, 174; of
    criminal justice system, 165; of
    joy, 203–4; of law, 9–10, 88, 102–6,
    108, 111–14; privilege and, 13, 120;
    structures of, 25, 96
power dynamics, 146–47
power relationships, 67, 152–53
"The Predator and the Jokester" (Ber-
    lant), 230n142
predators: "jokester" versus, 155–56,
    230n142; sexual, 150, 193–94
predatory sexual assault, 163
presumption, of innocence, 106, 107
Price, Brian, 159
prison abolition movement, 168
prison industrial complex, 167–68
prison population, 167

prison sentencing, 163, 164
privilege, power and, 13, 120
"The Proliferation of Consent-Focused
    Rape Prevention Social Marketing
    Materials" (Beres), 221n139
prostitution, 3. See also sex work
public accusations, 17

queer activism, 15
queer critique, 136, 140, 160–61,
    227n79, 228n97
queer/feminist divide, 129, 136, 144
queer framework, 4, 93, 120, 126, 141,
    227n70; sexual harm and, 166; Sex
    Wars 2.0 and, 128–40
queer futurity, 191
queer intimacy, 138
queer of-color critique, 131
queer politics, 130–31
queer reparative justice, 176
queer theory, 129–39, 227n70;
    feminism and, 135–36, 228n92;
    paranoid, 141; photography and,
    153–54; Ronell and, 136–40, 149,
    228n92

racialization, of sexual violence, 169
racism, 93–94, 168, 194, 198, 205
radicals: feminists, 3, 43, 87; sex, 3, 4,
    43, 52, 55–56, 66–67
rage, 199–200, 201–2, 203
Rage Becomes Her (Chemaly), 198
rape, 20, 23, 80–81, 90, 163, 212n21;
    anti-rape movement, 38, 73, 82;
    date, 99; law, 183; pornography
    and, 45, 46, 48, 50
rape culture, 163–64, 230n3
reading, 228n113; paranoid, 141–43,
    148, 228n103; reparative, 141–44,
    145, 147, 157
Reading Sideways (Seitler), 228n113
recognition, for victims, 178–79
regret, 158–60
regulations, 5, 6, 161; of consent, 148;
    overregulation, 148; reparative,
    176–84, 191–92, 195; reparative

reading and, 145; of sexual harm, 145, 148, 162, 167, 184–85; of sex work, 192, 193; for Title IX, 189

Reinke, Rachel, 217n126

Reitman, Nimrod, 117–19, 123, 138, 145–46

remorse, criminal justice system and, 232n55

Remorse, Penal Theory, and Sentencing (Maslen), 232n55

"Remorse and Criminal Justice" (Bandes), 232n55

reparative justice, 160–62, 182, 184, 206, 232n46; queer, 176; sexual harm and, 166, 175; Title IX as, 188, 190

reparative reading, 141–44, 145, 147, 157; regulation of sexual harm and, 167; to reparative justice, 160–62; sex wars and, 197; of sex work, 192–93

reparative regulation, 176–84, 191–92; anger and, 202; laws and, 177, 195

Republicans, 157

resignations: Franken and, 229n130; political, 157–59

Resolution on Lesbian Rights, 51

respair, feminist, 203

responsibility, 148; from universities, 146

restorative justice, 171–75, 188, 231n30

retributive justice, 171, 177

"The Return of the Sex Wars" (Bazelon), 79

revenge, 200

revenge pornography, 70, 193

Richie, Beth, 168

Ricoeur, Paul, 141

Robbenolt, Jennifer, 173–74

Robin, Corey, 127–28, 129

Robinson, Sara, 199

Roiphe, Katie, 24, 37–38

Romero, Adam, 228n92

Ronell, Avital, 117, 121, 128, 129, 134–35, 226n52; letter of support for, 118–19, 122–27, 148; queer theory and, 136–40, 149, 228n92; reparative reading and, 143–44, 145–46, 161–62

Rose, Charlie, 19

Rubin, Gayle, 46–47, 51, 68, 129

Russell, Dianne, 47

sadomasochism, 3, 47

Saint Foucault (Halperin, D.), 227n70

Samois, 46

Schor, Naomi, 228n92

Scott, Joan, 122, 125, 202

Screw Consent (Fischel), 221

"The Second Feminist Wave," (*New York Times*), 33

second-wave feminism, 2, 18, 24, 27, 28–32, 37–39; third-wave feminism and, 33–35

Sedgwick, Eve, 5, 129, 130–31, 141–43, 175, 203; on paranoid reading, 228n103

Seitler, Dana, 143, 228n113

Senate Ethics Committee, 150, 158

Senate Judiciary Committee, 151, 159

serial sexual assault, 161

Serisier, Tanya, 178

sex discrimination, 71

sexism, 35, 36, 42, 66, 194

sex offenders, 133

sex panic, 93–95, 222n10

sex-positive feminism, 14, 79, 129, 137, 177, 182–83

sex positivity, 48

sex radicals, 3, 4, 43, 52, 55–56, 66; laws and, 67–69; on sexual harm, 83

sex scandals, political, 157–58

sexting, 192, 193, 234n94

sexual abuse: of children, 93, 132–33; gender and, 125

sexual agency, 9, 48, 50, 55, 60–62

sexual assault, 1, 80; predatory, 163; serial, 161. *See also specific topics*

sexual freedom, 23, 91, 133–34

sexual harassment, 1, 122–23, 136–37; on campuses, 3, 21–22, 71, 233n76; definition of, 233n76; laws on, 32, 182; policies for, 122, 185

Sexual Harassment Guidance, 71

sexual harm, 1–2, 106, 160; consent and, 140; definition of, 92, 166; as joke, 155–56; law and, 88, 107–9, 116, 223n38, 229n118; #MeToo and, 89; in politics, 157–58; preventing, 133; queer framework and, 166; regulation of, 145, 148, 162, 167, 184–85; reparative justice and, 166, 175; rethinking of, 189; sex radicals on, 83

sexuality, 82–86, 89–97, 116; criminalization of, 4, 165–66, 192; gender and, 129, 131, 227n69; "gray area" of, 100; overregulation of, 165; S/M, 51

sexuality hierarchies, 129–30

sexualization, of women, 96–97

sexual minorities, 137

sexual misconduct, 89, 109–14, 157, 160

sexual-offense charges, 163

sexual paranoia, 124

"Sexual Paranoia Strikes Academe" (Kipnis), 75

sexual predators, 150, 193–94

sexual violence, 1, 2, 22, 114, 176; on campuses, 70–72; condoning, 200; laws and, 102–4; male, 44; pornography and, 45–46, 49, 52–53, 65; racialization of, 169; workplace, 23

sex wars (1970s and 1980s), 2–3, 43, 66–69, 87–88, 115; Barnard Conference and, 52–56; beginning of, 44–52; Civil Rights Ordinance and FACT, 56–65; reading beside, 144–49

Sex Wars (Duggan and Hunter), 219n53

sex wars, campus, 187

Sex Wars 2.0, 2, 5, 15, 44, 69–82, 87; queer framework and, 120, 128–40

"Sex Wars Revisited" (Phipps), 234n92

sex work, 3, 70, 132, 234n92; abolition politics and, 234n90; abuse and, 193; regulation of, 192, 193; reparative reading of, 192–93

shame, 132

Shitty Media Men list, 24

Silman, Anna, 104

S/M pornography, 46–47, 61

S/M sexuality, 51, 54–55, 66

Snuff (film), 45–46

social media, 13, 17, 35, 83, 103, 126–27

social service surveillance, 169

Sommers, Christina Hoff, 124–25

Sontag, Susan, 153

Spacey, Kevin, 19, 134–35, 160

Stanford University, 1, 222n140

statutes of limitation, 222n10

Steinem, Gloria, 48, 58, 218n20

Stringer, Rebecca, 180–81, 233n67

Sulkowicz, Emma, 72–73

supremacy: male, 50; white, 205

Supreme Court, 32, 50, 59, 64, 157

surveillance: over-/under axis, 148; social-service, 169

survivors, 98, 176–77, 178, 184, 187; anger and, 230n10; Black women, 2, 17

systematic oppression, 109

Tagg, John, 153

Take Back the Night March, 47

Taylor, Chloe, 176

Teachout, Zephyr, 21

terminology, 14–15

Terwiel, Anna, 176–77

"Thinking Sex" (Rubin), 68

third-wave feminism, 33–35, 37–39, 216n100

The 13th (film), 167

Title IX, 20, 21–22, 71, 74–76, 82, 117; criticism of, 79–81; feminism and, 126, 191; Harvard University and, 184–86; *History, Uses, and Abuses of Title IX* (report), 122; Know Your IX, 72, 125, 187–88; regulations for, 189; as reparative justice, 188, 190; revisions to, 186–87

Tolentino, Jia, 24

Toward a Feminist Theory of the State (MacKinnon), 212n21

trafficking, anti-, 69
Traister, Rebecca, 96, 97, 100, 198, 199
transformative justice, 175, 176–77, 231n30
"Transformative Justice" (Cocker), 231n30
transitional justice, 170–73
trauma, 12, 96, 181–82, 204, 230n10
Trump administration, 187
Tudor, Steven Keith, 232n55
Turner, Brock, 1, 84–85, 191, 222n140
Tweeden, Leeann, 20, 149–50, 152, 154–58, 213n7
Tyson, Neil Degrasse, 160

UBC. See University of British Columbia
Udall, Tom, 229n124
United States (US), 186, 187, 190
universities, responsibility from, 146
University of British Columbia (UBC), 25–26
University of Maryland, 173
Unwanted Advances (Kipnis), 91
US. See United States

Vacchelli, Elena, 216n108
Valenti, Jessica, 104, 163, 195, 230n3
validation: from criminal justice system, 178; of harm, 184, 231n37
Vance, Carole, 52–53, 54, 91, 144, 218n41, 219n70
victim feminism, 181
victimization, 95–96, 178, 180–81; agency and, 97–102, 183
victimology, 22, 98
victim politics, 181
victims, 181, 184, 233n67; acknowledgement for, 178–79; anger and, 201–2; healing for, 171–72; justice for, 173, 174, 177; power back to, 174; recognition for, 178–79; wounded attachments and, 180
victim script, 182–84, 232n64
vigilante feminism, 105

vigilante justice, 26
vindication, 78, 173, 194, 231n37
violations, human rights, 170
violence: domestic, 176; gendered, 172–73; nonviolence, 199. See also sexual violence
visual evidence, 158
voluntary intoxication, 81

Walker, Rebecca, 33–34
Walters, Suzanna Danuta, 16, 197
WAP. See Women Against Pornography
war: generation, 29–30, 32, 39–40; metaphor of, 16. See also sex wars (1970s and 1980s); Sex Wars 2.0
"The War on #MeToo Will Fail" (Donegan), 229n125
War on Sex (D. Halperin and Hoppe), 4, 132–34
WAVAW. See Women against Violence Against Women
waves: of feminism, 33–37, 216n108; political movements, 41
WAVPM. See Women against Violence in Pornography and Media
Way, Katie, 28–29
Webster, Paula, 51
Weed, Elizabeth, 142, 228n92
Weinstein, Harvey, 17, 119–20, 161, 163–65; conviction of, 194; as villain, 19
Weiss, Bari, 21, 28, 119
Wexler, Lesley, 172, 173–74
What We Don't Talk about When We Talk about #MeToo (Wypijewski), 205, 222n10
Where the Girls Are (Douglas), 40, 217n126
white feminism, 205
whiteness, political, 204–5
white supremacy, 205
"Who Are You Calling a Second Wave Feminist?" (Dean), 31–32
"Who's Afraid of Third Wave Feminism?" (Dean), 216n100

"Why Should Remorse Be a Mitigating Factor in Sentencing?" (Tudor), 232n55
Wiegman, Robin, 203
Willingham, Kamilah, 77
Willis, Ellen, 49–50, 51, 54–55
Winch, Alice, 39–40
Winston, Brandon, 77, 78
witch hunt claims, 92, 94–95, 213n6, 222n15
Wolf, Naomi, 38
women: Black, 2, 17, 199, 203, 211n2; of color, 37, 194, 205, 211n2; control of, 95–96; empowerment of, 86, 98, 173; French, 23–24; marginalized, 194; oppression of, 65; sexualization of, 96–97

Women Against Pornography (WAP), 48–50, 58, 218n20
Women against Violence Against Women (WAVAW), 45–46, 66, 104
Women against Violence in Pornography and Media (WAVPM), 46–47, 58, 66, 104
workplace: inequalities in, 96; sexual violence in, 23
wounded attachments, 180
Wypijewski, Joann, 93, 205, 222n10

#YesAllWomen, 36
Yoffe, Emily, 21–22, 77, 91, 108, 111; on Franken, 149–50

Zander, Christine, 154–55
Zehr, Howard, 174

ABOUT THE AUTHOR

Brenda Cossman is the Goodman-Schipper Chair and Professor of Law at the University of Toronto. She is the author of *Sexual Citizens: The Legal and Cultural Regulation of Sex and Belonging* (2007).